here we are among the living

a memoir in emails

here we are among the living

a memoir in emails

Samantha Bernstein

Copyright © 2012 Samantha Bernstein
All rights reserved

Tightrope Books
17 Greyton Crescent
Toronto, Ontario. M6E 2G1
www.tightropebooks.com

Edited: Robyn Read
Design and typsetting: Dawn Kresan
Cover image: *Trapeze Artists in Circus* (1890 lithograph by Calvert Litho. Co.)
Printed and bound in Canada.

We thank the Canada Council for the Arts and the Ontario Arts Council for their support of our publishing program.

Canada Council for the Arts / Conseil des Arts du Canada

ONTARIO ARTS COUNCIL
CONSEIL DES ARTS DE L'ONTARIO

Library and Archives Canada Cataloguing in Publication

Bernstein, Samantha, 1981–
      Here we are among the living / Samantha Bernstein.

ISBN 978-1-926639-44-4

      1. Bernstein, Samantha, 1981–. 2. Bernstein, Samantha, 1981–
– Family. 3. Layton, Irving, 1912-2006. 4. Authors, Canadian (English)
– 21st century – Biography. 5. Fathers and daughters – Canada – Biography.
      I. Title.

PS8603.E762Z465 2012   C813'.6   C2012-901806-6

"is not the Distant, the Dead, while I love it,
and long for it, and mourn for it, Here, in the genuine sense,
as truly as the floor I stand on? But that same WHERE,
with its brother WHEN, are from the first the master-colours
of our Dream-grotto; say rather, the Canvass (the warp
and woof thereof) whereon all our Dreams and Life-visions are painted."

– Thomas Carlyle, *Sartor Resartus*

– For Mama, who believes

Prologue

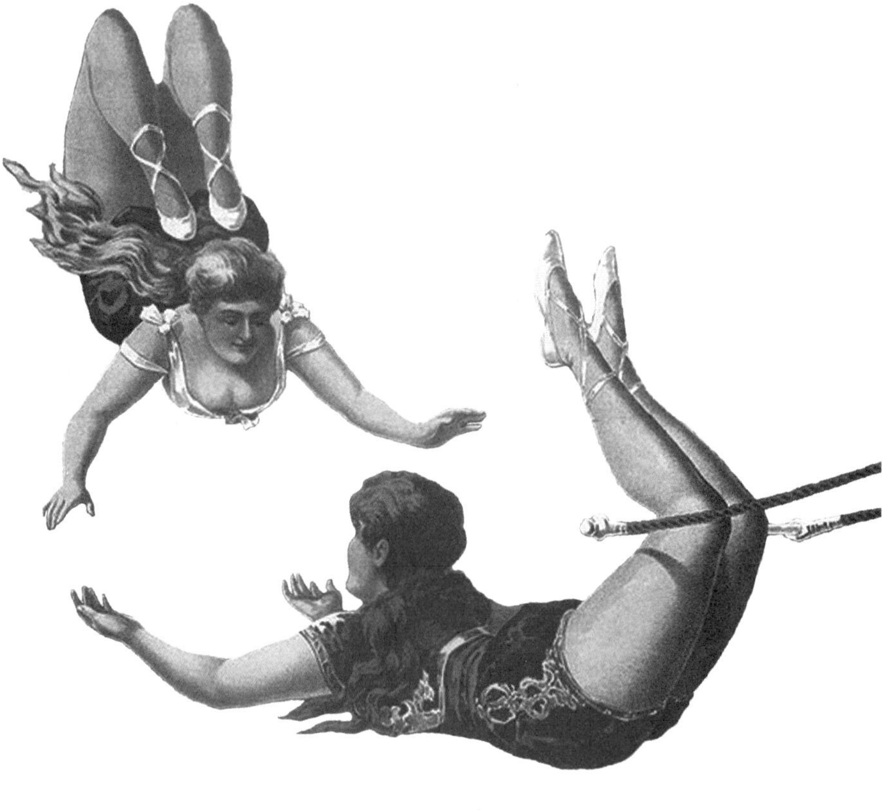

YOU'RE BEAUTIFUL, WHO ARE YOU?
11/01/1999

Eshe!

I should be studying my psychology textbook right now but it's impossible – I have to study myself instead, the weekend's been too crazy.

So of everyone I asked the only person available to go with me to Montreal for Irving's tribute was Michael Bobbie. Which should have been strange, considering we've only really known each other a couple of months, but it seemed appropriate. To do this weird thing with a new person, I guess.

I arranged to pick him up outside Hart House, where he was auditioning for a play. I had class in the morning, rushed home to pack, then over to Mom's office to say goodbye – where I realized I should book a place to stay, and so took the first convenient and affordable thing even though the lady told me all the rooms only had one bed. Since I was talking to her five minutes before I was supposed to meet Michael Bobbie, I said okay.

Into trusty and freshly-cleaned Mel (cigarette packs and tickets removed from the back seat), across clogged Bloor Street, down University to the bridge into Hart House circle and there's Michael. Under the grey sky and noble stone building in an old brown leather jacket looking pleased and slightly reserved as he always does, he flings himself lightly into the car and we dash north and onto the highway before dark.

Of course we got to talking about his audition, which led to his final year at Northern where suddenly everybody knew him because of all those plays he was in, and that one he wrote – do you remember it, the one about an insurance guy who wants to kill himself and a "secret agent?" How could we not go from that to his love that year for Hannah, which is after all how we come to know each other. Isn't it wild? Because he fell in love with Hannah in drama class, and because that happened to be at just the time that N. decided to love Hannah and she, inexplicably, decided to love him back (rather than Michael, who really would have been the probable match), Michael when he returned from China two years later went to sit with Hannah after Graduation (which Mike attended because he'd missed his own), and sitting with Hannah was Bri. Michael wasn't in love with Hannah anymore and anyway her parents had moved to the States, but he and Bri struck up a friendship; so this past summer when I finally got the balls to call her again and she miraculously forgave me everything and said Come over, there was Mike. And since N. "broke up with me" (I swear to god Eshe, he divined my infidelity in New Orleans – why else break up with me the day I come home? Of course we're still hanging out, but he didn't want to come to Montreal, and sex is rare and on his say-so…), there was Michael in my car rehearsing this whole history with me. Michael Chaste and Fair, as Bri sometimes calls him.

I'm glad Bri picked up the phone when I called her, I said to Mike, probing to see how terrible he thought me for the whole Bri – N. – me triangle and also because I was in one of those speedy, devil-may-care moods, 130 the whole way, cars getting out of my lane at my signal, the highway lights blurring beside Michael's head as I stole a glance and cast my choices before him.

Well, you guys were good friends, he said, Before whatever happened.

And "whatever happened" was just the kind of thing that simply does happen. The same way my contribution to the demise of N. and Hannah's relationship happened, and Michael Bobbie doesn't hold that against me.

What happened was I just had no motherfucking idea what I was doing, I said. It was that way all the way to Montreal: constant talk, not just my past mistakes and the labyrinth of our coming to know each other but all manner of things – parents, childhood, stories from his time in China, plenty of subjects to take us to Rue de Pins, which it delighted Michael to say with a ridiculous accent. The room was small, pretty, and, as promised, had one double bed.

Sorry, I said to Mike as our hostess shut the door behind her. I made the arrangements in kind of a rush.

No problem, he said, surprised but prepared to adapt.

We went out back and smoked a little joint, then I changed in the bathroom. When I came out Michael was there in an undershirt, and before I knew what I was saying exclaimed You're hot! (Which made him blush! He blushed and looked down, saying Oh, why thanks!). Sorry, I said, To sound so surprised it's just, you always wear such baggy clothes I didn't realize you had all that muscle under there (which explanation just deepened his pleased embarrassment). He quickly rubbed the creamy skin over his rippling biceps and gave a funny little hop, smiled at me then dove into the bathroom. We shared the bed pretty nicely, me by the wall, him on the outside, each of us with enough room to be comfortable without touching.

The tribute the next day was more difficult than I'd expected. Michael and I spent a pleasant afternoon meandering around the Plateau, smelling the dead leaves and ogling the old buildings. I told him about the first time I saw Irving since I was a toddler, that time in Grade Eleven when Bri and I went to Montreal over Christmas and house-sat for her aunt and uncle in Westmount. How surreal it was – one day Bri and I striding through the snowy streets in our combat boots, loving the grey sky and how tough and competent we felt; then the next, me paying the cabbie with money Mom had given me for that purpose outside Irving's tidy little house, patches of grass peeking through the windswept snow. The door opened by his friend and caretaker, nervous and pleased as she showed me into the dining room where Irving sat, white hair illuminated by the sun coming through the window behind him.

Beige, was my first thought. Beige, and the immediate impression of an old man. The table in front of him a mild disorder of papers, books, pill bottles, a pipe, a crumb-strewn cloth placemat over a tablecloth, which distressed me. The room was too warm, too used, strained by the immobility of its inhabitant. But he knew who I was and was glad I'd come. I played him songs on my guitar and showed him a poem of mine and one of Bri's, and he complimented each in its turn, spending time with the phrases he liked. Diana, the caregiver, took pictures. I asked how he met Leonard Cohen and he started saying something about Greece, and Diana looked at me and quietly informed me he was getting it all wrong. He asked me about Mom and not knowing what to say I said she was okay.

I hadn't thought much about that visit, so it felt sort of good to be ambling about with an amiable boy, one interested in people's stories. As I spoke I realized how the only time the strangeness of the whole visit really hit me was when I went to use Irving's bathroom, and Diana showed me down the light wood stairs and to the right. And turning on the light in the small, tiled bathroom, an old man's bathroom in an old man's basement with worn brown couches from the seventies and musty books, I thought, this could be the most familiar bathroom in the world to me. But it's not. Funny how I hadn't thought of that until now, I said to Michael, and he gave me this intent, sidelong look, rather pleased I thought.

And then we were getting dressed for the tribute – Michael and I grooming ourselves together in the little room, navigating our way to the Jewish Library. We found a good parking spot and followed some clusters of nicely-dressed people. There was a surprising diversity to the attendees gathering around the tables with Irving's books and following the red plush cordon into the auditorium, a high-ceilinged, angular sort of affair. Musia Schwartz, Irving's longtime friend, recognized me, though I had to struggle to remember who she was. She expressed her extreme pleasure that I had come and showed us to a seat in the middle of the second row, where we sat amidst the flowing crowd.

After a while, I saw Irving coming in through the same doors we had, walking with a cane and supported by a middle-aged man. They walked in without any fanfare; a few people gathered around them and Irving shuffled over to the first row of seats and sat down directly in front of me. The man with him sat down in front of Michael. I leaned forward to say hello to Irving but he didn't hear me, so I leaned back and shrugged at Michael.

The low hum of the room ceased as a well-dressed lady from the Library, who had planned the event, got onstage and welcomed us. Next, Musia got up and talked about coming to Canada after the Second World War and meeting Irving in an English class he was teaching for Holocaust survivors. When she sat down someone read Irving's beautiful poem "For Musia's Grandchildren," and I wondered what it was like for her to be sitting in this room as her young self danced lively and lovely before us. In front of me Irving leaned over periodically and asked the man with him what had been said.

Later Moses Znaimer, who Irving had taught at Herzelia High School in Montreal, took the stage and spoke of Irving's outrageousness, his passion as a teacher and as a lover of life. The first day of school, Znaimer said, This man comes into the classroom, picks up a piece of chalk, and writes the number ninety-nine point nine nine nine nine, and he keeps writing across the whole blackboard and onto the one on the other wall, fills both boards with nines. When he's finished he says to us, That is the percentage of people in this world who are philistines.

The audience laughed. I looked at Mike with a little grimace. On the big screen behind Znaimer's head a man appeared, saying nice things about Irving at an earlier birthday party; beneath him appeared a caption reading "Max Layton." I looked at Michael, and at the man in front of him. I looked back at the screen and, pointing to the grey-haired man in front of Michael whispered to him, I guess that's my brother.

Later on in the evening my brother Max took the stage. Irving Layton was a wonderful, devoted father, he began. I immediately thought of the book written by my other half-brother, David. His memoir, *Motion Sickness*, is essentially a chronicle of the horrors of life as Irving's child: his and Aviva's self-absorption, their rootlessness, the whole hedonistic experiment of the late sixties and early seventies that warped David's childhood. It was a good read, really, and I think won some kind of award, although Mom didn't like it because she said he got details wrong. She hates everything she feels emphasizes Irving's bastardly selfish side. Anyway Max talked about the pride Irving took in his children's accomplishments and activities, about Irving's pleasure in sharing his abundance of knowledge with them. My brother

David couldn't be here tonight, Max said, Although I know he wanted to be. I found myself full of pity for this grey-haired man in front of me. Irving seemed so alone in the world; only two of his four children were there, and only one he could pick out of a crowd. I wondered if Max had reconciled himself to his origins; wondered if I saw muted rage in his filial devotion.

Max moved on to illustrating Irving's love with selected poems about each of his children – each but me, that is. He started with "Maxie," a poem of mad fear about being supplanted by his son; and "Shakespeare," Irving admitting to a young son that his father will never write a greater poem than the Old Bard – but threatening that one of his "clan" might – eliciting literary giggles from the audience. Then he moved on to "Song for Naomi," which I had never read or heard. I loved it, the gentleness, the rhythm of it nothing like what I usually thought of as Irving's writing. After that I thought would come "The Annunciation," or "For Samantha Clara Layton," but it didn't come, and I suddenly doubted my paternity – it was like for a moment my name seemed an alias, a fake. But then, I thought, why should he read those? Irving fathered me, but I guess he wasn't my father, my Dad.

At the end of the affair Max was standing by the doors, and I figured I had better go introduce myself. When I visited Irving before he had told me I should meet my siblings, talked of it as if it was the most natural thing in the world. So I walked up, extended my hand and said Hi, I'm Samantha.

Max seemed surprised but pleased. You have hair just like your sister's, you know. Naomi has hair just like that.

Hm. I always thought I got my hair from my mother.

Max, 53, told me he lived in Caledon, and that he was a high school English teacher; he wrote his number and address on a little piece of paper and told me I should come by some time. I put it in my purse thinking I might, and made my way over to Irving, who was still seated and receiving a line of well-wishers. I slipped into the chair next to him and he turned to me with these delighted blue eyes – eyes that looked as though simply knowing they would be delighted – and said to me You're beautiful, who are you?

Ever the poet, I thought, Bacchanalian celebrant to the end. Your daughter, I said, and watched amazement spread across his face.

From Betty, he said, knowing he was wrong.

From Harriet, I told him and he said Samantha, yes, Samantha. He pulled me to him, his arm still surprisingly strong. His colossal wrist rested on my shoulder as a photographer snapped shots of us and other people waited in line to speak to him, eager and self-conscious. I realized that the wonderment in his eyes was not just that life-lust I'd heard so much about; it was the look of a man whose history is dwindling to forgotten photographs, found and lost, found and lost. He was marveling, surprised, his forgetting a sadness, a lightness across his face. Camera flashes almost continuous, and directions to lean in, smile, Irving smiling through it all, face brash and pugnacious yet; and Michael on the periphery, watching calmly. Then a woman standing before us saying, Hello Darling.

Hello, said Irving, bewildered.

I'm Anna, Anna. You remember darling we were married –.

She seemed slightly hysterical to me, this wide, crooning woman, and I couldn't help thinking This is who replaced my mother? She only stayed a moment, and shortly after I extricated myself and got outside with Michael.

As we walked to the car I was jabbering about the event, the people and whatever else; I got into old Mellow Yellow, leaned over to unlock the passenger side and started to cry. I don't know why, I said, apologizing. But I couldn't stop. In my head the lines, not for me, "My daughter, my lovely daughter"; the image of a father, all wonder at the passing of time, at watching his child growing. Irving on a summer's evening decades ago, in another era, scribbling down how his daughter is now taller than the tall grass by the water. Thought of the poems for me, a progression from the first knowledge of my existence to my first breath, and no farther. My being for him stunted at my two tiny fists and his head full of blessings.

Oh I don't know, said Michael, It was a lot. It seems pretty reasonable to me. Don't apologize, geez. You shouldn't be apologizing.

He was so unembarrassed by my tears – neither did he become overly familiar with me because of them. He just sat quietly, and when I stopped we headed back to the Plateau, and found a dark bistro, and ordered steak. I was feeling sort of raw, like I'd been through an ordeal, and it was a solid, secure thing to be there in the warm little circle of light cast by the low-hanging lamp with Michael Bobbie across from me. He is almost pretty, with his high cheekbones and full lips, but his voice is low, and his movements entirely unfeminine. Like a long, wise little boy, especially this one moment when he said something about how in high school he looked at everyone one day and saw how young and awkward they all were, and how he loved them so much better for it, for how hard they were trying. We're all caterpillars perpetually becoming butterflies, he said. It's cheesy, I know, but that's what I think sometimes.

I thought of how N. would snort and laugh if he heard a guy say that. But fuck, I thought, it's really kind of nice. It is the trying that makes us beautiful; I've thought that myself.

Back at the B&B we watched shitty TV for awhile, Michael making fun of everything. Then, with the lights off, we weren't so far from each other as we had been the night before. His body was hard and wary and I liked it. With his arm around me I fell asleep.

In the morning we lay quietly in the sunshine. On our backs, acutely conscious of each other, I listened to his breath coming harder, his effort to keep it steady. He's never been with anybody, never even kissed a girl – shocking, really, for a boy so good-looking, although I suppose he was scrawnier and geekier for most of high school, his hair in what he referred to as a Prince Charming Sweep. Be that as it may I wanted him, and I thought of N. and thought whatever, he's let me go, I don't owe him anything. After what might have been an hour, the hum between my hand and Michael's, between our two bodies, produced a sound, and that sound was Michael asking me, Can I... touch you... in places I wouldn't, normally?

What a question! It was so sweet, and serious, and almost childish that I had to giggle a little, although very gently and only as I said Yes and turned my face up to him. And touch he did, with hands less uncertain than I would have expected, and kissed me with a wonderful, knowing mouth; the bed was in shadow and the landlady knocking on the door before we realized how many hours we'd been there.

We gathered our things and emerged from our disheveled nook, the other guests in the dining room looking up with smiling faces. We drove the quiet streets until spying a place that looked good to have breakfast, a place with brick walls, wide unvarnished wood floors and an upright piano being played by a man in black leotard, green shorts, suspenders and a bowler hat. The waiters and waitresses were all dressed for Halloween: we were served by a weary young man with a five o'clock shadow, black and white striped shirt and black beret; a few tables over a tabby cat poured coffee. It seemed absurdly appropriate – our faux-Parisian waiter and the topsy-turvy atmosphere. The day was aeriform, hyperalive; my brain felt like a windy sky. We sat quietly, Michael rather grave, me delighting in the saloon-style piano, the good coffee, the jumble of colours and patterns in the shadowy room.

Our trip back to the city was quiet but relatively comfortable, although how little we really know each other was somehow more tangible. Obviously I was wondering what would happen, and if I would tell N. about it. Michael came by the apartment later – Bri and Flo had come to celebrate Halloween with Mom and me, light some candles and eat candy. It was a treat to see how much Mom liked him – she noticed the shine on me as soon as I walked in the door, and was none too sorry to hear the possibility of me transferring my affections to this young Michael Bobbie, polite and full of laughter. He only gave me a quick hug as he headed off, but that seemed in keeping with his character.

And here's the coda: today he found out he'd gotten the part in the play, and the preface to the play is "A Tall Man Executes a Jig," one of Irving's poems. Apparently the playwright is a big fan. Trippy, no?

So that, my friend, is that. I wish you'd been here for Thanksgiving, you would have met him – although, actually, I guess you probably have, since you know people in common. It was a fun night – a big buffet. I invited my new school friend Michelle (the girl N. was banging in the spring is Michelle's friend – connections, connections!); after people left, literally every boy there except Mike called me to ask who Michelle was and if she was single. Ty, I believe, has since been wooing her via email. She has a boyfriend, but that's no deterrent for Ty. Boyfriend shmoyfriend, he said to me.

Does she love him? You don't know? It's been what, a few months? Okay, well, I'll write her and if she writes back then we'll know what's what.

So the millennium is racing to a close, and the kids are thinking of love.

Sorry, I have been writing this for hours. I haven't written anything lately, no new songs, nothing, so I guess you have served as my creative outlet; thank you.

I'll write you if there's any deflowering to report. Write me because I miss you.

Love, Sam.

PART I:

In which the characters here contained,
who hope their stories will entertain,
understand that their lives are blessed
and yet experience much unrest.

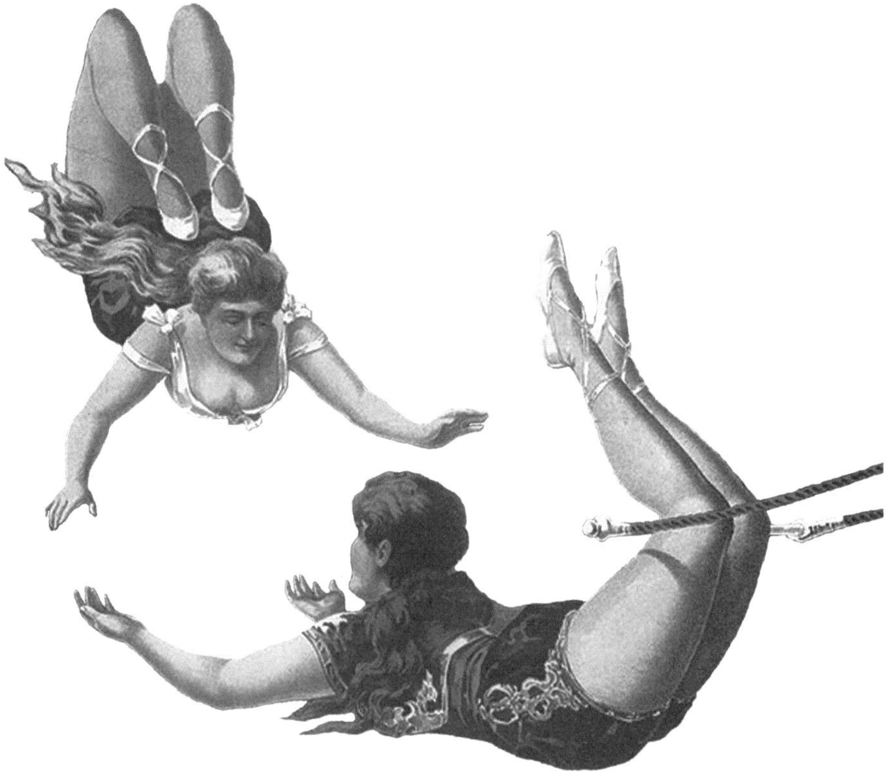

GENERATION BLUES (AND HAPPY BIRTHDAY!)
09/15/2001

Dear Eshe,

How have you fared in the first days of your twenty-first year, this strangest of weeks? How is your poor adopted city? It is crazy that for the rest of our lives, your birthday (and Bri's!) will be associated with the act that will prove the beginning of the end of the British-American Empire. The news coverage hasn't stopped and it's all appalling. I can only imagine what it's like down there. Patriotic speeches day and night? Orgiastic nation-lust in the dorms?

Yesterday I was standing in the kitchen after dinner, ranting bitterly as Mom washed dishes. This whole thing has made her sad, much sadder than I would have expected.

Why are you so angry? Mom asks me.

Why? The question is so fucking ludicrous, Eshe. Why? Because they brought this on themselves, that's what I told her. I knew I was being vicious, having a little adolescent moment, trying to say the most shocking thing. And of course Mom, poor Mom, was appalled.

How can you say that? She looked hurt that I could have even thought it, like she had maybe brought me up wrong that I could say such a thing. Those were innocent–

But Eshe I couldn't even let her finish – her outrage and compassion seemed so unreasonable, so poorly placed. I tried to explain that I didn't mean the people who died were guilty of anything, not all of them anyway, and obviously I'm not saying I think they deserved to die.

Mama, I tried to explain, This act was caused by other actions, it's not for no reason, and people are being told it's this incredible, inexplicable thing. But it's not inexplicable. It's perfectly fucking explicable.

I was nearly crying, spinning around on the linoleum in my socks, talking through my hair. All I could be was disgusted, and sad for everybody.

And Mom, so perplexed. My whole reaction to the "national tragedy" a mystery to her. I know she's rattled by my vengeance, the constant invective against everything that has obliterated "normal conversation." I can't help it. I am always simmering; at the dinner table or watching the news I boil into an unseemly rage, my frame nothing but a vessel for indignation. Every day there is some new horror we can do nothing about that will have immense repercussions; everything, down to the absurd conditions under which my mother works, is a product of avarice and stunted perception. What good is it to mourn New York's dead? I have to explain to my mother that if I'm mourning dead strangers, then I'm mourning all dead strangers equally.

But surely, Mom was saying, Surely you can understand why Americans are reacting the way they are –

– Like they're the only nation ever to get attacked by something? Three thousand people. Sure it's a lot of people, especially in the fucking States – but Mama, do you know how many deaths they're responsible for worldwide? Millions. Millions and millions of people dead, and for what? So the rich can further enrich themselves.

Oh, says Mom, So this too is rich people's fault.

(Poor mom, I can imagine her in a chorus of Jewish mothers, lined up since the time of Trotsky – *Oy vey iz mir*, my daughter is a Communist, now she'll never marry a nice doctor....)

Do you think, I asked her, It was a fucking accident they flew into the *World Trade Centre?*

Practical Mom: And the Pentagon.

The Pentagon, whatever, those aren't civilians. That's a fair target. The American military isn't some benign peacekeeping force, you know? The *rest* of the world knows America is fucking evil –

Excuse me, *evil* is a strong word. Who would you prefer to have running things? China, maybe? Germany, if, godforbid *they* had won the war? At least America has an idea of human rights, they have women's rights, I mean c'mon.

Sure they have the idea of human rights. Well, la dee-fuckin'-da. They can afford to have human rights. They just can't afford for other countries to have them. You think Haitians *want* to work for thirty-five cents an hour? No, you have to have dictators to do that. God, the hypocrisy of it, it's so *sinister*, don't you see? That's why I say evil – it's so premeditated, and it's all for money...

I was getting breathless, tripping up on myself, on generalities. But it seemed so obvious, so perfectly simple. Mom was pursing her lips over the dishwater like I was a fanatic.

Well, she said, I don't know where you get your information (she's always asking me where I get my information), but I think, she said (holding her hands out like I was a mad dog needing calming), I mean I'm sure America has its faults, but –

Faults? Mom, I told her, Read Noam Chomsky. Read anything, you'll like him, he teaches at MIT. Read about what the States has done in South and Central America and then talk to me about faults.

I had just finished Chomsky's *Turning the Tide*, so my brain was a splitscreen of headless Guatemalan babies and businessmen perusing figures, CIA fatcats sweating in the jungle, passing along their American wisdom.

And Eshe you know what Mom says to this, to this miasma of human misery and premeditated cruelty and blind stupidity? You know what she always says? So change things. It's up to your generation now. Every generation has its challenges. If you don't like how things are, make them better.

So I asked her How? But I didn't mean it because I don't think she has any idea. She only has her incredibly sweet but frustratingly absurd assertion that I, we, our group of brilliant friends now on the cusp of everything should somehow take the bull by the horns, as she would say, come into ourselves and change the world.

How should we do that? I asked her, too loudly. Conditions were way better for you guys and the world's no better, arguably it's worse. I knew I was exaggerating, yes yes feminism, gay rights, medical advances, whatever. Most hippies, I said, Were just nice middle-class kids who smoked pot and listened to Hendrix albums and had lotsa sex. That was a big deal, the sex –

I knew that would get her. She cocked her head, mildly offended: Yes, she said. Excuse me, it was a very big deal, the sexual revolution. And how about those nice Jewish kids who went down south and were *killed*, got *lynched* by some good ol' southern boys, trying to fight segregation. Young lawyers. People who felt they had to make a difference.

I conceded that point. In these conversations it seems to be Mom's habit to bring up these martyred white civil rights fighters. As though they were representative of what the Baby Boomers stood for, what the generation was capable of.

Mom was saying, Write letters. (It's always some personal take-action solution like that – as though I'm anyone to be writing letters about anything. And what do letters do?) You have all this passion, why don't you write an article for *The Star*, or hell, send something in to the *New York Times*, they need young voices.

Ah, moms. What is more timeless than a mother's tendency to grossly overestimate the importance of her children?

Mom, I said. There are undoubtedly better-qualified persons than myself to write for the *New York Times*. I dunno, it just all seems too big – whatsammater, something hurt you?

Mom had winced, was holding her side as she sometimes does. She sucked the air through her teeth and said, Oh, just got a little pain, you know… I'm very tired. It's been a long day, I think I need to sit down. She slowly pulled off her rubber gloves and laid them by the sink, shuffled to the couch.

Her little pains always seem a kind of remonstration. I should have done less talking, more dishes.

I asked her about her day.

Yeah, she said, You know, just the usual crap. It's trailer day, I had to fight with Cineplex to get more screens, Pat called me seventeen times, and she's doing ten things at once so she's all distracted on the phone… I had fifty-two emails waiting for me this morning and fourteen voicemail. Until eleven o'clock all I did was respond to email because I kept being interrupted by the phone. And it's all the managers from the theatres calling, where's my stuff, and I have to ask them the same questions, did you set up a promotion, did you fax the form… it's just so boring.

Oh Eshe, how I loathe my mother's job. I have always loathed my mother's job, even as a small child, but it's only gotten worse with time, become a festering vendetta. (I have Inigo Montoya fantasies of springing into Jerry Gorenfeld's office brandishing a sword, intoning You are killing my mother, prepare to die. I don't want to kill him of course; just for him to lose all his money and maybe a testicle). I hate her job far more than she ever could, you know how she is, she really cares about things. She also had a father who never took a sick day in his whole life; I think it gives her unreasonable expectations of how hard a person is supposed to work. Of course, his heart gave out at seventy.

And Baba called me three times, Mom was saying; I was on the phone with her in the middle of the day for almost an hour, you know, she just doesn't care. I tell her I'm busy, she keeps right on talking. She has no one to talk to, poor pathetic thing, she has no one; she needs someone to complain to – oh goddamnit.

Mom had torn a small hole in her pajama-pant leg. Uch, she said, bending down with a groan to inspect the piece of metal jutting out from the wooden trunk-cum-coffee table. It had seemed a cheap, rustic replacement for our old Art Shoppe coffee table, finally relinquished to the rust and grime of decades past. I still like the trunk, but it has turned a bit vicious. I shall try and whack the nails back in.

I have to go to bed, Mom said: her end-of-day declaration signaling the retreat to her room and her as-yet intact blond wood bedroom set. That set is inextricably linked in my mind with the snapping of tape measures, Mom at one end, me at the other, measuring dresser, highboy, night tables; and then in an empty room, empty master bedrooms in unknown apartments, our voices ringing against the bare walls as we speculate furniture arrangement, agree the set would or would not fit. The determining qualification for every new abode. It is a beautiful set, I would hate to see her part with it.

It's so solid and elegantly carved, reminds me of something Mom's beloved demimondaine would have had in their boudoirs. A present from Zaida shortly before he died, irreplaceable because he is gone, and because no one now can provide Mom with such luxuries.

Eshe, I am strung between wanting to make Mom not want these things and wanting to give her everything. It's all too hard, hearts on the Bernstein side are weak and I am afraid for her. Although I know life would be easier for her if she wanted less, it's too late for her to change. What baffles me is that when she was our age, she really thought her values were radically different from her parents. She thought she had rejected materialism, thought she knew the treachery of money. But now she wants to be living in the style she grew accustomed to growing up. She wants theatre tickets, vacations, pretty clothes. And why not? Those are nice things, everyone should be able to have them. But her life hasn't worked out that way, so I wish she could be content with less.

And can I be? What will I find myself wanting when I'm fifty-three? Can I envision a life I can have? And what will I do with this impossible need to describe everything, which you my dear friend indulge?

I may have to come down and visit you soon. Tell me when is good.

Love and more love,

Sam.

CH-CH-CH-CHANGES

10/03/2001

Dear Eshe,

you know me too well. Of course I've been seeing Michael, never able to stop myself from dialing the familiar numbers, and he, apparently, still compelled to pick up or call back. I had people here last night and he came, then bustled out the door at one o'clock sharp to catch the last train…. It is depressing. But how to avoid seeing each other? And then, too, that seems so silly. It wasn't an acrimonious breakup; how can you be mad at a person for not loving you? Or not loving you the same as they used to? Or for being, belatedly, terribly hurt and angry about your horrible duplicity?

He says it isn't the cheating. Mostly not, anyway. He says he had known all along that N. would still be part of the picture in the beginning, and had forgiven me over this past year – and he must have, to be so kind to me, or the human-shaped lump that was then passing for me. Last winter, when I tried to break up with him and he talked me out of it, we sort of agreed that at the end of term Michael would go tree planting, and I'd leave the city or something – godknows what I thought I was going to do. For no reason I can now give we somehow had this understanding that our relationship was simply to fade out. But then in the spring all I wanted was to be with him. His hours and hours "alone on the block," as he put it, of course did bring it all to his mind again, my wavering loyalty, even though he knew N. was gone, from the city as well as from my head. Michael said sometimes he'd be squatting beside a hole holding a sapling and find he'd just been staring a moment, then snap back to his work in a silent rage. And I can imagine his disgust, thinking of me in the city with a cleaned-up brain and new intentions for everything, eyes finally clear and full of the beauty of Michael Bobbie. I am a fucking idiot.

Also I guess his leaving was inevitable. The Two-Year Fear. The need for new things. When he was breaking up with me he talked about living different places, learning more languages. He reminded me of our first mushroom trip when I had a vision of battling a dragon which he slew; he said that since we met I had seemed unmoored and in pain, and that it seemed he could help. And now that I'm less fucked-up – my words, not his – we can part, both better equipped for our lives ahead. It's so strange, I never thought of myself like that, as needing help, but when he said that I realized how true it was. He was a blessing.

Well, I was his first; I guess I wasn't going to be his last.

On a happier note, I seem to have made a new friend. A lovely boy at the 'bucks, here from England. Funny, he's been at the store since January or so, but we hadn't talked much, rarely worked the same shifts. And, I guess, I wasn't really talking to anybody for like the first eight months I was there, until – I remember so clearly – one spring day it occurred to me as I was leaving to tell the people I'd been working with that it was nice working with them. I feel like that was the day the haze of the past year started to lift. Anyway as the weather got warmer, this boy Joe and I started smoking on the stairs together for longer. Leaving for the East Coast with Flo in May I said to him – or rather lilted, embarrassingly, an accidental imitation of his accent perhaps – that we'd go for a drink when I got back. A group of us did, a couple of times. One day in August, soon after Michael broke up with me, Joe was rollerblading around the city with Tyler Bratt, a chestnut-eyed kid recently initiated into the Barista trade. They wheeled into the store in the late afternoon: We've been all over the city, Joe said – and from behind his back sprung forward an arm extending sunflowers. For me.

Still we hadn't really spent much time together, but in the past month we've had some long day-shifts – how strange it is not to be in school! Sorry, but it just made me think. It has been an odd fall. Everyone I know headed back, Michael taking more courses now, and Florence too. And me donning my apron, arranging pastries, slurping tea and reading *Ghost World* on my smoke break. I'm sure it will get old but right now man I'm so fucking happy not to be in a cold sweat scouring some building for a room, dodging well-heeled kids who always seem to know where they're going; thrilled not to be crying into the phone trying to enroll in courses, or writing an essay on verb use in Seamus Heaney's *Sweeny Astray*. There's the guilt, of course: Mom and Baba worried I'll never go back, will squander my life over a coffee urn. Actually I don't think Mom thinks that, she just doesn't want me to waste too much time, "disadvantage" myself. There are moments I am surprised at myself. I mean, it just seemed the thing we'd do, go to university. I didn't even look into what school to go to, just thought U of T, it's the best, it's downtown, what could be more obvious. Fuck. It just seemed so horribly pointless. I guess it's my fault I can't see the big picture, that I let myself get rattled by how the professors talked to us – like doctors hired to cure us of our imbecility. I haven't gotten over the triumph of thanking that film prof for making my decision to leave school so easy, and the thought of his disgusted face as he collected my exam rekindles my joy at being free of it all.

But how is NYC, and how fareth your fellow Columbians? What are you reading these days? I'm so glad you are liking your writing class – will you send me something? And boys, are there boys?

Oh yes, boys – my new friend Joseph. On Rosh Hashanah we'd been chatting for a bit after work; I had to go home and change for supper with the family, but for some reason I felt like our conversation wasn't done, so I called him from home and we talked a while longer. On a whim I said, Could I drop by?

Of course, he said, his lilt encouraging, We'll have tea.

So down I went to Crawford St., a charming old low-rise where he and some other Brits he met when he first arrived in Toronto have a three-bedroom on the top floor. We sat on the tiny patio overlooking the street and I noticed how very nice he is to look at – watched him as he thought about fair Tyler Bratt, who has become his inseparable friend. I divined it might be more than that, watching Joe's face after he'd described to me a day they'd recently had together – sitting in a park, strumming a guitar, quipping Smiths lyrics, afternoon into evening, liquor in a bag. Loopy feelings of youth, hearts open and racing like boxcars through the night.

You are a little in love with him, I said; I think, if you don't mind me saying.

He smile-frowned and knitted his brows. Winced a slow O God, it's true. It's so fucking cliché.

Smiling into his hand, rubbing his head.

What can you do, I said? Cliché or no cliché we feel how we feel. And patterns have reasons.

He liked that, and so we talked for awhile about stereotypes and how clichés happen; and a little more about the torment of loving straight boys. I liked his quiet self-consciousness, he was graceful in it. He seemed shyly pleased to be able to speak about himself, and I felt I was being of service.

And since then we've hung out a lot – going to the park after shifts, or back to 420 Crawford for joints and tea, poetry at his kitchen table beneath a bunch of daisies. He reads a lot, and it's nice to have someone around who's not in school but who likes to think about words. We lie around listening to songs and wondering about the lyrics, where they came from, who has loved them. We went to Lava last Friday, the first time in who-knows-how-long that I've been out dancing. He's a great dancer – used to study I think – but there's no flash to him. Calloused hands, clothes often rumpled. The girls in the store all have crushes on him. I do not have a crush on him, exactly, I just seem to deeply enjoy having him in my line of vision. And I have to say that when he, Mike and I were hanging out one night after I closed the store, Mike's leaving was easier because I was still there with Joe.

So that's the news, my friend. Give my regards to Broadway and yes, I shall check schedules and see about coming down....

Huge love, Sam

NEW MILLENNIUM NYC

11/25/2001

Dear Eshe,

thanks again for putting us all up – it worked out so well that your roomie was out of town. It really is kind of a great room, despite its tininess. The way your bed is so high up you can sit in it and see out the window, Broadway up beyond Harlem and down to downtown. Truly it brought smoking in bed to new heights of pleasure. The only thing that could have made it better is if we could have opened the windows fully and leaned out. This is maybe a weird thing to say about a city that's just been attacked by "terrorists," but the whole trip sort of made me think about how things just get safer and blander by the minute, and it doesn't really do anyone all that much good. Like, I know I'm supposed to be happy that Giuliani has cleaned up New York City, but I would have liked to see Times Square before it was Disneyfied, or the Lower East Side the way it was in the '70s or '80s – after all, the junkies and artists living in tenements were part of what made New York iconic. Now the city is still being idolized for a grittiness it has mostly abolished.

Or take Greenwich Village. It's still cool but now it sort of feels like an Epcot Centre Cool People Pavilion, you know? It's too much what it is, without all of what made it that thing in the first place. Of course, I could just be feeling the fact that I was a tourist there, walking around trying to get the Greenwich Village vibe, looking for a certain thing and unable to find it because it's not my city. Whatever happens there has nothing to do with me, whatever scene exists there I don't have any right to by virtue of birth or circumstance. I would have to choose it very deliberately, decide, *I am the sort of person that must go to Greenwich Village.* But then I expect that most people who are part of that scene have come there because it is Greenwich Village, drawn by the same myth as me and other tourists but determined to be a part of it. And that's what is destroying its authenticity, yet also what maintains it as the thing I went there to see. It's hard – we don't want things to change and we don't want them to become replicas of themselves, which is the only way they can stay the same.

As though any of it could be the same. It's like when I was a kid and I'd try not to imagine things that I really wanted to happen, because I knew that once I'd imagined them, they'd never happen quite that way. So highways, the Brooklyn Bridge, Harlem, the New York subway can never be experienced again the way they were forty years ago; and staying up all night, and drugs, and jazz clubs, and stumbling from jazz clubs at dawn – who knows how we might have experienced these things if there had never been a Kerouac or a Neal Cassady? (And then again would they have done what they did had there been no Rimbaud, or whoever those starving Parisian absinthe-drinking people were?) But no dearly departed artist can stop us from going to the jazz club, chasing the ghosts of Bird and mad Mingus, and the crazy shake-ups of the late fifties. Or from having moments of complete happiness stoned on a stoop, smoking in jeans and leather jackets, or poised on benches in the decaying grandeur of a New York subway. Isn't it amazing – although New York City means all of what it does, has been sung, filmed, and written into something beyond itself, I can still experience a personal kind of joy there. Yet it's shaped by all my prior knowledge of it – there is a template, maybe, and the degree to which I'm happy is the degree to which my experiences fit my expectations. But then, did any boy ever buy himself a bunch of purple orchids just to walk around with them on a sunny afternoon, the way Joe did on our last day? Maybe, I don't care. To me, that day, it was perfect, and the picture of him on that classic stoop smiling at Bratt, orchids in his hand, is irreproachable.

All of Joe's pictures are great, pure New York iconic in glossy black and white. He even got a good one of me, in my leather jacket and wool hat, smiling up at him from the sidewalk. I wish he wasn't leaving – so soon, too, in less than a month. He doesn't want to go. This is the first place he's ever wanted to stay, the first place, he says, where he feels at home. He looked at me the other day – I'd been talking to Mom on the phone, and when we hung up I was a little upset – he placed a big, rough hand on the side of my head, and said, I wish I could bind you to me.

Though I have to say, sometimes I worry that mostly he wants to be here because of Bratt, and that once he gets home, gets wrapped into a new life again, he'll forget all about Toronto. Which reminds me, don't worry about having monopolized Bratt – you can't help chemistry, and anyway perhaps it's best that his heterosexuality is brazenly displayed, the better to quell impossible hopes. I did commiserate with Joe, though, and say you two had been prattling selfishly on! Poor thing, he feels things so deeply. He's a proper Romantic, should be letting his tears drop into a limpid pool somewhere, the breeze cooling his knotted, feverish brow. He almost makes an art form of suffering, yet it feels uncontrived.

And now Jamie has taken a shine to Joe, but Joe's far too messed up over Bratt to know much of anything else. You remember Jamie – he was two grades ahead of us, had long dark hair; he was in the play with me that Ariel directed. They're roommates in that dental office at College and Palmerston that Ariel turned into an apartment. Joe has come with me to visit them a few times after work, Jamie moving stacks of comic books, philosophy books off chairs in his bedroom, talking all the while; in the time it took Joe to get out five quiet words Jamie told us Barthes' life story while crafting a joint and tapping his leg in time to a Grandmaster Flash song. Pricked to even more vehement exertion than usual by the fascination of Joe's quiet body. I think Joe knows the effect he has on people, but has no ego about it – I suppose because his childhood was spent feeling so strange and miserable. No wonder he is dreading the return to his little Yorkshire town, though I'm sure he won't stay there long.

Last time Joe and I visited Flavour Hall, as Ariel and Jamie's place has been dubbed, they were telling us about being in Quebec for the IMF and World Bank protests. It's hard to believe that all that went down not four hours from here; it looked like a war zone. (Has it been in the American news?) They said it was amazing, the protesters looking out for one another, partying together at night – so many more than they expected. Maybe Seattle really did light a fire under people's asses. I feel a bit silly for not trying harder to go. Like a hippie who missed Woodstock or something. Of course, Mom would have been beside herself if I'd gone. (She was so worried about us coming to NYC. I was like, What, the terrorists are going to attack the same place twice?) How would I have explained to her what I was going to Quebec to do? What the purpose is of protesting these particular institutions, what we hope to accomplish?

Anyway here I am, glad beyond glad I have you to write to. Soon you'll be home for Christmas and we'll smoke in the car while you regale me with stories of crazy rich Americans.

Lots of love,
Sam.

P.S. Speaking of Americans, Mom is sending Bonnie and Thor gas masks for the whole family. Bonnie asked Mom to; they tried to buy the masks, but the store was all sold out: apparently Charlotte is a big potential target because it's like the banking capital of the States. I told Mom they should all wear the masks in the family Christmas card....

FIRST VISIONS OF TORONTO WINTER

12/15/2001

So it has finally snowed, my Dearest Joe. I wish you had seen it.

This afternoon was brain-matter grey, messy and brutally cold. Then around four o'clock, just as it was getting dark, giant dollops of snow started falling and suddenly a blizzard! And not just any blizzard, a thunderstorm blizzard. Ty was changing a headlight on Zippy at Canadian Tire, and it got so dark, snow collecting on our hair and jackets and then this smack of thunder, blue lightning through the snow-heavy clouds making the city uncanny, people bracing against the storm, cars valiantly chugging through. Especially great at Davenport and Yonge where the girls who work at salons are tottering in their heeled boots and the rich patrons pull their furs around them, peer bewildered through the fogged windows of their BMWs. And the Canadian Tire Christmas shoppers like stereotypes of Christmas shoppers dragging bags, children, carts through the mounting slush, concentrating, contained in their tasks.

I should tell you I've been awake for like twenty-five hours now. I opened the store (the whole eight hour shift, fuck me gently with a chainsaw, or with the raw humid cold of 5:15 this morning and the wretched vomit-smell of those cheese bagels you end up wanting so badly to eat three hours later); then after work Mom and I picked out our solstice tree; we needed some nuts and bolts to make it stand up so when Ty dropped by we went to get some and also to fix my light. After that it was up to Bri's for a little gathering – some people there I had known in high school and haven't seen for maybe two years. They already seem older, you can see so much more how they're going to be. I guess the same is true of me.

The ever-mysterious Ty sauntered in a little after I arrived, the room halting a moment to his salute and wary, eager grin, Michelle in her tall boots statuesque behind him. And then there was Bri looking happy, drunk and delightful, all dimples in pink cheeks and bare shoulders flitting through the room. I knew from the first the evening would be a flirtatious one. Later Bri wanted to play in the snow so she and Mike and I went to the schoolyard across the street and Bri took off like a terrier around and around and Mike running after her in his massive Chinese army coat. I was in five-inch boots so flopped down and made snow angels until Bri's face was shining familiar and pleased in the clear night above me. Then I got up, tackled Mike and was thrown back where I started.

We're still hanging out quite a bit, but he's quiet. I think he's sort of depressed. He's certainly not the happy-go-lucky, laughing guy I first met. He still has his goofy moments, they're written in his DNA I think, so nothing in the world could keep him from making weird noises when he drops something or imitating the cheesy voice-over guy in movie trailers (he does that really well); but sometimes I think he gets even goofier when he's unhappy. So I want to see him of course but when I do it's hard. I sit at his parents' kitchen table and watch him pet his cat. His cat hissed at me for the first time ever. Monty, his fat black walrus of a cat who is Mike's grouchy but sweet feline alter ego has always liked me fine but the other day I saw fangs. I think he can feel Mike's ambivalence toward me, or Mike's bad mood.

Anyway, it was a good first real day of winter. I smiled thinking how if you were here we'd sit in Zippy (the door is sticking again and I have to climb in from the passenger seat – in Mom's old grey sheepskin coat) and it would all be magical and twinkling and we'd listen to Lamb, Gorecki over and over for that crackling witchy voice ascending…. Too bad you can't really say things like "magical" anymore. That makes me think of a drawing Bri did years ago – it was a dryad speaking to a unicorn, saying No one believes in spirits and legends like us anymore.

I wanted you there for the weird mystical drift through dark silent streets – that wonderful isolated feeling of just floating, navigating through three unobstructed feet of windshield, hemmed in by snow. The world beyond frost-bound, completely still.

Now it's after five and I'm in flannel pajamas, I have Spike purring on my lap, orange tea and this as-yet bare, round little tree over by the window, a few high rise lights twinkling through the branches. I don't want to go to bed, I want to stay up writing to you. Earlier Mom was talking in her sleep but now she's stopped.

Thank you for the email. I'm very sorry to hear you didn't want to get out of bed. I am glad you listened to Bob Dylan with your dad. I don't think it's strange that nothing seems strange but you wish it did. Only a few weeks ago you were here talking about people from your "old life" like it was so far away, because it was, and now there you are. Writing to me of an earlier Joseph, your lines the thread sewing that shadow to your present self.

It seems so much of what we do is tell stories about ourselves. Sometimes it seems that we can't open our mouths without telling a story about ourselves and that no two people ever have a conversation about one subject, but that we are just sending stories about ourselves back and forth, and "getting along" is the degree to which the stories are understood.

    Maybe I should go to bed. The traffic on Yonge St. is already getting louder. I have to be back at the 'bucks in ten hours. But it's alright. I'm closing with Jesse and Katrina, we can holler about politics all night. I have to say, though, that consumerist and awful as the whole holiday season is, there's something heartwarming about the people and their packages, all hectic and full of plans. There's some illustration from a Dickens novel (or Disney movie thereof) in my head that superimposes itself on the shops, the slushy sidewalks and irritable people, and makes them sweet. In my gaslamp lit brain they're all going somewhere warm and full of good-smelling things to eat; there's children and sweaters and fireplaces. Stoned and swilling stolen gingerbread hot chocolate, I can almost imagine I wasn't in a Starbucks staring at a dizzying corporate mural and a wall of five hundred dollar espresso machines. Of course, if this were Dickensian London, we'd be choking on soot all day long and the snow would probably have fallen black.

    Awful that you're not up the street, won't just come through the door at 12:25 and start stacking chairs for me.

    Beautiful to think of you with my songs in your ears all the way to London. I'm glad now I got Ty and Jed to help me make that recording – I didn't know why I was doing it at the time, but now I do.

    xo

NEW RITUALS FOR OLD TRADITIONS
    12/ 21/2001

Here's to Light in the Darkness, Dear Joe.

    Thank you for your letter; I loved it – not that you are so unhappy, obviously, but how beautifully you write about it. Don't ever think you are taking advantage of our friendship by putting your brain into words; you do it rarely enough, Joseph, I feel privileged to be the one receiving them, and so glad that anything I say gives you solace. And why apologize for your so-called craziness? You are in fine company: centuries, maybe millennia of humans pacing, flinging themselves down and weeping, scrawling out their desperation to someone dear or no-one at all. It's fascinating. How could you explain to your mom why you are like this?

And why wouldn't you be smarting? That must have been awesome, your dad asking all day if you'd called Bratt back, meaning so well, only wanting to see you happy (and with parents there's always the guilt of making them unhappy by being unhappy); and meanwhile your grandfather there wanting to know if the Canadian girls are pretty, and if, for the life of you, you have a girlfriend yet.... Never mind. There will be a boy someday Joe, better than any Bratt I swear on the ghost of winter and all its clearest, sharpest nights.

I am glad, at least, to hear of your fine communion with the year's longest night; it's nice to imagine you on your roof, face to the sky. I think anyone who can be delighted, in the midst of torment, by two shooting stars will be alright.

As for me, Flo came by after dinner and we sort of celebrated the solstice with Mom. Lit candles and welcomed the four directions and the dark. Flo is good to have when you want to celebrate something, she puts herself into moments so thoroughly. Though I feel the solstice should be marked I always feel slightly ridiculous when trying to. I mean, I'd like to celebrate the day, have a feast, exchange gifts but it's the 25th everyone's got off and is busy preparing for. And any "ritual" we might do... what would we do, where would we have learned it from? Is it possible I could dance around a bonfire, bless the solstice with light and heat and music without feeling like I'm making a mere spectacle for myself? At what point does a thing we do become a tradition? This writing to you, for instance, already feels like one.

x

TONIGHT IN THIS GREAT METROPOLIS
12/ 29/ 2001

Dear Joe,
congratulations on getting the record store job even if it does pay worse than the 'bucks! It was lovely to hear from you. There's no need to call yourself a fucked-up runaway, however. I wouldn't have called you exactly that, even if the email you sent last week had said what I feared when I saw

it – your subject line did worry me – I hated to think of your heart getting harder, and was afraid, as I opened it, you might simply be saying goodbye. But wanting to write less – as in, not almost every night – because you don't want to be thinking about Toronto all the time isn't hardening your heart, or at least, it doesn't have to be. Though I love the phrase, I don't believe you are experiencing what you called "a flourishing indifference" – maybe just a new kind of contentment; adaptation, at least. So don't abase yourself, sweet Joe, for not being a good friend to me. We're just learning.

I've been down to the loft a few times to see Ty and Michelle. I had been neglecting them in the last weeks you were here! I am glad we got down to my beloved Eastern Avenue before you left; I think it's the dearest place in the city to me. It satisfies some deep-rooted desire I have for decaying old structures – at least what we consider old in this adolescent town. And, ridiculous as I know it is, when I'm there the impulse to write everything down feels less crazy; if nothing else, then just an expression of delight – like singing in the shower, snapping a photograph. I don't know if it's wrong or weak to give such significance to a stretch of chain-link fence, a steel door, a glossy expanse of wood floor imprinted with the ghostly footprints of departed working-men; when I was there earlier this week, an image of you and I reading Ginsberg sitting on the car in the vacant lot out back sprung on me like a premonition of all the poetry we shall read each other in times to come.

Ty and Mike came by tonight. They had been at my place an hour when I got there, having gotten entangled after work talking with Ariel who dropped by as I was cashing out. But the boys were fine, chatting with Mom when I came in. It's nice how she's adopted my friends, it brings us a little closer to having the large family she always wanted. A house full of people, *freilach*, as we would say in Yiddish – cheerful, boisterous, warm. Even though home is just yet another rented rectangle in the sky, it's nice to come in and see Mom relaxed and ruddy, sipping her tea and asking questions of my friends. Ty has spent so much time at our place, he's started calling her Mama B.

Mike is looking good and not at me. I don't know, I catch myself with deluded fantasies that he will fall in love with me all over again. This grown-up Mike with new subtleties and capabilities and confidence. Or so he seems. Perhaps it's viewing him from a distance, better able to assess what I have lost. But of course he is growing up, too. His jaw seems more defined, and the dimple in his chin was, this night, driving me to distraction.

They turned my room into a studio for the evening, tried to soundproof it by draping my duvet over the bedpost and putting blankets on the floor (after the downstairs neighbors rapped on their ceiling). They played for a good forty minutes, Ty on tarbuka, Mike on his oud. He's taken Ty seriously (he said I'll give you the instrument but you have to learn how to play it) and has a lesson every week up in Richmond Hill. It was lovely to watch them play together, so different but complementary: Ty cocky, driving the rhythm, self-effacing at just the right moments; Mike's eyes lit up and almost severe. He took some time to get going and then suddenly his wrist clicked into time and his fingers mastered the unmarked frets. Michael Bobbie and the oud suit each other. His long arms easily enfold the body's unwieldy bulge; the very strangeness of the instrument is appropriate. Mom says he is an Old Soul. Well, whatever he is I still find it sometimes unbearable that I cannot touch him. I look at his smooth neck and think, I used to have the immutable right to touch that neck.

Aw shit.

Anyway I wish you could have been here. I was sitting on pillows and a sleeping bag, candles lit, multi-coloured fairy lights on the mirror, blankets everywhere, joint-smoke a thick curl around my head, streetcars whining below; a thoroughly Torontonian decadence you would have loved. I glanced at the black-and-white photograph of you by a New York subway stuck into my mirror and wasn't sad. Joy instead that you are at all, and the thought of you was like a happy secret, a gift reminding me of something about myself. But I longed to see the enjoyment on your face as you appraised this scene, your never-ending lashes meeting in appreciation, a slow kiss for your world.

Mom poked her head in and had a toke, smiled approvingly at the music and at me. She loves these little gatherings, and I am glad, because so few things seem to make her really happy. She has been stressed as usual, and now with you gone I have nowhere to sleep but home, and see more closely her exhaustion. But she has had a few days off and we've spent some time, saw *Chicago*, watched *The Young and the Restless*. I have been eating too much and lying around, getting flabby. That's the holidays, I guess. Nice but hard. Mom loves to be very generous with gifts but then freaks out about having no money. We always take a drive through Forest Hill to see the lights on the old mansions (or the gaudy new horrors, as the case may be); and Mom delights in the decorations like a child but then says, Why are there so many rich people and why aren't I one?

Fucking Money, Joe, I don't understand. These colossal lots, homes large enough for four families and you can just imagine the four people that are probably in there, sitting in Holt Renfrew lounge clothes among expanses of marble and dark rooms full of expensive shit. And outside my mother in her 1987 Saab, creeping by with tears in her eyes for what she doesn't have. But she didn't choose to have it; she could have been rich, if that was what she wanted – could have been the wildcat, artsy wife of some decent neighborhood Jew. She could have married Luciano and moved to Rome, had a palazzo overlooking her beloved Spanish Steps. But no, she married Irving, had me, and got stuck in miserable Toronto, a city she always despised as cold, boring and lifeless. If only the whole poet's wife thing had worked out better; if only she could have been soup-cooking muse, homemaking debater forever, scribbling poems in her spare time. Maybe they'd have stayed in Niagara-on-the-Lake, had a garden, more kids. Though of course, from the time I was about fifteen she would have been a full-time caretaker to aged Irving. I wonder if she ever thought of that, as they were falling in love. Probably not; she always talks about how very vigorous he was. But he was in his late sixties when they met – he was more than twice her age. She talks about it like it didn't matter, but everything matters. Anyway, love of this man got her this life – although, you know what she often says, when speaking of the marriage and its consequences? Well, you had to be born.

I think she means to make me feels special, like a marvelous cosmic necessity, but I always just think, wonderful, so I'm the reason everything has worked out this way. Makes me think I'd better do something good with this life of mine. Though tonight all I want is for Michael to love me, for us to have a house and a couple of kids – that's something good, I suppose.

Happy New Year, if I don't speak to you before. And much love, Sam.

GUIDING AN OLD HIPPIE THROUGH MODERN LOVE (and other stories...)
01/15/2002

Hello Sweet Joe,

thanks again for calling on my birthday, it was so good to hear you. I can now legally drink in the States, woohoo! Mom gave me an album that she's been working on for months – a photographic retrospective of my life, with captions. Which made me cry, of course, partly because I felt bad that she'd been staying up late to get it finished – she's been working on it for months; I'd been wondering why her bedroom door was closed at night, and it's because she was in there, gold pen in hand surrounded by photographs of me as a child. But it's a lovely gift. The cover has that quote from Thoreau: "Go confidently in the direction of your dreams! Live the life you've imagined." Which sort of distressed me, in a way, because I know that's what Mom wants me to do, and I don't know if I can or should. Turn my eyes toward the writing dream, that is. Sometimes her encouragement feels like a spell, making me want things I shouldn't. And then comes the guilt, for I am questioning the value of what my mother prizes most in this world.

In the New York park on our last day, when I said Moments are illuminated like particles of dust in the attics of our minds – and when asked told you I had written it, you laughed and said you liked that I quoted myself. You sounded so decisive; I remember thinking then it might be possible.

But then immediately it gets too big, and I know myself absurd for thinking I could be a writer. Isn't it funny that my mom is more of a willing idealist than her kid? She believes so passionately in the value of art, in "getting your voice heard." Ah, the generational divide – evident also in Mom's response to finding Mike at our place on New Year's morning.... Where he'd ended up after a party that was much as you'd expect: Led Zep, Flo getting stoned to Janice; Bratt happy drunk, slopping over to me with his pained smile groaning Where's Joe?, his hands on my shoulders. Meandering off in his undershirt to start a mural on his bedroom wall with Z (looks like a naked girl, big surprise). Mike fell asleep on the couch right after midnight. I woke him up when I was leaving at about two, and he seemed not to know what to do with himself, and I guess I was just like, I can take you home, you can come to my place.... And then he was just there, I don't think we even said a word in the car. Through the freezing night good little Zippy purring along all warm and blue, with Mike next to me there in his big green coat and it seemed so natural. Quiet and together in the orange lights of the 1980s panel display, strange in our own ways and even with each other, but knowing and easy with how we're strange. Then we got home and he was in my bed and I felt triumphant that he was there. But sad because he seemed sad, or worse than sad, defeated. Reaching for me but weary, his long limbs seeming tired out reaching for me and it was so good to be tangled up in them again but I felt like I was taking something from him. But he'd asked to be there, he'd wanted to come, so what can I say? I wondered if he'd stay the night and he did. Too late, he was too tired, the bed was so familiar. Falling asleep next to him I had the weirdest feeling that we were two siblings who'd had a fight but were forced to sleep in the same bed. The intimacy, the sometimes stifling yet beautiful intimacy of two heads beside each other; the sense that tomorrow the person belonging to that still, quiet head will provoke you and everything will be irritation, complication and discord, yet now in the warm darkness that person is your companion, someone you can trust with the vulnerability of your unconsciousness.

In the morning he beat a hasty retreat and I spent the day shuffling around the apartment, watching *Breakfast at Tiffany's* with Mom and hoping for snow. At first she didn't say anything about Mike being here (and taking off), just gave me that eyebrow-raised *what is this bullshit anyway* look, before we settled onto the couch to eat Cadbury's Fingers and call Cat! Cat! with Audrey Hepburn and George Peppard in the alley in the rain.

Later in the evening Mom could no longer help herself. So she starts, I'm just curious, but –

Oh lord, Mama I don't know what I'm doing.

Well, okay, you don't have to talk about it, but I just wonder because I thought you were broken up and then I see him here –

We are broken up.

Okay, so then why –

I don't know, it was New Year's. Nobody likes to go home alone on New Year's if they can help it.

Well I understand that, but if it's supposed to be over between the two of you don't you think it confuses the issue a bit for him to be coming around? I understand you want to be friends, you've explained to me that you're not going to stop hanging out with him and whatever, but there's got to be some kind of line. I mean honey, how can you tell if you're "going out" or not. ("Going out" in a goofy voice to connote her sense that this term is idiocy.)

Yes, it confuses the issue. The issue is confused. He's confused. I'm sort of confused but, I don't know. I probably should have just taken him home.

Well, she says, all mama lion instinct, What did he want to come here for anyway? He *says he doesn't love you* anymore (this not said to be hurtful, though it is because that's truly what he said; Mom drawls says he doesn't love you with disbelieving scorn, dredging *love* up from the depths of her chest to display for the world the pettiness, the uselessness of Mike's understanding of this concept love if he can't love me); your relationship is done, so what does he want to come here for?

I don't know, Mama, out of habit?

Well! Habit! I don't think that's –

Not habit, not habit, but, it's familiar, he seemed sad, he was sitting alone on the couch and fell asleep, he's been all quiet lately. I don't know, I guess he just thought it would be nice.

It would be nice. Well honey, it just seems to me that if someone, a man, is coming around a lot, and he's staying over, and you're the person he goes to when he's sad or whatever, then, by your definition anyway, that's going out!

Well, sort of, but we're not. I mean, it's not, there has been no agreement that we are dating, we're not together.

No agreement. So that's how you define dating? I altogether don't understand your use of that term. Dating, when I was a young woman, meant a man came to your door, he came and got you, he took you somewhere, a movie, dinner, theatre, and then he brought you home. And if you liked him you saw him again. You say dating and it means the guy comes over and hangs out in your living room. There's no, I don't know, there's no delineation, it seems to me, that you're "going out" as you call it.

Well, the delineation is, if you're sleeping with one person on a regular basis you're going out.

So that's it? It's just sex.

Well, sex and the acknowledgment that you like each other. I mean, Mike and I were just one day like, So, I guess we're going out now.

And now you're not.

And now we're not.

Well, whatever you say honey, I just think in my day –

In your day? In your day people were just having sex with everyone as I understand it.

Well, that really depended, I mean some people were like that, for sure. It was free love and all of that. But even the Living Theater, like I told you, Rodd, when we were together he said I could be with whoever I wanted but it would change things. And that was the most anarchist of the anarchist. The Living Theater I mean, they were not exactly playing by conventional rules. They were crazy, man.

Okay, so Rodd said sleeping with other guys would change shit that's one thing. But I mean was it really all I'll pick you up at seven o'clock and we'll go see a show? That's so, like, 1950s. I mean did you ever get in a serious relationship that way? There's Irving, that sure wasn't like that, there was that dude, whatsisname that followed you home in his car.

Oh yes Michael Schwartz she says, a twinkle in her eye at the memory. Who saw me in my little silver convertible and followed me home. From tennis lessons at the North Y. Me, in a little tennis outfit, can you imagine? I guess I was trying to please my father.

By the end of it I'd convinced Mom that there was no reason for dating to mean being taken somewhere by someone and having it paid for. A funny thing to have to convince an old hippie of, don't you think? She's all for women's lib and all that in one sense, you know, she's very proud of what women of her generation have accomplished, down with mean old patriarchy, etc. She was a businesswoman in the '80s after all. But at the same time she still thinks a woman ought to wear makeup, that not shaving your armpits is gross (unless you're French), and that men should pick you up for dates.

As for our generation and coupling, the night before Eshe left to go back to school we parked Zippy in front of her house, talked about husbands and sunny kitchens and how it would be. My husband would sit shirtless on the counter and read the newspaper to me while I cooked eggs; with Eshe it would be the other way around, and she declined the infants (though I think she'll change her mind).

God, I said, We have a surprising amount of faith in marriage given the current divorce rate.

Bah, the pendulum has to swing back, she said.

In our hats and mittens, sealed in by the frost I thought what a tradition this has become with us. Lighting the last smoke of the evening, "You Can't Always Get What You Want" came on the radio and we howled along to that and when it ended I said, When we're forty we'll be doing the same thing, sitting in the car like this, except I'll be like Fuck this is my one cigarette of the week, better enjoy it.

And Eshe said, We'll go home to our husbands all stoned, tee hee. And he'll find it cute and give you a good shagging and you'll wake up and have tea in a sunny kitchen and get breakfast for the kids.

That sounds like bliss, I said.

What conventional dreams, hey, my sweet Joe?

And you shall live next door and on summer afternoons we'll shell peas on the stoop listening to Bob Dylan or Muddy Waters, watching our kids play out in the road.

xo.

I miss you.

WHATEVER HAPPENED TO GYPSY JO?

01/27/2002

Dear Joe.

Mom came home from L.A. today, another grueling trip done. I was supposed to go out dancing but decided to stay in and hang out with Mama. As I brought her tea, she started again with how I should go back to school, how I'll be "handicapping" myself by not going. And I found myself suddenly raging that I'm not that kind of person, I don't want those things you get by going that route, I don't want that pampered student life. Memories of U of T lectures, the cold sleepiness of Convocation Hall at ten a.m., rich kids in MEC gear clutching their coffee cups, embroiled in their important little worlds. All it made me want to do was come in my pajamas, chain-smoke at the break in my shedding sheepskin coat while staring down the chattering girls in those stretchy black pants everyone was wearing; I'd darkly contemplate their straightened, highlighted hair and how much time it must have taken them. Wondering about what seemed to me their incomprehensibly simple lives, about what it must be like to live in residence, go out to pubs at night, do your make-up in the bathroom with a bunch of other girls, call your parents once a week. People whose parents load their cars with their children's stuff and drive it to the dorms, pay the rent. Girls with hard-working Daddies who adore them.

But of course all this is very silly; I was just as much embroiled in my own little world and the pleasure I took in showing up gruff and scruffy to my classes only confirms it.

In any case I conceded to Mom that someday I'll have to go back, once I've decided what kind of program I need to do. Some kind of social work, I suppose, since the only thing I'm really good at other than writing is listening. I can't be a shrink because I can't go through med school and I won't be a psychologist and charge a hundred dollars an hour. Mom just kept sounding kind of skeptical, like I was missing the point, and all I could see were the massive lecture halls and the shit jobs one gets with a B.A., so finally I told Mom I want to see the good my work is doing. I don't want to work for a corporation and bust my ass to make it money and I don't want my accomplishment at the end of a day to be getting a trailer on some movie and I don't fucking care how good I am at it or how many perks the corporation gives me, I don't want it. It will never make me happy.

Which I guess is a good thing to know. But I feel awful now, because it's obviously not the thing to tell Mom, and especially not the night she comes home from a business trip.

Well, she said, There's lots of other things I would rather have done too. I would have liked to be an interior decorator – I wanted to go to OCAD, your grandfather said No. I used to think about teaching – but I didn't, I got a job in the industry because I could, and, I suppose, in a misguided attempt to please your grandfather. I was good at it. I didn't love it, but I was good at it, and I took satisfaction from it. Which did please him. He liked that I could be tough, and that I had brains. But I left to go back to school. Then I met your father. After that ended I had to earn a living and this is what I knew.

I pressed my knuckles into her tired feet, thinking of her life, and was flooded with a mixture of rage and admiration so potent I got kind of dizzy.

How well she had adapted, and what she had consented to adapt to. I silently damned my grandfather for his tyranny over my mother's life – thought of Baba telling me how, during my parents' divorce, Zaida had made Irving a proposal: no child support, no visitation. He was a genius with numbers, your grandfather, Baba has said on multiple occasions; He calculated right there, quick, how much your father would pay until you were eighteen, and said to him, You keep that money, and just stay away. And your father did.

I always thought Irving was just a cheap cad, and maybe he was, but maybe, it occurred to me tonight, it wasn't Zaida's place to be bargaining with my father about how I would grow up. I never even considered the story of the divorce from Irving's point of view until I was eighteen – that was the first time I ever had a good solid cry about the whole father mother family thing. Mom and I were moving to Madison (our one brief, failed stint of Annex living, in a tiny apartment that flooded, owned by landlords with rage problems); I was standing on a chair taking down Irving's books from the top of the bookshelf and leafing through them. I opened *The Gucci Bag* which I know Mom hates because Irving wrote it during their divorce and it's mostly a scathing diatribe against the bourgeoisie. The book's title refers to a bag my grandfather bought for Irving which, during the divorce, he nailed to the front door of his and Mom's house in Niagara-on-the-Lake like a manifesto. In the book was a letter from Irving to my Mom, I can't remember now all what it said – his disappointments, and how Mom had changed or perhaps just what she'd been all along. The dedication to the book is FOR GYPSY JO, A wonderful flower child I used to know.

And that just got me. That and the desperation I felt in the belligerence of the poems, the bitterness of the letter.

So why am I writing this now? I guess because when Mom gets on me about school and all that, and when I see how viciously her work preys on her, I think of that dedication and wonder what happened. She would say, of course, that she still is a flower child, that those lines were written in anger. That when they were married Irving used to call her bourgeois because she liked clean sheets always and restaurants sometimes, that he used to fling the word at her in argument, notwithstanding his perfect enjoyment of his bourgeois acquaintances' fine Scotch. We would have these arguments, Mom told me once, As he sunned his belly in Florida when we were staying at your grandparents' apartment.

And I'm sure that's all true. But I can't help, seditiously, sympathizing with Irving a little. Because that dedication makes me wonder if maybe Mom's values were never quite clear to her. It's like somehow her parents' ideas and expectations became a film across her vision of her own life. How awful of Irving to fling her overbearing parents in her face – calling her false when she was only confused. And really, as if being a "flower child" after the '60s was really contradicted by liking to eat in nice restaurants, or wanting a comfortable home. (Michael and I once had a prolonged and heated debate over whether it was possible to be a rich hippie – I said yes, he insisted no. I still say it depends on one's definition of "hippie"….) If only Irving had been kinder, or more sane. Which I suppose often comes to the same thing.

He carried that damn bag until he nailed it to his own door, so what does that say about him?

Anyway. Reading your email I was thinking that your mom sounds like my mom, talking about using your gifts, not wasting your life and all that. And it's infuriating but also frightening, because how much can we fuck around waiting for something we believe to be purpose until we've been floating too long, have forgotten our way back to the pier and been condemned to tread water forever?

I had lunch with my grandmother today. I like to see her when Mom's out of town – I know she's even lonelier when she can't talk to Mom for an hour a day and anyway it's kind of interesting to see her alone. She was talking about decisions and my mother's lack of good ones, and said to my surprise how Mom had been caught between two things – between a father who wanted to send her to finishing school in Switzerland and wanting to be a hippie. Why did she want to be a hippie? my grandmother asked me.

So I told her, Oh lots of reasons, I'm sure. I mean for one thing she saw these parents who had money but didn't seem happy, and she said that's not how I want to be. And you know, she never felt… fully understood and all that… she wanted to take jazz piano and Zaida said classical or nothing… and you had your career and your amazing gowns and jewels, and I think it sort of… *alienated* Mom a bit.

It was strange to be telling my grandmother how I think her daughter sees her upbringing, but Baba was listening. So I said, I don't think Mom ever really thought it out. I mean, if you want to say I renounce materialism, well fine, but then you've got to think how do I want to live and what kind of job will I hold and what will my life be?

And Baba says, Well I don't think your mother was thinking like you are.

I felt like I should have wanted to defend Mom, say well, she was figuring things out her own way, and things were different back then, but instead I was happy that Baba had said what she did. As though she could see how my aimlessness is different than my mother's was. It was good to be sitting there in The Coffee Mill in Yorkville where we've been going forever (a brown and beige place run by well-preserved Hungarian women), but speaking for the first time like two adults that have something in common. The careless familiarity you get in conversations with family was absent; there was mutual interest and respect. And she's terribly critical and pessimistic – no bias toward me, like Mom has – so her approbation is satisfying. Maybe I think she can identify people who have a shot at, you know, making it, having done it herself. (I told you she was an opera singer, right? She was successful, but would have been more famous if she'd been less crazy – she turned down singing at The Met, and La Scala… she could never stand to be away from my grandfather, and was always terrified about her health.) It's like if what I'm thinking about makes some sense to her, if something about the way I'm seeing the world and what I'm extrapolating from it is meaningful to her, then maybe something I would write could be good, maybe I have something to offer.

I think I will make my bed just to get into it. x

TIRED OF MYSELF, TIRED OF THIS TOWN
02/14/2002

Happy Valentine's Day, Dearest Eshe;

Congratulations on being crowned Miss Dance Marathon 2002!! You fucking blow my mind, you really do. For all my griping, when was the last time I went out of my way to perform an act toward the betterment of society? And you just helped organize – and danced for twenty-eight hours in – this awesome charity thing which, being you, you hadn't even mentioned until days before it happened….

Your email cheered me up and depressed me in one paragraph. It is heartening to think that our sense of expectancy might be for something good, that this suspended animation is momentary, and can give way to something useful. I have memorized your line: "The exciting thing about limbo is that heaven could be anything." I love that even this sincerest of metaphors reveals your obsession with *Seventh Heaven*…

But your description of the poetry movement your class is studying – a movement that just came together out of a shared set of values, or questions, because the right people happened to be hanging out in the right coffee shops – these things always make me feel sorry for myself (and, hence, disgusted…). Stumbling into the magical coffee shop that's germinating the next poetry movement seems about as likely as finding a unicorn on which to ride there. But, re-reading your email just now made me a little hopeful: just to know you are in the world, looking at it with your kind eyes. This, dear Eshe, is our coffee shop, our university classroom, our bookstore – the one I believe in, even on nights I have nothing useful to say.

Like this one. I did a stupid thing, a few nights ago. I slept with Bratt. You know how these things happen – I was at 420 and when I went to leave something was wrong with Zippy so Bratt said stay over and I thought why not. We drank some vodka on his futon by the window, the ridiculous New Year's mural still half-finished on the opposite wall, his long lean body next to me but why not is the betrayal of Joe, obviously, who would be so hurt to know I did what he couldn't… and I did mumble something about him before that old "what he doesn't know" instinct kicked in and I thought it shouldn't matter. It was fun at the time – he is like a charming cipher, I see what you mean (I hope you don't mind I borrowed him) – but the next day I felt horribly guilty. What they don't know always matters. I came home to an email from him with the subject heading "Got to Keep Moving… On" – so of course freaked out thinking that somehow he knew. But he did not; it's just that writing is making him miserable, because he wants to be here.

And I had no comfort to offer him; couldn't think of anything I had to offer him at all. It has been that kind of week, careening back and forth – terrified of dying, wanting to die, wanting to write, wanting never to think of writing again. But when I think of you and I on the carpet with the atlas open between us, our fingers tracing where our bodies will soon go, then invariably I am happy.

THINGS I'M NOT AND THINGS I DO
02/25/2002

Dear Eshe,
other than emails to you and sometimes Joe I'm not really writing, so

thanks for giving me a reason to sit at the keyboard; I'll try and do something with this brain of mine, which is of late rather having its way with me. Joe did write to me recently, and said he found the writing helpful. It looks like he's going to work in a hostel in the Lakes. It makes sense – he'd be somewhere pretty for the summer, making food, being pleasant to travelers.

So, yes. I wrote on Valentines' Day and neglected to mention Michael Bobbie. We are (against Mom's advice) still hanging out. Sexlessly, confusedly, insatiably. Watching the news. We've been miserably enjoying the announcement – five months into the "first war of the 21st century" – that the reason we went to war is no longer the reason we're at war. So have you heard, Mike said yesterday, Finding Bin Laden has been proclaimed "not a primary war aim?" We watched Rumsfeld explaining to the press why there must be more military spending, world domination schemes visible like cartoon gears through his Frankenstein head.

Weren't we supposed to be the first generation to grow up without war? Michael asked gesticulating 2D Rummy; Cold War finally over, the U.S. on top, keeping global peace with its enlightened sense of justice…?

It is all enormously incomprehensible – Michael and politics. I threw Mike a surprise birthday party (he turned twenty-four) which turned out better than I'd expected. It was a little haphazard – we walked into the apartment and only Ariel was there, talking to my mom. So I was like, Oh, look who's here! Then other people started showing up in bunches and we had a delightful time. I was worried about how Mike would like it considering how glum and quiet he's been, but he seemed happy, talking and laughing almost like his old self. We got him good and riled up about the bulldozed runway at Gaza airport, and we toasted with a joint the fifty-two soldiers who refused to serve in the Occupied Territories (To the conscientious objectors: if everyone were like you there'd be no more war.) Also we toasted good old Chrétien, who's never been a better politician than now, when his political career is done. He might decriminalize weed before he goes! People stayed late, Jamie talking semiotics and Flo giving backrubs and me hollering to my heart's content about Bush and Enron. We had a laugh over Mike's birthday present: Rummy's announcement that the propaganda office has been shut down (a gorgeous piece of propaganda…). Mom walked around rosy-cheeked, smiling at our loud, fast talk saying I wish I had a video camera. Look at you all, look at you all, we should be recording this.

Indeed, my friend, we should be recording everything.

HUNTER S. SAID IT TRUE
03/13/2002

Dear Joe,

never come here. Or rather, come here for two days then leave. What you'd like is driving in from the airport and seeing the city rise glowing out of the desert like a neon paean to the gods of money. What you'd hate is everything else. You might get a brief kick out of the gaudy grandeur of it, the absurdity of taking taxis across the street (we did that today, Mom had to be at a meeting at Bellagio and we got a cab in front of our hotel – the roads are so wide and the hotel grounds so big that walking would literally have taken twenty minutes). But really, two days is all you need.

This trip was a mistake. The first time I was here, on the road trip with Bri, Flo and Mike, it was just like a massive anthropological expedition and I loved it (which is why, when Mom proposed this trip, I happily assented). But then we'd been driving for three weeks, hadn't been in a city since Santa Fe. The sudden enormity of Vegas was mind-blowing, and it was hilarious pulling onto the strip in dusty mismatched clothes, gawking at the flashing everything. Somehow that first time gambling seemed like so much fun – high on oxygen pumping quarters into slots at the Holiday Inn with greasy-haired men and desperate, vicious little grandmas was so iconic, I didn't want to leave. I was fascinated by the girls bringing drinks on trays, by what it's like to do that job, and then after to go back to a desert-fringe apartment and roll down stockings, light a cigarette, unhook garters. But this time I can't see anything but the sheer, exploitative absurdity of the place. When I passed through as one member of a little pod zooming gaping through the States, all was art. This time though I'm in the belly of the beast, waiting eagerly to be shat out and regain my rightful identity.

I am trying to hide my disgust from Mom, as this is, horribly, my birthday present, and she's doing everything she can to make it fun. I don't think she can understand, though, that as hellish as this place seems to her, to me it's twice as heinous. She keeps saying, Now you see what I have to deal with, now you see why I hate it so much. Every year, ShoWest, same bullshit. And it's true that now I can see firsthand what she contends with year after year. She's been coming here for this conference since before I was born. At first I could find it funny – the film people rushing around in black talking on cellphones, totally oblivious to how mass-produced they look. Like a Robert Altman satire of film people. Someone stopped Mom and asked her, Is this a convention of undertakers? Mom said No, why? The person said, Well it's just that everyone's in black and looks kind of anxious.

But it's quickly gone from funny to terrifying to plain old sad. Mom running from meeting to meeting, exhausted, talking about promotions and tie-ins and free advertising. I'd like to say As though she gives a fuck, but she does. I want her to do her job with the minimum effort required – to do it knowing the industry's wastefulness and total lack of respect for human life, and investing herself accordingly. (DreamWorks doesn't even pay the interest on the credit card debt she has to rack up for these trips.) But she can't, she has to go all in, all the while lamenting every way in which the business is not what it was when her father was the President of Famous Players.

All I can see is greedy fuckers killing my mother, an Armani-suited army under the DreamWorks standard – a little boy whimsically fishing off a crescent moon – pillaging her life.

Today as she was changing between meetings she told me that she did quit once out of principle. *This is Cinerama* had come out in the early fifties, and had some great technology that made you feel like you were in the movie; Ambassador Film, who Mom worked for in the seventies, re-released it and sold it like the technology was still really hype. Mom had a fantastic marketing plan so it opened really well. She went to see it that first weekend to gauge audience reaction, and found herself sitting behind a family that obviously didn't have much money; she could tell that going to the movies was a big outing for them. And when it was over they were so disappointed, because they had been expecting this great movie event and it was crap. Mom said she felt terrible, like she'd been responsible for conning these people. So she quit. Went to Spain, fell in love with a Jewish Flamenco dancer named Antonio and had a passionate affair in Madrid. But that was then, when she was in her twenties, and this is now, and now she can't quit.

On the first day we were here, before the convention kicked in, Mom rented a red Mustang convertible and we drove out to the desert. Of course there is something terribly classic and exciting about driving through the desert in a red convertible, dry wind whipping at you, whizzing by cacti and dusty desert plants. We got out at one point where there was an almost-road that seemed to lead nowhere; I walked, pulled forward by the vacant space. I left my shoes behind. I passed a dead tree, low and gnarled, branches bleached by sun, a skeleton returning to dust. Also being consumed nearby were a pair of shorts, some beer bottles and a formerly white sofa giving itself over to decay, all lying in a sandy heap by the side of the road. Then before me the low hills, dreamy taupe tinted pink by the late-afternoon sun, and above them a pale turquoise horizon that grew stronger with altitude, into a blue so blue it was almost shrill, a high-frequency hum. The cars on the highway behind me were dwarfed, silent and surreal. In that parched silence the smell and taste of the Marley I lit was preternaturally vivid, the sound of the match loud as a flare. I took out my little book and for a moment the whole world was my hands and the glaring cream-coloured pages.

As I walked back I began to hear a sound. It was Mom yelling Samantha, Samantha. I walked faster and called back I'm here, I'm coming. When I saw her she was red as a bordello bedcover, puffing and gasping and furious. I had been gone, she said, a long time. (It could not have been more than fifteen minutes.) She had started walking the road I had taken and had seen the abandoned couch and things and become hysterical. Who knows, she said, What kind of crazies live out here? She had been marching toward me through the sand and dust believing I had been abducted by convict survivalist Nevada wackos. You can't just walk off like that she said. How do I know where you've gone or when you might come back?

I apologized, still bewildered that what had seemed so natural – a few minutes' exploration – had caused this disaster. I alluded to the fact that she would not be able to know my exact whereabouts when I'm in Europe with Eshe, and suggested to her that it would be better for her health if she didn't allow herself to get so worked up without a reasonable cause, but she wasn't having any of it. It was my duty to be more considerate; and indeed, it was.

Yesterday Mom sent me for a spa treatment at the hotel. It was very nice of course, to be wrapped in thick white terrycloth, massaged, facialed. Nice middle-aged Russian lady efficient with my pores, wielding dental-looking utensils. But extremely strange too, to be flipping through some celebrity rag alongside sleek twenty- and thirty-somethings sitting self-possessed and silent, critically perusing the spa's Cosmo magazines. Next to them I felt like the ten-year-old in a party dress awkwardly sipping her Shirley Temple at a table full of well-groomed adults. Padding back to our room in spa-loaned flip-flops, I thought of Cleopatra, princesses through the ages, servants attending their preparations. It was like I had fulfilled some feminine obligation, some ancient tradition of bathing and oiling and scenting. To be presented. To a prince? In any case to be shown, appreciated in my femininity, and that part was nice. But, I thought, so unlike that; so unlike any communal bathing in any culture where it might be good to clean oneself in the company of other women, to attend to bodily things… I don't know. In the spa women were ranged against the walls of the waiting room like patients, all privately engaged in the ministrations necessary to more smoothly inhabit the colossal money-consuming emporiums downstairs. Everything money and business and spending and getting; shoes poised on glass shelves, hideous handbags for hundreds or thousands of dollars, souvenir decks of cards, Christmas ornaments, booze and commemoratory booze glasses; positioned within all this, the spa felt cold as the clack of heels on tile, the smell of creams and oils making an odd little zone of over-rich cleanness, like a scented candle in a roomful of alcohol and smoke.

Unfortunately I tried to explain this to Mom. She had come back to take a half-hour nap before dinner. She asked me how the spa was and I said it was lovely. Lying on the grey satin bedspread, staring at the hotel dresser's faux-cherrywood sheen and the big TV I did feel very indulged: I was smooth, clean, smelled good, there was nothing I had to do. But I had that feeling a body gets when traveling, the vaguely disorienting sensation of using strange facilities, hotel towels, those smooth-rolling hotel drawers. You feel not quite yourself. Though I knew this was sort of myself, too; I remembered other times with Mom in hotels, that strange but luxuriant feeling of being away, but I wasn't sure I fully liked it. I felt aimless, pampered but antsy. So foolishly I told her that I liked the spa, but that I wouldn't want to get used to that kind of thing. I felt out of place, I said, And I kind of preferred it that way.

And do you know what she did, Joe? She started to cry. Exhausted body in bra and underwear, pretty china beads around her neck, her face crumpled and she sobbed.

I apologized, trying to explain that it had been very enjoyable, but just that I felt I wasn't exactly like the other people there. I didn't mean to be ungrateful, it was a wonderful present, my shoulders were like jelly, etc. But she just kept on crying.

You just seem to have such low expectations, she said. You don't want… anything nice… So vituperative… and I don't understand. . .

I tried to explain I do want nice things, but there are other things, other kinds of luxuries. I wished she could see, but couldn't explain, the life I imagine, in which spas or expensive clothes are simply absent. I was angry at myself for making her cry, and angry at her for crying; her sadness seemed so unnecessary, I couldn't understand it – her desire for me to like the spa like her father's wish for her to go to finishing school in Switzerland (which she refused to do), or his presents of fantastically expensive clothes (which she often loathed). But still I am denying her the pleasure of giving me certain things, a certain type of life.

Finally she looked at me, and rather than the forgiving look I was hoping for there was a dark sorrow, an exhaustion so complete it frightened me.

And as though uttering a prophesy, she said, I'm just afraid you're going to have a very hard life. Then she crawled into her bed.

Horribly, the thought I couldn't keep down as she pulled the hotel blanket up to her ears like a forlorn child was, Look who's talking.

But I so wish that I'd kept my stupid mouth shut. Why isn't it good enough to just quietly know what we don't want, and live accordingly?

See you soon, sweet Joe. xo

CAREER COUNSELING

03/18/2002

Dear Eshe,

I've never been so happy to walk through the doors of this apartment as I was last Friday. I gleefully smoked a joint while organizing my room, making everything neat and pretty. Then I moved on to the living room, throwing out old newspapers, putting *New York Times* Magazines into the bathroom where we'll actually read them, lining up the candles on the coffee table, vacuuming; then I got into bed and read a few pages of *Mind and Brain For Beginners*.

On Saturday we saw Baba, went to the Four Seasons for dinner because it's next door and Baba didn't want to have to go anywhere. I think it's insane to go to the Studio Café for convenience while Mom struggles to pay bills, but such is my family.

So Mom recounted our trip, Baba groaning and *oy vey iz mir*-ing in all the appropriate spots. Truly, nothing unites my family like a tale of woe. If you're sick, or suffering at the hands of someone else's stupidity, you're sure to have an interested ear.

And then Baba asked me, as she does every now and again, Can't you do your mother's job?

Now, I know Baba feels guilty sometimes about her, let's say, parental lapses of judgment. Sometimes they are justified by, I was a diva, I didn't know from children. Wagner, Puccini, that I knew. Cooking? Looking after a household? Listen, I played the violin. What did my parents know? Poor, immigrant people, what did they know from a child like me? I did my homework, I'd cry it wasn't good enough. But my Daddy knew I had a talent, and he loved me the best for that talent. I told you, I was a *little*, little girl and I saw the violin in the window and I had to have it. My parents didn't have any money, what money? But he saved up, a penny here, a penny there, and he got it for me. Then I went to lessons with bundles of wash under my arm, can you imagine? A little girl, going on the streetcar with her violin and a bundle of laundry that Mom would have done for my teacher? But I was excused, you see? It was, Mary doesn't wash dishes, Mary has to practice violin. Rose will wash the dishes. And my poor sister, she was so good, she never complained. And your grandfather. If he was on a plane and saw kids sitting near him, he'd ask to be moved to a different seat. I mean he liked children, you know, they're very cute and you make funny faces like that (and she'll stick her curled tongue out of her ruby-red lips) but when they start crying and fussing, feh. Nosir, *that* wasn't for him.

But sometimes she'll seem genuinely sorry about not being a better mother. Poor Harriet, she'll say. We used to put her on the balcony if she wouldn't stop crying. Poor little thing. We were stupid. And she was the cutest baby you ever saw. After she stopped being bald.

And Mom will chime in with, Yeah, when I was an infant, if they couldn't get me to shut up they'd put me out on the balcony, the snow would pile up on my blanket. I guess eventually I'd get too cold to cry. Whatever. They were very busy, you know, with their careers.

What, I asked once, to clarify, You'd just like put her in a stroller or something on the balcony until she stopped crying?

And Baba nodded sheepishly, like a little kid standing in a puddle of pee she couldn't keep in, hoping you might think it's funny.

Then sometimes she just becomes blinded with torment over what she sees as her daughter's ruined life. At those moments I think I become a little less real to her; I am just some person who might be able to make her daughter's life easier. What are you? Your mother is sick. Her life is too hard. Help her.

And though there are times I feel something whirring violently in my chest like a motor propelling me out of the churning orbit called Bernstein, there are times when I think she's right: I should do anything, give up anything to help Mom, and I hate myself for resisting.

But having just come back from Vegas, branded with the sight of Mom sweating in an enormous convention room full of two thousand distributors, exhibitors, and vendors working their ways around the different stalls, toting their little loot bags, getting their pictures taken with a life-size replica of Scooby Doo, enthusing over Sony's theme-park-worthy Spiderman display, I was in no mood for taking on my mother's business. My revulsion an itchy scab over the wound of knowing that my mother actually has to *do this shit*, and care about it

So, in response to Baba's suggestion that I do my mother's job, I just said, I don't think I'm qualified. And chewed my gorgeous steak, stared at the blown glass vases on their immaculate white shelves above the rich old Jewish couple my mother never wanted to be until maybe now.

And Mom said, You're more qualified than most of the people in the business. Nobody has film sense anymore, the business is all these stupid twelve-year-olds with their chirpy voices, their heads up their asses – they wouldn't know a good picture if it dropped – well you saw them; there's no creativity, no artistry brought to it anymore. The whole business has changed. If Father were here –

Oh, Baba said, as she is wont, *Well*, if your Father were here, none of this would be like this. He was a king of a man; he could move mountains. I mean he would just not allow the film business to be taken over by these –

Yes, said Mom, If Father had lived he would have taken Famous in a whole other direction. That generation is all dying off, you know, all the old guys, it's very sad. And you – her dark eyes fixing my face – have more film sense in your pinky finger than these kids will get in their lifetimes.

Maybe so, I said, But in that case I guess the companies aren't looking for film sense, they're looking for vicious little twelve-year-olds who'll be happy to work sixty hours a week for peanuts and speak good Corporatese.

Shortly after that we moved on to discussing the pain in Baba's groin, and I was left to nod sympathetically and hope dinner ended before the conversation turned Mom into a small jagged thing defending itself against the devouring world.

This morning I worked, happy to wrap the apron around me and get back to being the server rather than the served. Although sometimes I think if I see one more casually well-dressed thirty-something couple window shopping, pushing one of those all-terrain-vehicle strollers and sipping their decaf Americanos in the College St. sunshine, I'm gonna start ranting like the scary homeless lady with the moles. You know the one I mean, she sits on the steps of the church at Palmerston, and spat on the guy I was opening with one morning. She has some lucid things to say about capitalism and foreign policy and all that, and she likes to say them to the pretty stroller-pushing couples. I've seen her screaming at them at like seven a.m., You don't even care! That's right, walk away, walk away, but it's on your heads!

I'd like to tell her she's got the right idea, but I'm afraid she'll spit on me too. After all, there's not much on the yuppies' heads that isn't on mine.

It was so good to get your email, to think of traipsing Parisian streets with you nine weeks from now. It shall indeed be a Grand Tour – we will wring our full measure of meaning out of this middle-class rite of passage! Isn't it wild to think that our grandparents, at our age, could hardly dream of doing such a thing?

Write soon...

DREAMS

04/10/2002

Dear Eshe,

tonight I came in and thought I'd drop a line to Joe, though he's not writing much lately – ensconced in his new life at the hostel in the Lakes, where the Internet costs money and everyone spends their time off work riding bikes around the countryside. I hadn't written in a while, and was percolating some description of something.... which I thought might be pleasant to pour out before writing you the unhappy news contained below.

Mom won't be meeting me in Rome after I leave England, so we have to rearrange where and when we are meeting.

She had a blood clot. She will not be able to fly in May, and can't get time off work later in the summer. So now one of her greatest dreams, to show me her favorite city, has become another impossibility. Last week her right arm started to swell, and she complained that it was heavy-feeling and hard to lift. It was hard to tell at first, because of her weight and also because her right arm has been bigger than the left ever since the anaphylaxis. She went to her doctor who said keep an eye on it. It got redder and more swollen so Mom went back to the doctor, who got her an appointment to see a vascular surgeon. Mom drove herself to Sunnybrook where the vascular surgeon took an ultrasound and said she had no clot. Maybe something was pinched, he didn't know. Later that day she went to her dermatologist with whom she happened to have an appointment. Dr. Ricky (that wise old lady my whole family has seen for decades) told Mom to have another ultrasound. So the next day Mom went down to Western and had another ultrasound and she knew something was wrong when the technician kept running over and over the same spot, then called in the doctor.

I'll be damned, he said, You have a blood clot in your arm. That's when Mom called me, and then they whisked her off to fast-track emergency and stuck needles with blood thinners into her stomach. I rushed over to Western and with immense gratitude discovered that Mom's dear friend Francezska was there with her (a better surrogate aunt I could not ask for). All the doctors who saw Mom were very confused as to why she had a blood clot, since she is young and swims four times a week. Nonetheless they said she was very lucky. If she had waited any longer she would have lost her arm, or worse, the clot could have traveled to her brain and killed her.

She has been giving herself injections of blood thinners into her stomach, and she has to go to the hospital every day to have her blood checked. She almost passes out with queasiness when she injects herself, but I can't help her because I'd pass out for sure. I can barely stand to stand beside her with my eyes closed and my hand on her shoulder while she does it. Pathetic, hey? What would I do if I had to give her the needle? Well I guess I just would. Like the time when I was ten and a bee stung her foot so she asked me to take out the stinger.

The really horrible thing is that in a way I was relieved at first that she wasn't going. I think I was dreading listening to her tales of passion and adventure from when she was my age and knowing I'll never match them; feared the irritation I'd feel at the look of approval in her eyes if men holler as I walk past. I've always wondered at that – how a self-proclaimed feminist can value looks, and men's appreciation of them, so highly. You see what a beautiful girl you are, she'll proudly say when she catches a man staring my way. I wonder if I get as much notice as she did with her made-up Persian eyes and pouty lips. I doubt it. I've always felt a little inadequate looking at pictures of her and Baba in their youths. Baba in her publicity shots with her brilliant smile and 1940s film star hairline; Mom in the professional photographs my grandparents had taken of her when she was nineteen: porcelain face tilted slightly downward, dark eyes raised to the camera, the guarded, knowing, slightly devilish look she's giving the photographer is something I could never replicate.

Now I'm just sad; my impatience for the youngwildandfree part of the trip feels monstrous. The printouts from Mom's hours and hours of internet research on ancient countryside villas and day-trip possibilities lie on the kitchen table, a tragic pile of pleasure denied her. Baba thinks I shouldn't still be going but Mom insists I should. To me, it simultaneously seems selfish not to give the trip up, and absurd that I should. She will be fine; there's nothing my staying could do. Except not leave her alone.

Though ambivalent before, now that she's not going I realize how lovely it would have been to see her happy, walking down a fragrant Italian street, on vacation. I keep envisioning her excitement, her delighted generosity in pretty little Roman shops and gorgeous restaurants, which I would no doubt have silently pooh-poohed as extravagant folly she couldn't afford. But I'd have loved it, too, putting on makeup and going out to dinner, half-embarrassed half-proud of her perfectly pronounced but limited Italian.

She's afraid now that she will die without showing me Rome, and so am I. Oh Eshe I know that almost everybody on the miserable planet has it worse than us and I don't mean to complain but holy fucking christ couldn't life just give my mother one lousy fucking break already? It's been thirteen years since my grandfather died and it seems that every year since then things have only gotten harder. While I was putting on my pajamas tonight, the kettle started to whistle; I ran to the kitchen and poured my tea. From Mom's room I heard a high-pitched hum, and I thought Oh no, I've woken her up, and she's... imitating the kettle? But the sound grew louder, higher, punctuated by gasps, a panicked, muffled sleep-scream. I rushed in and sat on the bed, put my hands on her shoulders. Still crying she opened her eyes and, terrified, said Things were falling on me. There was this woman, this horrible woman. I don't know if it was me or someone else. But there was this ceiling fixture and pieces started to fall and things kept falling on me and there was no safe place. I'm so tired, she said, her face crumpled and hot beneath the tossed sheets.

Well, go back to sleep, I said in what I hoped was a soothing voice. Hoping I wasn't betraying my impatience, my desire to get back to my tea, this keyboard, my rightful role as daughter. Why isn't it rewarding to look after parents the way it is to take care of friends? Ever since the diverticulitis and anaphylactic shock three years ago, I have felt this responsibility toward Mom – or a new sense of how she needs me – and I wish I could carry it gladly.

Find some pretty visions, I told her, Fill your head with something nice and drift back off... rubbing her back, hoping resentment wasn't seeping through my fingers.

Mmmm, Mom said, There are no pretty visions anymore. No pretty visions. Because I don't get to go anywhere nice, or see anything pretty. Pretty is gone.

Well, I said, pushing down a sea of desperation like bile, I like to think of a sunny kitchen and some kids, you, friends, people around noshing out of the fridge.... Hoping this vision of the future would calm her, that this beautiful life I hold in my head like a scared child holds on to her mother's leg could offer some succor, some hope for better days to come.

That's for you, she said. You have them. I'll find something to do with my head.

So I stroked her hair for awhile and now here I am, at the keyboard. All I can think of is Mom's exhausted, terrified face, and how tomorrow morning she'll haul her body out of bed and drag it to the toilet, the kitchen, the car, the office.

It's five in the morning and I should go to sleep. Lately I've been compulsively listening to that Radiohead song that goes *after years of waiting nothing came. Does your life flash before your eyes…* Tonight on my way home from work I played the song over and over, trying to let it sink in that I'll never be able to save my mother, never write the books I think I'll write, never understand or do for the world the way I'd like to. Instead of the acceptance I hoped I'd find, I hit a horrified panic, hauled on my smoke trying not to start crying hysterically while I was driving, afraid I'd crash and die and really be responsible for killing what's left of my family.

And I don't want to go to bed because in every unoccupied moment I feel raw, exposed, like trying to sleep with no blanket and I don't have the energy to try and feel otherwise. I want to be sediment settling in a riverbed. It's strange to me that these words as they appear before me are my thoughts.

Farewell for now my oldest, dearest friend; I'll be seeing you soon.

NOTE FROM ACROSS THE POND
05/15/2002

Holy Crap Eshe The Trip is Beginning.

I am here at the hostel where Joe is working, an old converted farm in the Lake District. It is very good, and a little strange, to see Joe again. He picked me up from the minuscule train station in Doncaster, a half-hour's drive from his parents' house. The car, named William, is a Vauxhall Nova – a teensy blue two-door hatchback from 1989. Joe is extremely pleased with himself – he has never been a good driver (so bad that in his lessons, when he didn't know what to do, he'd just throw his hands in the air above the steering wheel) but has suddenly discovered that he loves it.

As soon as I got into the car, something about Joe made more sense to me than ever before, and at the same time became more strange. There he was beside me, on the same side as usual but for the first time with his eyes fixed on the road ahead, and so competent with this retro-looking gearshift, in his lived-in car with its tapes and maps, cigarettes rolled and waiting in the change-holder. And suddenly the boy I've known mostly in three rooms, mine, his, and Starbucks – four if you count the dancefloor at Lava – is careening with haphazard familiarity around roundabouts, navigating lorries and turn-offs, smoking and saying little, as is his habit, but staring without wonder at a vista of which I know nothing. I worried that I might not understand this Joe, that it had been a mistake to think we could simply pick up where we'd left off; then I worried at my lack of faith.

We stayed with his parents for two days in Maltby, in the tiny house where Joe grew up. The first night we didn't have much to say to each other. I saw the cramped desk in the living room from which he wrote me his tortured nocturnal emails before he moved to the hostel. I saw the roof outside his bedroom window where he's climbed out to smoke since he was sixteen, and his brother's shoebox of a room, football trophies lined up on the white shelves. I tried to remind myself that it was only the first night, that it might take a couple of days to re-acquaint ourselves with one another. But it's hard to say how our relationship will pan out in the long run. Joe has had so many close friends, so many people he spent all his time with until moving on to the next place where he spends all his time with someone else, and maybe writes letters for a while until that drops off and all ties are cut.

And we had so little time together – three months, really, that's all. It was like falling in love, those three months. Not that sex ever came into it; but the sight of him pleased me the way a lover does. Even showing up to open the store and seeing the note he left when he closed would give me a shiver of pleasure to know that five hours ago he was standing where I was standing, thinking of me. But you know how he fascinates people – it's something in the way he moves, the rueful-mischievous smile displaying the pointed canines and inward-turned eye teeth, the slightly tragic cast of his eyebrows; the brief glances of complete shining happiness he bestows upon his friends. There is something – it's like life is coursing through him very tangibly, violent and unpredictable, close to the surface of its slight frame. This is why to watch him wake up is such a beautiful thing. The endless golden-brown lashes open and he looks at you from those deep-set brown eyes; they close again, and the lashes flutter very slowly, for all the world like a butterfly keeping its balance. And while he struggles toward consciousness his skinny body is coursing, pulsing with life: his head is hot, cheeks ruddy, a storm of consciousness whirling in his brain like a motor; he thrashes around in the sheets half asleep, moaning occasionally, laughing at himself a little, until finally sitting up decisively and flailing an arm toward his puffer. Then the spray and a long, hollow-sounding inhalation of Ventolin. Afterwards he rolls a smoke and drags on it with deep satisfaction.

We slept in his brother's old bed because it is bigger than Joe's, but we kept to our separate sides. Used to be in the mornings we'd end up in the middle, bodies fused; in our half-sleep I'd feel him clutch my hand and fling it around his middle and that is how we'd greet the day. But I've always felt it best to wait for him to invite me near. He is a reticent creature, easily imposed upon by too much love. And everyone loves him too much, they can't help it. It is one of the reasons he first liked me, I think, that I could see that and keep my distance.

The next day we drove to the slag heap that Joe used to sit on in his youth, and I pictured him scrawny and tormented, smoking with his two good friends on this pile of mine refuse reclaimed by vegetation, the countryside rolling away grey and green behind them. And now here we are in the Lakes. It is the quaint England, Romantic England, the England for vacationers. Stucco and Tudor buildings, flowers everywhere, merry shopkeepers. When I arrived I stayed in bed for three days. I don't know what was the matter with me – I conceived an absurd horror of going down to meet Joe's co-workers. I stayed in bed and he brought me food, the soups he'd made in the morning, thick slices of bread. I felt like an invalid and couldn't help it. I couldn't get out of bed. I was stupid, ugly, useless. What does Joe need me for now, I wondered. I realized I had to be happy that he was no longer living only to come back to Toronto, heart rent over Bratt, over the fact of his Bratt-rent heart. I had to be happy he was here in these pristine hills, flying up and down them on a borrowed mountain bike, getting on with the next phase of his life. He was up by 6:30 every morning, up and out before I knew he was gone. I would wake up hours later, my first thoughts bringing me to Mom alone in the apartment, Mom in the hospital with her swollen arm, Mom dying. Saying goodbye to Mom as she slipped away, closed her eyes a final time. I couldn't get out of bed. I read the *Portable Beat Reader* I gave Joe for Christmas and wondered why there are no bands of what Mom would call "great talent" anymore, no groups of artists to embody our age; no writers who make their readers fall in love with them or their friends. Then I wondered at the Beats' misogyny and messianic drama, and how I had never realized. I read a David Lodge book and started *The Road to Wigan Pier*. I thought about writing and decided against it, stared at the strange life proceeding outside the open window. Slept. Joe worked, came in and talked with me awhile, went back to work.

Finally I ventured out (had to call Mom), and of course everyone's lovely – they assumed I'd been jet lagged and were pleased I was up. I remembered that Michael has noticed how, when I'm feeling bad about something to do with Mom, I hate myself more; which was helpful, because I saw I probably am not the nightmare I sometimes think myself. Although, I never do feel fully comfortable with these hale-and-hearty types, these world-travelers so active and independent. Joe fits in here because he fits in everywhere; it's a good job for the time being, but I doubt he'll stay long. Tomorrow we go to Wales to see Dave, the boy Joe may be in love with now. They met at a training course a month ago. Dave has never been with a boy before, never even thought about it, but he saw Joe and that was that. So tomorrow we drive to the Brecon Beacons. I am excited for the journey but nervous about meeting the boy. Afraid, ignominiously, that he will supplant me in Joe's heart, render me superfluous. But I'm excited to see Wales again – when Mom and I came to Britain when I was eight, Wales was my favorite place. The gnarled little trees all seemed like Merlin would pop out from behind them. I wonder if it will still seem that way.

In breathless anticipation of your arrival,
Sam.

WATER

05/18/2002

Dearest Eshe,

we have just returned from the Brecon Beacons, four hours rattling through the hyper-green, sheep-dotted hills separated by hedges or stone walls, me smoking hash and mulling over my excellent, sleepless night (more on that later). Our first day there we went to a waterfall nearby the hostel, where Dave played as a child. It was on a winding river with short, crooked trees that Mom would say were witchy-looking. They were witchy-looking, the roots like a solid extension of the river cascading into the earth, branches a raised chalice. I used to conjure places like this as a kid, I told Joe, as I bent to caress a tiny white flower shimmering in the phosphorescent grass.

I had never seen any waterfall but the Niagara Falls, which Mom took me to as a child. I had never been to a waterfall small enough to walk around in, to come close to. I stood by the falls fingering the bright green, earth-smelling moss, breathing in the water's breath. When I turned around Joe was watching me from the middle of the river. He was very still, his face shining toward me. I felt immensely beautiful, ageless as the river, as the stones, full and knowing as the corded, twisted trees. Though I was some Canadian girl in a foreign river with her Adidas shoes and bell-bottomed jeans, I did not feel out of place. Crystallized in Joe's gaze in that moment I felt the perfection of my body young and strong, most of all was conscious of my eyes, green as the moss and bearing witness to everything, witnessed by Joe. Come over here, he mouthed. I skipped across, settled beside him. He was indescribably dear to me, the boy sharing this flat rock; I submerged my hand in the river, enveloped myself in wonder to contain the joy of being near him.

Lives irrevocably entwined, Joseph said, quoting the letter I wrote for his plane ride home from Toronto. Hearing those words filled my mind the way air fills lungs after a long dive.

His uncanny face was brimming with love. I've been watching you for the last fifteen minutes, he said. How did I find you?

When Dave came ambling back through the woods he found us looking at each other, eyes creating our own little falls down our cheeks. Alright? he queried. And we could only nod, crying and laughing.

It is strange to write about it all now, truthfully. But never mind, it is done and I'm glad.

As to the sleepless night… there was a lovely, slightly alcoholic boy at Dave's hostel named Jim; we all went to the beach the next day, Jim very competent with the hash between his long drummer's fingers in the backseat of the swerving car, letting himself be rolled toward me. And then exploring the caves beneath the cliff as Joe and Dave chased each other beneath the vast, windy sky…

Oh dear, it seems someone is waiting for the computer.

The rest in person! I am going to practice my new song….

Have a great flight, see you at King's Cross!

Yours, in all anticipation, Sam.

A CITY FULL OF OTHER PEOPLE'S HISTORY
05/31/2002

Maman;

I'm sorry you haven't been receiving the emails – you are on the list, and also I sent one just to you two days ago. So I apologize for having worried you. But was that last email of yours necessary? If you are trying to make sure that I keep you and your health in mind, rest assured that you are. You don't need to drive the point home by alluding to your imminent... what, hospitalization? incapacitation? I am already unable to sleep most nights, tormented with images of your death. I hate to be so blunt, but I don't think I can take another email like that. I'm glad people have my contact information in case of emergencies, but if you could possibly minimize the alarmist nature of your emails, my psyche and I would appreciate it.

Now that that's out of the way…. Yesterday we climbed the steps of the Sacre Couer in the freezing wind and rain, saw grey Paris laid out before us and were slightly moved by its oldness and hugeness, marched over to L'Arc de Triomphe dodging four lanes of frenzied Parisian drivers to stand beneath it, traipsed to the Eiffel Tower and then collapsed into bed. Eshe lent me Jonathan Safran Foer's book so I read that until Eshe woke up and we drank what was left of our wine and watched the narrow little street below as she told me the dirt on all the old Northern people I never hear about any more.

I don't know, Mama, I'd like to be able to tell you that I feel all the cool old ghosts of this city, that I'm captivated by its beauty. But somehow, even eating bread and cheese in a park, I feel like I'm only doing it because that's what you do in Paris. It wasn't such good cheese, and it cost like six euros. We were just two more backpacking girls on a patch of Parisian grass trying to figure out which part of the city might yield up some of this legendary French Romance. Feh. This is a city for rich people. Or maybe I'm just not looking in the right places and don't know from cheese. I'm sure if you were here you'd find the city's three last authentic poets in a corner of the Latin Quarter, and they'd smoke you hash while discussing Voltaire in the courtyard of their 18th Century apartment, or take you to hear jazz somewhere tourists never go.

But I can't find those guys. We did stumble upon a quiet little nargila bar run by a couple of Algerians. We had a nice chat with them, drinking mint tea and smoking apricot tobacco in the almost-empty café. That was my favorite moment here: reclining on a low cushioned bench, the misted window-pane framing the dark street in which a drunken couple giggled past, arms flung around one another; our host poured more tea, said, Ah, Paris. It is a city for lovers.

Though for now we are but lovers of the world, I think we shall take a walk along the Seine, and then be on our way.

I hope you get this one, and that you're feeling well, and that you know I'm always thinking of you.

Love and More Love,

Daughter.

P.S. We went to Le Procope for lunch yesterday – thank you so much for that. We sent you the postcard that came with the bill. What a trippy old place!

ESHE SUMMONS THE SOUL OF PARIS

06/02/2002

Hi Mama, I'm glad you're getting my emails again. And Paris gave us a proper Paris ending: walking on the Seine, some young musicians in suits were playing jazz under a bridge. We stopped to listen, and when they finished their song they started talking to us. They were packing up, so smoked us a hash joint and told us about being impoverished music students in

Paris — and all the while, the ringlet-haloed trombonist couldn't take his eyes off Eshe. (She of course loves trombonists, as she used to play herself.) As the light started to fade they walked along the river with us, and beneath a bridge the suited jazz-man with his untied tie bent down and planted a perfect kiss on Eshe's smiling lips.

When we got to the station, we saw him running frantically from train to train; Eshe walked toward him and he came up to her thrilled, abashed, fumbling with a pen. He gave her his address and said if we come back we must stay with him. Then we boarded our train, Eshe literally waving goodbye as we pulled out into the night. If only she'd had a handkerchief.

Madrid is full of girls in skimpy clothes and the high-fashion shops that sell them. We're staying in the apartment of a mean matriarch with saggy boobs and gory-Christed crucifixes above every bed. Perfect.

I'll call from Seville. Love love love,

the girl.

FAMOUS LIKE COCA COLA

06/10/2002

— What Moukhtar told us he is, swilling illicit beer on the roof of our hostel last night. (Moukhtar is the Mauritanian Tom Waits of a turban-selling tour guide who's befriended us — I wrote about him in the mass email, if you haven't read it yet).

Mama, I'm in Fez and so happy I can't even tell you. You mustn't worry about us here — we don't even go out at night — there's nothing better to do than hang out at our hostel anyway. Traveling with Moukhtar and his friend Mohammed keeps other boys at bay, and traveling with people who live here makes everything easier. But it's all in the other email....

It's funny what you said about girls and jealousy of each other — I was thinking about that at the hammam earlier today. For fifty dirham we had a large, mostly naked woman forcefully escort us through the tiled, high-ceilinged, ancient building, throw water on us, stick our arms between her breasts and scrub while saying Dirty, dirty in French, as dead skin rolled off our soapy flesh. We were shampooed, massaged, while all around us women of every age scrubbed, shaved, talked, washed each other. It's a central part of social life here, and very interesting for us to see women who we mostly don't see at all, and very little of their skin if we do, naked and chattering away, taking care of these usually-hidden bodies. I noticed how different it felt from, say, a change-room at a gym – that is, charged with hidden glances, tabulations, envy, every inch of other women's skin a potential condemnation or redemption. Here bodies are just bodies; nudity isn't utterly branded by sex. Eshe and I were comfortable at the hammam, despite the occasional glances toward her fairly black and my ghostly white skin. And now we're so clean, full of tagine; the muezzin is calling and dusk is falling…

But no, to answer your question – Eshe and I haven't had a moment of tension, about anything. Ever, if I think about it, in our eight years of friendship.

We're leaving tomorrow for the Gnawa festival, with a stop at some giant waterfall to pick up another of Moukhtar and Mohammed's friends. I'll try to write when I get my bearings in Essaouira. Did you know Jimi Hendrix played a concert there once?

As Moukhtar would say, Take it easy lemon squeezy, before you get crazy. Love, Me.

P.S. Thank you so much for looking after my school stuff. Here are some more lyrics – it's a new song, and should bring us up to their requested page count. I hope York finds the portfolio acceptable; the more I think about it the more I want to get in. I am glad you have convinced me to try.

Untitled:

Crumbling beneath the weight
of everything I maybe could create,
potential laid out in some sombre finery
I am on my way to the silent cemetery
To lay it all to rest finally

Ch: I just want a good man
Who won't mind
Sweeping up shredded bits of my rhyme
I just want a good man who knows my mind
I just want a good man who knows

Daddy you don't come around
It is that way with people of your trade I've found
I don't want to follow your lonely ghost around
I just want a little plot of land to settle down

Terrified of everything I'd like to say
I'm terrified that my mind works this way
Most days I wish I'd never taught myself to play
I'm tired of the thought that someday I may
Yes I'm sick of the dream that someday I may

TRAVELING

07/30/2002

Dear Joe,

    I hope this finds you well, and that your recent silence is only attributable to your being too busy with pleasant things to write me back. Meantime here I am back in T.O., and although it's hard to have my Big Trip behind me, and as much as some part of me wants to hop the next plane to anywhere, it is wonderful to be home. The joy of traveling is being constantly thrown into new settings and situations yet finding one's consciousness continuous and familiar; the joy of being at home is meeting my 16-year-old self standing on the street-corner at Bathurst and Bloor, the lemon-juice of the location manifesting the invisible ink of my memories. Everywhere scraps of myself, secret messages from the past.

    But I shan't clutter up your inbox, since I don't know how often you're checking it these days; I just wanted to say Hi.

    x

THE PIECE AND THE WHOLE

08/01/2002

Eshe! Come back from New York already. I wake up in the morning and still expect you to be next to me and it takes me a minute to realize that life is back to normal. A lot of the pictures didn't turn out – the one of us and the German boys at the Gato Negro is four dark blobs and a terrace with brightness beyond.... Some were good, though: you by the medina wall in twilight; me on the Spanish Steps. Mom said it was a trip to see me where she had such vivid memories of being. I told her that, standing on those Steps I'd always heard about, I had imagined her there when she was my age. I did, too. As you squinted into the camera at me in my slightly grimy jeans and torn shirt, the day around us a nondescript wash of brightly coloured tourists milling through streets of chic shops encased in grey stone, I conjured Mom there on a hot night – the long, straight auburn hair, that impish smile I'd seen in photographs – high, radiant, decadent as a Fellini character in her audacious youth, every man's face turned toward her.

Michael had dinner with Mom while I was gone. What a sweet thing to do, eh? I'm sure he knew she would be lonely, missing not only me but everyone that comes around. But that's the kind of thing Michael does. Of course I am also hoping that maybe it was because he was missing me, a little bit. I mean, who goes to see the mother of his ex-girlfriend if he's not still at least somewhat interested in the girl?

He was the first person I wanted to see when I got home. Being away seems to have made me value Mike even more, unfortunately. (Another nice thing about being home – freedom from the stupid men and drunken men, cars full of leering men. Men on the street whispering into our ears. Men telling us everything about themselves, or asking the same questions, having the same responses to our answers. I wish I had your knack for ignoring these people, could make my face into a mask of untouchable serenity the way you do, rather than lurching through another one-sided conversation I'm too polite to end. I don't know where Mom found all her fascinating lovers, these artists and dancers and so on. Although, I wouldn't trade our two weeks with Moukhtar and Mohammed, crazy as they were, for anything. And Hannes was lovely – I don't remember anything about the Alhambra except him! But he got me thinking about Mike again – wasn't Hannes rather like a German Mike? Passionate about human rights, kinda reserved around girls….)

When we got together, the day after I came home, Michael sat on my balcony playing his oud for so long I finally said, So, are you gonna talk to me, or…? He put the oud down, looked at me somewhat doggedly, and sighed a short Yeah.

Eventually he came out with the fact that part of his being so tongue-tied was, at long last, he had slept with Hannah. Can you believe it? Michael's first love, the girl responsible for my knowing him – sleeping with her was the final stage in something that had to be completed; balance for my contribution to the demise of her and N, at least. That's great, I told him, glad he had not thoroughly retreated to his monastic ways.

But once he'd been with her he was sorry he'd done it. All his desire for her was gone, and he felt awful, like every get-off, get-gone jerk in history.

Why? I asked him. There were no arrangements, no expectations, she lives in the States for chrissakes. So why feel bad? You both got what you wanted out of it.

Well, he said, It was kind of a big deal for her. Afterward she was talking about, you know, staying in touch, and the intensity of being with someone again…

Essentially she's sort of into him, and he's not really into her. Which suits me fine, obviously (means maybe his heart is elsewhere engaged?). He feels bad, because he's a sweet guy like that. Man, men of the present age have it tough. Especially those like Mike who were really affected by what they learned about the women's movement in high school, who took feminism and all modern criticisms of patriarchy seriously. As a boy like that it must seem there are pit-falls everywhere, the desire for sex an obstacle-course of possible ways to be an asshole. Despite being raised by a Mom as lusty as Janice (there is a tiny figurine couple copulating in her bathroom), Mike always felt his desires to be an imposition – when he met me he told me what a relief it was to find that women really do want sex, that they don't just endure it for men (I guess he though his mom was an anomaly). What progress! From Victorian ladies who are supposed to be terrified of sex, to Boomer women who appear to be angered by it. Making the kindest, the most decent men ashamed.

We're going up to Flo's cottage this weekend, so we'll see how it is with us. (Meanwhile, a muscular young man appeared in the laundry room yesterday, and tomorrow I shall have him up for tea....)

In other news, I got into York's creative writing intro course! I'm actually pretty stoked to be going back to school. And I'm not the only one returning: Mom has been diligently working on getting back to York to finish her M.A., which is a whole big hassle since she left in, like, 1976 (fleeing from Irving, before being reunited once again sometime soon after). But she has succeeded: determined to write a thesis on Gertrude Stein, she'll be taking night courses, and hopefully eventually she'll get to work on this project. Crazy, eh? But that's Mom for you. She says she's dying for some intellectual stimulation.

Her friend Andrea came up from New Hampshire and was still here when I returned. It's always good to see her, and it seemed right that as I'm off in Europe for the first time, Mom's here with the person she first went with. It's wonderful that they're still interesting to one another, different as their lives are. Only thing was, she sort of suggested I smoke less pot. I guess, since I've not been in school and just working at the 'bucks and all, she thought I'd get more done if I weren't smoking so much. I started to say it wasn't really like that, that pot helped me put things in perspective, helped me to do the things I have to do, but to my mortification got a little emotional as I was trying to explain. I know things are hard with your Mom, she said. But that's why I think it's important to maybe get involved with something; your Mom was saying you're pretty outraged about the political climate these days, maybe there's something that could use that energy. Or when you go back to school, there will be a paper, or groups who feel like you do. It's worth investigating and you know pot, it's not the best for motivation.

Mom came out of her bedroom then, dressed and ready to go with Andrea to dinner. I don't begrudge her saying what she did, but I didn't think there'd be any way I could explain to her that when I smoke I become motivated to do all kinds of things – clean, read, write. And that the reason I haven't yet joined any organization is a wholly separate issue....

But I have joined Ty's samba band. At a party at Ariel and Jamie's the other night Ty decided to play out on College St; not all the band members were there, so I grabbed an extra surdo and tried to follow along. Fun! Surprisingly not baffling; and so entertaining to see the bar-hoppers stopped by the sight of a drum band which had suddenly materialized like a giant many-armed genie on College St. Ty strutting chest forward, sticks purring on his drum's skin, looking up devilishly at the ladies in the crowd; the mysterious force field his body exudes drawing each of us into the rhythm. I went to my first rehearsal the next day, and it made me even happier than I'd expected. Looking up and seeing these lovely young faces beating out their patterns in harmony, my drum one of twenty or more subsumed into a vibrating whole. Light was flooding into the loft, spreading across the honey-coloured floors, reflecting off our metal rims. With that big drum strapped to me I saw why Ty had started the band, was immensely pleased that I had stepped over whatever *michegas* was keeping me from playing with him. To have missed out on a year of this for fear of looking stupid! Never mind not being as good as him, or Jed, or any of the experienced musicians in the band. That's the point of this thing, what Ty has been trying to explain to me – the music that gets produced is greater than the sum of its parts.

Missing you bad, Sam.

AUGUST AND EVERYTHING AFTER
08/06/2002

Dearest Eshe,

my friend, it is good to be young. I came back yesterday from Flo's cottage, three gorgeous days, two nights. We were staying in what they call "the toolshed" – a little cabin across from the main cottage where Flo's dad works when he's up here. Also where Florence and her sister came to play when they were kids; it has the airy cheerfulness of somewhere young girls lost themselves in summer reveries, feels like a livable dollhouse tucked away at the edge of the woods. There's a platform with a bed, very cozy under the white sloped roof, and that's where the three of us slept. At least, the first night. I lay between Flo and Michael under the hexagonal window, candles burning on the ledge, smoking a sloppily rolled joint. I remember thinking what a childish thing, to be piled in here on one little mattress, our rumpled sleepy faces inches from one another, and how lovely the comfort of these friends. Dozens of hours of shared sleep already between us. Not too many years left of this, though; I thought how we'll soon grow up and have separate rooms, and there won't be time for these days like be-ins, hours stretching in peaceful wisps of smoke and sun around our unkempt heads (full of John-and-Yoko images in whites and grays). Beached on a big bed amid tossed sheets, ashtrays, cookies, books, apple cores, guitars. The charged serenity of hours spent with nothing in particular to do but be together, talk about the world, inspect it, taste it and love it. Notice our own bodies as we abuse and please them. But maybe we don't have to lose all of it. Falling asleep I thought of camping trips with our kids, shared tents, shameless peeing, skinny-dipping. I thought of collective breakfasts, the perfectly feasible glory of early coffee in bedclothes with good friends. Even if we're older. Even if we have kids and jobs and all that. It doesn't have to be all bustle and nuclear isolation.

Breast-stroking through the fresh, heavy water I felt so clearly what it is to be me, here, at twenty-one: felt my toes, calves, inner thigh muscles pulling me through the reflections of trees and sky, ribs to the lake-bed, water on my lips, sun in my eyelashes and everywhere the pines, and birch trunks rising straight and white as bones.

Having traveled has made Ontario seem more like home, has made my Ontario-ness more evident, even this rural scene that in some ways I barely belong to, having never known family cottages or overnight camps like so many middle-class Torontonians. But in another way I do belong to it – Zaida's parents had a summer resort in Orillia, just south of Flo's parents' place, long before I was born. My grandparents were married there.

As I swam toward shore I saw Michael sitting on the rock watching me. Resting my feet on the rocky bottom I waded toward him. Florence had removed her blood-red lace bra and gypsy skirt and was resting in only her tattoos against a tree, her face in sunshine. I grabbed the camera off the shore and snapped vivid Flo against the blue sky, and Michael leaning back smiling at me. In that moment I thought there's no way a man can look at a woman like this and not love her. In the picture he has that look I love best to receive – full of sweetness and goodwill, lips slightly pursed and smiling, a silent "my oh my" at what he's seeing. The way he's leaning back looking right at me, veins running down his forearms, triceps bulging, is like an invitation.

That night Florence, very stoned, fell asleep in the cottage living room. Can I tell you what I felt when I saw her newly-shorn hair peeking from the day-bed's patchwork cushions? What hopefulness and apprehension and bliss when I realized she was fully succumbed to sleep, was staying the night, that it would be only Michael and I in the toolshed, in the white-painted coziness of that little bunk in the pines. I of course made nothing of it. Just donned my pajamas and climbed beneath the sheets, kept my eyes mostly off Michael as his torso then boxer-briefed bottom climbed up the ladder and in next to me, face ruddy and brown in the candlelight. In the close cot I drank in the mixed smells of his body and smoke from our extinguished candle-flame, his familiar earthy smell and his hair retaining a breath of lake-water. Lying next to him wildly awake, bodies not touching but close enough to hear him breathing, I let one finger rest on his arm. Heat pulsed through that finger into his shoulder, sucked his body's heat into mine. My whole body thrumming, the centimetre of skin in contact with his sending its frenzied signal cartwheeling through my nervous system.

Sam, he said into the darkness.

What? Breathless and giving myself away.

We can't.

Why not?

Because –

And the next thing I know he's on top of me, and my whole body is relief. Except the niggling worry at the repercussions, for a moment.

In the morning Mike looked at me slightly guiltily, not without tenderness, shrugged his shoulders and I was suddenly beneath him again.

Happy as I was afterward, I couldn't get the image of that shrug out of my mind. As much as I wanted to think, I have him back, all will be sorted out, I saw him shrugging as though to say well I've transgressed once, I may as well do it once more before I start feeling bad about it.

Which is, of course, what happened.

We left the cottage early to miss the 400 traffic, and because I wanted to make a Samba barbeque Ty was throwing. Florence was staying up north; Michael and I listened to tapes, commenting on random things, ignoring The Talk that dangled like invisible dice between us.

When we got back to the city it had settled into a lovely late afternoon, as hideous Toronto summer days will do, so we decided to walk down to Ty's. I would never have known how to go but Mike being an east-end boy had a perfect route right through the Don Valley. South to Riverdale park where Mike has played since he was a child, down the big hill where east-end couples were watching their dogs dash through the sunlit grass. We followed the river south as it burbled along dragging its smells of ragweed, car exhaust and freshwater. It was very pleasant to be walking, fit from traveling and so wearing a large bandanna stretched over my torso and tied at the back, red Moroccan satchel over my shoulder, feeling the sun make jade of my eyes, golden threads of Michael's hair. When I think back on that walk I'll remember Michael's lean face listening to me as we pass tall shrubbery, dusty, dark-green August leaves flying by his head as we stride forward and I argue that we can't know anything, we can't know anything, but we know we like to have sex, we keep coming back to each other and why try and deny it? What sense does it make? When it needs to end it will end, I proclaimed with absolute confidence, with blind, stalwart assurance, But that doesn't seem to be now. Now we want to have sex, so let's have sex! (Picturing simultaneously us going separate directions, the many varieties of man I could fuck, love, marry, seeing Mike with another girl, happy, ensconced in another life and also Mike and I in our little home, married, united, raising children, sex with him at forty-five, debating the meaning of life creaking with arthritis in our rocking chairs....) Thinking for one brief moment, why am I presenting this argument? What a ludicrous position this is! And for what am I choosing it? But arguing right along, staring into the sun and at his sweet, guarded, clearly captivated face as he let himself be persuaded.

By the time we got to Ty's Mike seemed satisfied. As to what I'm not too sure, perhaps just that he wasn't doing anything wrong by being with me despite his feelings not being what they were when we were together before. Ty was outside the front door standing over the little round barbeque Mom and I gave him when we last moved, unable to use it in the high-rise. He was happy, grilling things for people. Upstairs someone was thumping on a djembe and I heard Michelle say Okay, guys, we should open a window 'cuz it's getting pretty smoky.

I could see Mike was feeling antisocial so mostly we just sat in the driveway watching the sun filter its way through the poplar leaves above us, dapple their reflection on the cinderblock wall opposite.

By the time we were walking home Mike was unsure again.

Just wait and see how it goes, I told him, tired of the conversation. It's mildly uphill all the way and the humidity was building again as we trudged back through the city. How much more can be said about all this? I thought, head starting to hurt in the dampening air, the grit and fish smell of Broadview and Gerrard. By the time we reached Logan a misty drizzle was falling and I stood on the porch wondering if I should go in. I did of course, Mike pulling me to him with the same sense of relief and doubt I had felt in the toolshed.

An hour later, satisfied, troubled and pleased, I got into Zippy and drove home.

So that, my friend, is how things stand. I still haven't heard from Joe, not since I left England – I suppose I am joining his collection of happysad photographs of former life, to be mused over briefly in times to come.

If there is such a thing as uncomplicated love, I send it to you. You are maybe the only person who makes me think such a thing exists.

08/13/2002

Joe oh sweet Joe. Well, who knows if you'll read this or not, but I figured I may as well try. It's unfortunate that writing me took your boyfriend "abandoning you" and forcing you to put fingers to keyboard. Do thank Dave for me, won't you?

You tell me you haven't read my emails, have tucked them away for who knows when. But it's not because you're a fair-weather friend, as the "good friend" you haven't spoken to in years called you; you saw me through some rotten weather when we were on the same soil. If you miss me like you say you do (shall I call you Mister Misery?), what stops you from writing? What is the "something better" you think you could say months from now? You know it would be worse, too bad even to think about, and then it will be years, and I a tiny fetish you unearth now and again to invoke your worthlessness.

Only you can know what is preventing you from weaving together the threads of your life. You want to be a butterfly and flit from one flower to another, you do it, baby. You'll do it gracefully, absorbing more beauty than most. But I can't think of you saving for your plane ticket to T.O., or of the song about us you are coming to play me, and yet never hear from you. Why tell me these things, while depicting for me your profound reticence to write? Though I am glad you hit send and not delete before running from the computer.

Always, Sam.

P.S. Thanks for sending me the pictures. I am shocked and delighted, and I await them eagerly if with trepidation.

NICE LOCAL BOY TAKES NICE LOCAL GIRL...

08/14/2002

...to the ledge of tolerance, reason and faith.

Eshe, I've just read an email from Mike and I'm writing you to avoid writing him and telling him that if he drank cat piss and belched it back up it couldn't be more gross than what he did in that message. No. I should feel pity. What a raw display of how really fucked up he truly is at this particular moment.

It doesn't even sound like him – it sounds contrived, and maybe that's because this bullshit he's saying plainly contradicts the facts: I'm in fucking Europe and he's eating dinner with my mother; I come home and he gets his paws on me first chance he's given; he has one twinge of guilt, one hiccup of confusion and he's at the keyboard, full of his own sense of decency and Doing the Right Thing, telling me he's "grateful," and someday perhaps we'll be great friends.

I'm so glad.

I should have known better. But this is how it's been for a year. Sorry for all the Drama, he says. I'm not sure he is. He appears to have a penchant for melodrama I somehow hadn't expected. I thought he was just sensitive. But this seems something else, this tormented rambling, surely written to Radiohead; his "I feel different" and "things have changed but what a waste this world would be if everything stayed the same." Aw my god that's just lame – What doesn't change, I'd like to know. Genius. Why does he think I'm asking him to stop time, that being with me is antithetical to progress, to his development as an individual. If that is the case, he should say so, instead of abstractly holding forth as he explains to me, yet again, about how this last time we had sex was *really the last time...*

I'll write him back. More rational message to follow. Thank heavens you're coming home soon.

SUMMER IN THE CITY

08/31/2002

My dearest Joe! Thank you for writing me back – it has made my night. I did not expect to hear from you so quickly, but then, you see, we are always changing. I'm glad you aren't cross with me. I reread my email a few days ago and winced, thinking, what right did I have? And then here you are, telling me what right I do have. And no, of course nothing is ruined; our friendship is like Fantasia, in *The Neverending Story* – it exists if we believe in it.

So, life these days, you ask. Well, Eshe has returned from New York for the rest of vacation, so I have been enjoying the T.O. patio craze with her and Bratt (yes, they are seeing a lot of each other – I'm glad it doesn't bother you now. Anyway it's definitely not love, just summer fun – they closed Ted's the other night, were making out on the pool table until finally a bartender kicked them out). She picks me up from work some days, and we drift through the Annex with the same eyes that so recently beheld each other in foreign beds with foreign boys, on beaches and trains, on pavements tinted with strange light. I'm sorry you didn't get to know her better. In her company, life is never frightening – never malevolent or unmanageable. And, like you, she makes my Mom happy – even though Eshe was more of a badass than me in high school (minus the drug-dealing boyfriend, I guess), Mom always believed in Eshe's good sense – and rightly so. I don't think there's anyone else Mom would have let me drive to New Orleans with at eighteen, or anyone who could have made her less anxious about my traveling for three months.

Friday Ty knocked off work early in the afternoon, picked me up on the bike and took me to some garage out in Markham to buy a part, then down the DVP to the St. Lawrence Market where he knows all the people in the stalls and jokes with them, asks after business, shamelessly haggles, eats proffered slices of cheese, flirts with the ladies. Back at the barbecue in the quiet, Valley-smelling lane, I told him how I enjoyed dodging through the crowd behind him, watching him go about his business in his self-contained way. Really? he said; I'm glad. It makes Michelle angry how I just go and don't look back.

Well, I told him, I can see how it might be annoying if you were my boyfriend. But as it is it only makes me happy – I can just stand on the periphery and watch.

You make me happy too, Sammy, he said, his deep-brown eyes – clever simian eyes is how I sometimes think of them – aligning themselves with mine; and then he swiped my nose with his – once, with purpose – like he does now and again and turned back to the barbecue.

I wanted to know him, I thought. Not the very first time we met, when I was fifteen and Jed brought me to the party at Ty's grungy high rise in the east end – it was all too unknown and I got crazy high and was just about to start dating Jed, and Jed was Ty's oldest friend; he seemed like something between a street-urchin and a mad scientist – full of cunning and adventure. But the second time, later that year: Mom, Eshe and I ran into him at Word on the Street, where I had just read a thing I'd won a prize for from *The Star*, and Ty was on a stoop nonchalantly thwacking his djembe. I told him it made me want to dance and he said So do. I didn't of course but I liked how he'd said it. And then the third time, in Ariel's place on College before she moved in, when it was still an empty dental office. There was Ty again, catching my eye as he pulled his chin to a shoulder, his drumming habit; talking later, faces close in the Ariel party throng and me thinking I want to know this boy. Feeling so beautiful when I went home I didn't want to go to sleep because I knew when I woke up the vision of myself that way would be gone. We saw each other constantly that summer, at the end of which he had a bad motorcycle accident, and had to move back home to his Dad's, with whom he has always fought terribly. Then Ty got arrested for hacking he'd done maybe two years before; he dropped off the radar a while, working some low-level corporate job, horribly depressed. He called me one night that winter and I sat there debating with him about whether his hatred of everything included me.

 Leaning against the cinderblock wall of the factory he has turned into a home, I marveled at how much less rootless he has become, and wondered if he might stay in Toronto, make a good, stable life as the doctor he has wanted to be since he was a kid. Until he started university, I always thought one day he'd vanish from the city – to return to Israel (he once almost joined the army), or who knows what.

 He watched the trout on the barbeque, and I watched cars ascend the overpass thinking how it's not even a year since you left, but your time here was such a totally separate thing from your life now. Funny how I've always been terrified of change, yet love restless people.

 I've joined Ty's samba band, and a couple of weeks ago we played Reclaim the Streets. Some media collective asked us to march in the parade and dude, I didn't know I could walk for two hours playing a twenty pound drum that's hanging off me, but I guess I can. We started in the park in Kensington Market, and it didn't seem like all that many people as we set off along Queen. This was an unplanned parade – it's amazing that the police didn't stop it, although at one point they tried. Just south of the Eaton Centre, the parade had gained some kind of critical mass; we came to a parkette and a lot of cops on horses appeared at the north end, trying to fence us in. Bicycle cops amassed to our right. Suddenly Ty calls Rai, our most frenzied song, jubilant-serious. The band pounded its first shots and the horses starting backing up. As we charged into the song Ty turned around, powerful little body drilling rapid-fire beats from his battered steel-rimmed drum toward the spooked horses; the cops saw we weren't stopping, that there would be pandemonium if they tried to contain us, and suddenly we were moving again. At Yonge St. we managed to play one more triumphal Rai before the cops began to close in and Ty called us to a halt. In the newly blue evening I waddled toward the sidewalk, unhooked my drum, and sprawled on the sidewalk beneath the Eaton Centre glass, immensely satisfied.

The cause of public space is a manageable one, I feel. At least it's something people can have an effect on; certainly it makes for good theatre. In Kensington yesterday the guy that owns that pretty French restaurant La Palette bought a bunch of parking spaces on Augusta and had a street party, called it Car-Free Day. I walked by and people had put down blankets, sand, astroturf and were sitting around in the road playing music and having picnics – a proper hippie scene. A statement of intent, I suppose; a living out of values.

Hard to believe that next week I'll be back at school. Harder still to believe that I'm actually excited about it. Maybe it's just that I couldn't have borne coming back from traveling just to work full-time at the 'bucks again, but whatever the case, I think school might be fun. Get some booklearnin', why not?

Yours, Sam.

HOME SICK HOME
    09/18/2002

My dear Eshe,

I want to share with you the front page of yesterday's *Globe and Mail*, lest you are having halcyon visions of dear, progressive Canada: below "Iraq Scrambles to Avert War," "Bush Steely Resolve Pays Dividends Again." The article had a picture of him in profile, another jowly white man in a suit, in resolute pose, slightly better looking than some if you fancy a dim reptilian twinkle in the eyes. The contrast between Scrambles and Steely is wonderful – Iraq a headless chicken frantic beneath the unwavering glare of Western superiority.

Meanwhile the rich get richer. Mike and I enjoyed an article on the Tyco fatcat's expenditures, his ten thousand dollar umbrella holder and so forth. (Oh, yes, we're hanging out again. What can I tell you? I tried with the lovely boy from Côte d'Ivoire, my neighbor; it was too sad. His lovely body so eager to please and me only able to think of Mike. And then planning Bri's birthday party: filling balloons, Michael's long body stretched out on the couch, bluegreen eyes beaming at me, banishing the world, making a strange eternity of my living room. Two weeks ago I defied my mother's exhortations to let him be and wrote back, a very understanding and encouraging email in response to his last email – one of his less infuriating, which at least explained his actions and said kind things about me and our time together. So I wrote back saying good things about him and the future generally and then we saw each other at Flo's, and this is how it goes.)

Anyway we thought it was hysterical how in the same paper there are articles righteously debasing this rich, corrupt old bastard, and articles deifying Bush and Rumsfeld. As though it weren't all connected, as though one was a moral question and the other a question of "politics." Good old mealy-mouthed Canada: where being ostentatiously rich brings you more scorn than being an ideological war-mongerer.

And Mom saying Write letters, write articles, how can you get your opinions out there?

I'm not surprised you freaked out upon returning to NYC. It couldn't have helped that the "Fuck Canada" guy was the first person you met at your residence; nor would being stared down, as you wrote your last email, by the guy from the Black Students' Association for not joining his cause.

Fascinating and, I guess, unsurprising that the whole being black thing would be more of an issue there than here. Here, at least if you're middle class, it seems like we just ignore the question entirely.

Your epiphany made sense to me (how could you worry your email was too long? It was marvelous); yes, I think you do get told things because you're comfortable with yourself, and are not trying to obliterate your fear of yourself by working incessantly. (Though yes, you should go to class more.) And yes, I'm sure people do wonder why you and the odd band of people you've found to love hold yourselves apart from campus life; but at the same time, people find you interesting because of it.

Anyway, more in person – I'll call you next week. Counting the days 'til you're back for Thanksgiving. With much love, Sam.

THE STATE OF MODERN WOMANHOOD (or: Men Have No Sense of Timing)
09/26/2002

Okay, Eshe, as a thoroughly modern and enlightened woman who knows me as well as anyone on this earth, please tell me if the following scenario justifies the rage I am currently feeling:

Mike and I were in the car on the way to watch Ty play a gig for Sukkoth (he's in a new band, Shakshuka; they're sort of klezmer fusion). Mike and I spent a lovely afternoon together, culminating in some great sex. All was well. We were driving up Bathurst, me freshly-showered and very content, and we got to talking about this cd that Ariel has forced me to record (a friend of hers, Dean, has that new music-editing software), how it would be done soon, etc. And he says, with a suggestive little smile, I think Dean's got his eye on you. You should go for it.

I'm not interested in that, I said (sincerely, to my own surprise).

Well, okay, but you know if you were, you totally could, he said.

Now Eshe, to say to the girl you've just slept with half an hour ago, *Why don't you go fuck that other guy...?*

Only in the past thirty years, my friend, could a man and a woman have this conversation. Only in the wake of the Glorious Sexual Revolution. And thank god, or rather, our forebears, for the Sexual Revolution; I'm not saying

I would want to have lived in the fifties. Though sometimes I think so – oh the sweet ease of being a housewife, husband off to work each morning; the simplicity of traditional gender roles. High school sweetheart arriving with corsage for the prom, exchanging promise rings. Of course this is ridiculous, because if I'd lived then I would certainly have been the town slut, later heard to have taken up with "bohemians."

Man, what a rotten time to get all wholesome. Is that what love does, makes you wholesome? Yes, love, that's the problem, or really the fact that he knows I love him. That is what caused his pro bono pimp moment, it was a self-defence move, a brazen demonstration of how little our being together means to him. Not even as canny as a two-year-old testing his parents' limits; just an id-ball knee-jerk response to whatever spasm of concern for his freedom he was experiencing at that moment.

It's my own fault, for having unreasonable expectations from a boy I should know full well is with me for convenience. Waiting until something better comes along, or he gets out of town, off on his precious adventures. And I have said, again and again, that I am fine with that. So now fine I must be. Goddamn him. I still say his timing was tacky.

THE STATE OF MODERN WOMANHOOD PART 2
09/27/2002

Dear Eshe, thank you for your astute and humorous response. What's up with Columbia's strange sex rituals? The poor girls trying to fit into two eras at once: uterus rooted in the 1950s, dangling a thong into the frightening sex-scape of the new millennium trying to get the boys to notice. And hoping, as girls ever have hoped, that one of them will marry her based on that enticement.

The end to yesterday's tale of woe is that Mike sent me an email apologizing for what he said. He wrote out the dialogue we'd had, and inserted subtext indicating that he was aware of why he said what he did, and why it pissed me off. Included in this exhibition of consciousness was the understanding that I "don't want to be looking for an acceptable mate in every man" I meet, when I've got a perfectly good version of that sitting right next to me. Indeed. He then interpreted his Dean comment as an attempt to begin a conversation with me about our situation.

Which, in the end, I suppose I must be grateful for, since his response to my displeasure in the car led him to finally, at long last and to my immense satisfaction, admit that HE DOES STILL LOVE ME.

It was qualified, of course, by how his feelings are different: the "raging river" has become a "small tributary" – touching, eh? But read on – "the valley cut by the waters runs just as deep." So will a deluge of emotion ever swell that tributary? Who knows? I think so, but I'm not telling him that.

When we spoke he told me how he'd had a conversation with Ty, as Ty was driving him home after the Shakshuka gig. Apparently serious conversations in the car have become a sort of tradition in their friendship. So Ty asked him What's with you and Sam?

And Mike said something stupid like Well, the sex is so good, we just figured…

Ty was like, So you're just in it for the sex?

And Mike said I guess.

Ty shot him one of those sidelong, cocked-eyebrow Ty glances, a *Mikey, that doesn't sound like you*, and Mike said he felt the old guilt-hound gnawing at his heels.

So he went home and thought about it some, and realized that yes, he does love me, and that a relationship can't be turned on and off like a tap, so we may as well admit the truth of what's between us. Which is what, you might ask? Well love, familiarity, ease. Things, anyway, that can't be ignored out of existence. So he finished off with "If we can both handle a relationship like this, cool; if not, it'll change. I have faith."

Oh well, a point has been gained. He loves me. He has relented to this obvious fact. I should sleep with Dean out of spite, to see what Mike does, to prove it will hurt him. No, never mind, that's just mean. Tempting, but mean.

And so, despite all Revolutions of the past hundred years, I am still clinging to that most cherished of womanly virtues, Patience. And maybe

Charity. I am patiently and charitably waiting for my darling to pull his head out of his adorable ass and see that I am the best partner this world is going to offer him, and that he's not the lone wolf he sometimes thinks he is.

What can I say? I'm twenty-one years old and all I want is to be the angel of his house. Not a chaste angel, though.

Love, love, love,

Sam.

"I COME IN FROM THE WILDERNESS, A CREATURE VOID OF FORM..."
09/29/2002

Oh, Dear Joe, I think I like school.

I have my books, my schedule written in the daytimer Mom bought me, nice new pens she stole from her office. It was sweeter than I imagined to be organizing my school-things the night before my first class, an almost-painful throwback to being a kid, when each September meant the possibility of new beginnings, orderly progress, the safety of routine. I remember loving the night before the first day of school, all clean, hair braided, labeling my binders in my pajamas. Grateful that the summer, with its demands to wear shorts and meet new people at camp, had finished. Though I like summer much better than I used to I still had a delicious, almost visceral expectation of the coming cool air and warm sweaters, of unpacking my books in a room full of other students and waiting for a teacher to begin.

Although York is ugly and planted in the wilds of North York, it is so far infinitely better than U of T. (I'm sure some of this just has to do with my attitude; for instance, the mob-scene at the bookstore was horrible, but not panic-inducingly so.) York feels less like an old boy's club – seems more ethnically and economically diverse, has more left-leaning courses. And though U of T's old stone buildings are sumptuous, and there's something satisfying about walking through those hallowed halls of learning as people (well, white men) have been doing since the 1800s, York's hideous 1970s bunkers are less self-important. I don't feel quite as much like a privileged little girl wrapped in the protective folds of my class destiny. Though I guess that's still what I am.

My writing class is in the same building where Mom and Irving first met. Mom thinks it's a trip. She came to York for Irving's class after having worked in the film business for a couple of years, quitting, going to Spain and having that affair with the flamenco dancer. Actually, I came across a photograph the other day of a really skinny Mom holding up a large bag of weed in the basement of my grandparents' former house. I asked her what the story was with that, and she said, That was when I came home from Spain. Your grandparents had gotten me to come home saying Baba, my Baba, Minnie was very sick. (Was she sick? Well, yeah, but it wasn't as bad as they made it sound). So I came home and Antonio was supposed to come meet me here, but the months went by and he didn't come, things weren't working out for this reason and that reason and I got kind of depressed and lost a lot of weight. And smoked a lot of dope, obviously. That was when I heard that Irving was coming to teach at York. I'd admired him for years, you know, and had quite a few of his books so I got very excited and decided to go back to school. Moved up to the graduate residences on Assiniboine Road, looking out over nothing, the winds would howl against the buildings across the wastes of Keele and Finch – I mean you think there's nothing there *now*, you should have seen it in, what, 1974? There was *nothing*. But I wanted to take that class. In fact, there were too many people enrolled in it, I remember the first day students like packed against the walls. Irving said he would interview each of us, and cut down the class size that way and by reviewing our manuscripts. He asked everyone to leave and said he'd call us one by one. So everyone left but me. I just stayed at the desk and he said, Well I guess you're first.

Mom, too, is grooving on being back up at York, although it's weird for her, and also it's exhausting to commute up there twice a week after her long days at work. She still has time to get me presents, though: yesterday I came home to a framed poster for a smoke-in almost exactly thirty-five years ago to the day – "Sunday, Sept. 31." She had shown me the bill once before and I loved it – the black 1920s-on-acid writing and swirling designs and the enticing words "Music.... Bring Grass." So she'd had it framed for me and left it on my bed – so Mom thoughtful – to commemorate the anniversary, she said. What a time it must have been, Mom and her cousin Bonnie, and Andrea, and the Boston Commons full of stoned students in 1967.

Today I woke up at Mike's. He told me as I was falling asleep that it was fine if I stayed but in the morning we had to get up. We couldn't have another day lying around. I agreed I had shitloads of stuff to do, and slept. It's still a bit strange to sleep in his bed again – we don't exactly sleep tangled up in each other's arms any more yet there I am naked in this familiar bed. It's sort of distantly congenial. We woke about ten minutes before the alarm. Facing each other our eyes opened and we recognized each other calmly and not without pleasure. He switched off the alarm and lay back down. He sat up again and I rubbed his head and he fell toward me, let himself be pet for a moment like a cat torn between pleasure and watchfulness. Then he went to the bathroom and I heard the shower being turned on. I lay in bed, cold under the thin blankets. Half-sleeping I heard him come in and rolled over, looked admiringly at him as he unwrapped the towel from his pert little *tuchus*. Mmmm, clean, naked Mike I said and kissed his stomach as he stood at the foot of the bed.

Sammy, he said sternly.

What? I said, innocently.

I'm just not feeling it.

That's terrible, I said and fell without thinking onto the bed, hid beneath the covers more humiliated than I'd expected to be.

That really is terrible he said, laughing; You're hiding your head and everything.

He was feeling bad and I wouldn't have that; thought, No, I will get up. A minute later I fastened my bra and he asked me what I wanted for breakfast.

Downstairs I noodled on the guitar and fought a powerful urge to cry. Stupid, stupid stupid Sammy, I thought. No point to this, none at all. I went into the kitchen where Mike was making chai in a pot. I looked at the newspaper. What's going on in the world, he asked me, so I read some headlines. Decided to just add some honey to my tea, read aloud the tragicomedy of world news. I asked Mike about the political system in Canada, about which I know embarrassingly little, and he explained it over cheddar-on-bagels. Proud of my restraint I drank my tea, urged him to eat so as not to be late for class, joked about our progressive Senate and left. He took me up on a ride to school and we rejoiced at my ticketless car, whisked down grey, muggy Bayview and he said he felt uncomfortable in the leather jacket he was wearing, a dark-brown 1970s beauty inherited from his wild uncle. It looks too much like I'm trying to be something, he said. That's a shame, I thought, but said nothing, thinking I was happy to be messy-haired and wearing mine – it made me think of you. I drove him to College and St. George, and told him I'd be working if he wanted to drop by for a tea after class. He leaned toward me to say goodbye and I kissed his cheek; then he turned and gave me one quick, soft, full kiss on the lips, a kiss like a promise, shot me one swift glance and got out of the car slightly flustered for having not unlocked the door. I drove south to apply for court dates to fight my many tickets feeling the meatiness of his lips in mine, the perfect texture of them, wondering if he had caught the confusion in my eyes as I met his, then realized I had been smiling too and I drove completely happy, listening to a weighty Chili Peppers song, feeling myself at the beginning of a useful day.

One sad thing though – I had to give up Zippy, and now I'm driving Mom's Saab. This is because it has been decided that my grandmother doesn't need a car anymore, so Mom's driving the Boat. It makes sense I guess, but Zippy is a good little car and now she's just sitting in the weeds out back of Ty's loft. He doesn't want to sell it because it was his Mom's, but he's just bought this new Volvo, so we don't know what to do with it. And Mom hates the Boat. You need the Lincoln hood ornament to navigate the thing, it's so big. But mostly the problem is that it's Baba's car, and Mom doesn't want to be living her life in more of Baba's old stuff. Which I understand; I feel strange driving the Saab – it's the car Mom has driven since I was six, and it seems too grown-up for me. But tonight on the way home from work I listened to Bob Dylan for the first time in a long time – a kind of perfect evocation of both Mom and you. Howling *She walked up to me so gracefully and took my crown of thorns, come in she said I'll give ya shelter from the storm* I thought of how you'd look at me and we'd be pulled along by the round rhythm of Dylan's acoustic, the happy-sad chord progression a lesson in how we fail and save and create each other.

    Mike did indeed come visit me at work. Altogether a good day.

    xo, Sweet Joe.

PART II:

What is real, what is fake,
what to leave, what to take?

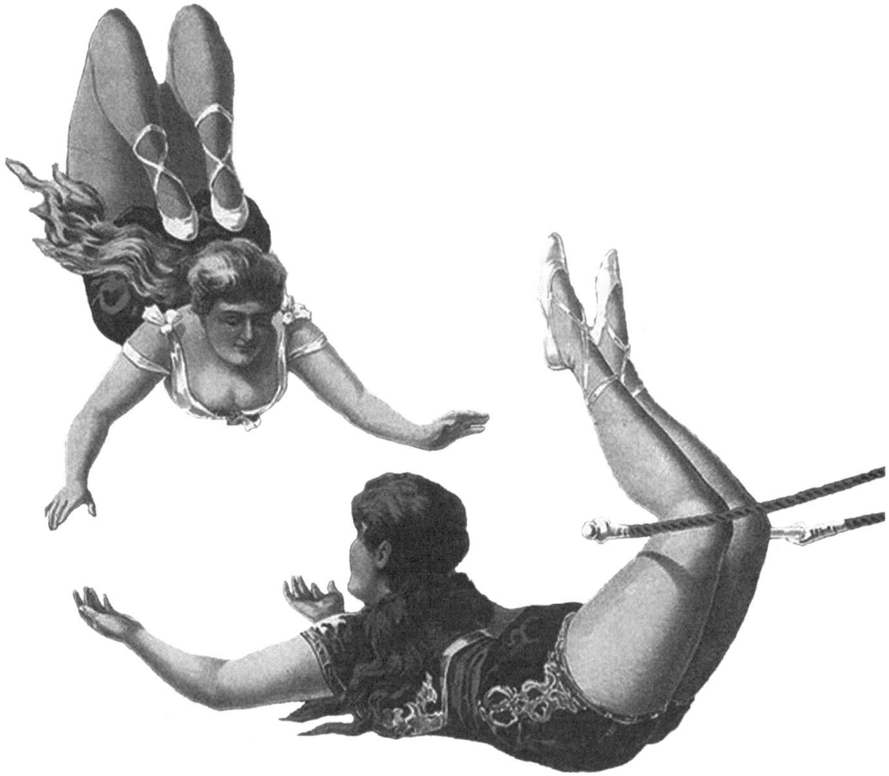

WE'VE ALL GONE TO LOOK FOR AMERICA...
                    10/15/2002

Dear Eshe,

tonight when I came home from taking Joe to the airport Mom was yelling into the phone, at Baba of course. *Okay, so?* You always were miserable, so you're still miserable. I'm very sorry, Mother. *Tse maisse frum drek, e medaf lecken de finger.* (The world is a bowl of shit and you have to lick your fingers: a favorite expression of Baba's grandmother.) That's right, Mother, if all you do is sit and worry, then you're going to feel sick. Mom rolling her eyes on the couch amid a sea of newspapers, TV on mute. Walking in was like being pushed from a height in a dream, my futility ringing in my ears as I plummeted. For six days when Joe was here I felt young, beholden to no one; suspended in the melancholy peace of his eyes I was just a long-haired kid with a car and a pack of smokes, music blaring and adventure everywhere. I imagine that's what it felt like to be young in the Sixties. When being young was what was going on, and your jeans, weed, music all signaled freedom, all meant infinite possibility, radical choice, the indescribable magnitude of Right Now.

In that spirit, Joe and I hopped into the car on Friday night and, to Mom's distress, headed for Detroit (Oh, you have to go look at the poor people? Smiling rueful love as we nodded and laughed. Oh well, she said, Joe's with you, you'll be okay). So off we went to find the ghost of America's golden years, though we got lost on the outskirts of Buffalo, where the all-night gas station clerk laughed at me and said the fastest way to Detroit was back through Canada. But we didn't mind covering a lot of road. I drove as long as I could stay awake through the subdivision-sown fields, Joe horrified and fascinated by the size, the immense pre-fab impermanence of millennial Ohio. On a dark misty patch of highway, a deer appeared and we watched its beautiful, terrified head vanish into the bushes at the back of a strip mall.

Approaching Detroit, Joe balanced his torso out the sunroof and took pictures of the skyline: the city ahead, and to the north a pile of mangled industrial shit that looked like the steel skeletons of a thousand dinosaurs. We parked beneath an empty building – a miniature castle – and started walking. I got a shot of Joe by a boarded-up garage that someone had spray-painted, in green, WITH OPEN EYES. If I were going to get a tattoo, I said to him, That's what I'd get. The sun very white reflecting off the dirty building, Joe squinting at me, legs apart, hips slightly askew: a portrait of motion, as always.

I took another shot of Joe standing in the middle of a six-lane road by a steaming sewer grate because we thought it would be iconic, but the street was too sunny and leafy for what we had in mind. Still, it looked as sad as we expected as we got to the heart of downtown. Everywhere garbage, boarded-up department stores, forsaken restaurants, ornate hotels ghostly as sacked palaces, the tattered remains of awnings flapping from their rails. The sunshine making strangely sweet the dirty bricks and flaking gilt shop-signs, we had our flitting visions of post-war American families congregating outside diners on a morning much like this one: ladies in hats entering department stores, bright, chrome-rimmed cars rolling down the streets, a war just won, factories a continuous hum except on Sundays. You can still feel what it must have been like. American cities seem to have changed less, there's a thicker residue of decades past; downtown Toronto feels so deliberately polished in places. Scrubbed so meaninglessly clean.

What is the meaning of looking at dirt, that's a question. Driving home at twilight, looking at the ragged fields I wondered what stories I am always looking for in dereliction. History, sure, but there's something else, too, and less disinterested. The desire to look feels cruel, like taking pleasure in pain; but is not wanting to look more ethical?

Anyway, my dear Eshe, it was good to be on the move again, even for two days, what with that post-trip travel bug still gnawing at my gut. Though it's excellent to be in school, learning new things. I've had moments taking notes on maquiladoras or discussing the causes of Bipolar disorder that I am so completely happy I actually smile to myself. Just being a proper student, taking in facts, ideas.

We missed you at Thanksgiving. We did a colossal thing, must have had forty people over the course of the night. It was maddening at times – for a while people were constantly coming and going, there were plates, bags, shoes everywhere, the phone unceasing with people needing buzzing up. Of course it was a buffet, people perched on sofa arms, cross-legged on the floor, leaning against the kitchen counter, but that was rather satisfying – it seemed people were eating for hours, in every corner of the apartment. As usual the preparations were all stress and horror at how much everything costs, Mom harrumphing into the fridge wishing she lived in a big house with a big proper fridge, muttering about how when Baba had the house there were two fridges but she had to go and sell the house.... But when people arrive Mom is rosy-cheeked and beaming, perfectly in her element bearing massive trays of turkey, ladling out steaming sweet potatoes. A basic, primal thing, to feed and be fed. The ritual of shared food. I've always particularly liked Thanksgiving; Mom first decided to do Thanksgiving dinner when I was maybe nine, and I remember being so excited, making little place cards for everyone, acting the cheery sprite of a child I wasn't by nature but desired to be. Which I suppose means I was naturally that way in some sense, but I had to work at it; at least, I remember pondering the lives of Pollyanna and Josephine March, those lessons in feminine virtue, in gaining strength through hardship. I realized it made me and others happy when I emulated them, bustling around in a little apron, humming a tune, arranging gourds in a basket or tidying the house.

Though I always knew, giving thanks at the laden table, that it wasn't the same as in olden times; that bounty meant something different since I had never known real scarcity. We'd bought this food like we'd buy anything else, from the ever-full supermarket; there were no winter stores being put away, no cellar full of pickles and preserves for the lean months. Arranging store-bought gourds in the wicker cornucopia I adored, I knew that image – food tumbling from a cornucopia – had become purely representative for us, not quite false but fundamentally unmoored from the original meaning. Nonetheless it always made sense to me to take the opportunity of Thanksgiving to thank the earth for what we have, though I've never so much as harvested a tomato. So that is what we did. Mom's work friends talking shop on the couch as Bri carved her tofurkey, Flo gave Joe a backrub, and Ty rolled joints and hollered gleefully about anatomy. Wonderful Franceszka washing dishes, insisting Mom sit down, putting things to order in her bossy, smiling way. A properly modern, haphazard celebration.

Tell me when you're coming home for American Thanksgiving, maybe I can pick you up from the bus.

Love always,

Sam.

BEWARE THE (IMPULSE TO) REVOLUTION!
10/19/2002

Dear Joe, thank you for sending the photographs – I love the one with the city reflected off the hood of the car; and the one of me in the side mirror, pumping gas – my hair has gotten crazy long, eh? Why do I always look best in pictures you take?

Yesterday I did my first real assignment for writing class. We were to go on a walk and describe what we saw. Mike picked me up from work after I closed and we went to the Market. We walked around and I took notes; a girl sitting outside a shambling garage-door store came over and told me to touch her hair because it felt "like a baa-sheep." Mike pet an orange cat outside a bicycle shop. I asked him, Why can't the city be a conglomeration of neighborhoods like this? Instead of what will happen instead, a bunch of rich people taking this place and turning it into a fake version of itself with "loft living" and "boutique shops."

There needs to be a change in the middle-class consciousness, he said. There never really has been. That was supposed to be the big shtick of the

French Revolution – well part of it – but then you had, like, Robespierre, killing priests in the countryside, we believe in the Church of Reason and all that. Saying this is better for the people. But it's their way of life, you can't just take that from them. It's very tempting, though, to talk about, well people don't need this or that and they're greedy and someone has to make them understand. So that's what we'll do, take their cars and their televisions and make them change their lifestyles and we'll force them to be free.

Smiling at me he says this, an old man in a young body giving me the long view, warning against righteous anger. For a moment there on Kensington Street where fifty years ago my great-grandmother haggled for beets and live chickens I envisioned a new generation of Canadians walking to the market with their canvas bags, buying local produce; I saw self-sustaining suburbs with small businesses, parks, convenience stores. CEOs living in normal-sized houses and sending their kids to public schools, where teachers are paid fairly and children aren't zoned out on computer games and Ritalin. It doesn't seem so hard, I thought, just a few changes in perspective, a radical but sensible reshuffling of priorities. Walking with Mike through the Market, contained microcosm that it is, I thought about the life we could lead, the small steps we could take toward the changes we want, our children growing up and continuing the work.

I had better learn how to sew, I thought. How to bake bread. How the economy works. Then, as always, it started to get away from me, look too big, everything controlled by uncontrollable forces, by people I can't know and desires I can't understand. The UN just reported that there's an "ever-mounting hunger crisis," and it's not as though it's a surprise. But people want Hummers. They want hamburgers. I want hamburgers. I want fruit in the wintertime. I and ninety-five percent of all women, on some days if not all, no matter what our political ideals, marital status or religious doctrine, feel we would be more worthy of love if entirely smooth and very thin and this requires energy either to control or to accomplish. We all know people are dying in horrendous and preventable ways, we know there's prejudice and injustice and so maybe we give to charity or have a bake sale for Afghan schools for girls. We institute political correctness and teach ourselves the proper terminology. Perform the MarineLand Dolphin Dance of Freedom that is life in the Western World.

It's hard to believe I've only been back for three months; it seems like life has been like this forever. To school most mornings, to work most nights, Mike dropping by, lunch breaks getting stoned at Flavour Hall – part of which Ariel has just turned into a mad little shop, a clothing store selling her creations and other local designers. She replaced a section of the wall facing College St. with an orange and pink Plexiglas door, which looks like a kind of gorgeous synthetic fungus colonizing the old brick. Lights with FLAVOUR HALL are scattered over and around the door, and the letters light up in succession to make the words. It's delightful – I see it and remember her at sixteen, a buxom waif in bright polyesters gliding through the halls of Northern Secondary.

And so life weaves each day into the next and makes a pattern. I suppose some people find that horrifying; most days I don't. Perhaps it's because I'm only young, but I find it fascinating, this strange, palimpsestic becoming. That these hands stacking patio tables – rough, intuitive hands, pale peasant hands – have rested on a brown steering wheel down through the whole Delta, made a thousand lattes, are typing these words now. Puerile, eh? Sometimes it does seem wonderful that my hands and their ways mean something to other people, something particular to them and unknowable by me yet that is how I exist. Because my hands create a pattern in your brain, you will know me well, I will have a history. As yours, sweet Joe – the fingers' sturdy knuckles and broad round tips, honest as a parsnip, and the slightly bulbous, implicitly rural thumb – tell me things I cannot know about your childhood, your Yorkshire town. Always slightly outstretched, your hands, ready to examine, they make me think of Courtney Love singing *I have a blister from touching everything I see...*

What will they learn to do next, those eager, gentle, capable hands?
xo

ALL ALONE AT THE FAIR

11/03/2002

Dearest Joe,

I wish you'd been here for the Night of Dread March, a Halloween thing organized by a community arts project called Clay and Paper Theater. I met Ty at Hart House, put half the Samba instruments in the Saab and tailed him across Bloor, arriving at Dufferin Grove Park just before dusk. In the late autumn gloom the park was a fantasy Underworld: clusters of forms in dark cloaks conspired beneath susurrous pines, while huge demons and death masks borne by dancers on stilts loomed above mutilated businessmen, Elizabethan ladies and their little fairies, skeletons, witches, animals, two tiny pink-haired punks. The march up to Bloor, over to Christie and back to Dufferin was grueling carrying the surdo, but worth it. When we got back to the park we stopped playing and walked carefully through the damp grass to a large bonfire around which people were gathered for the Burning of the Fears. We started into a slow samba, a polka, as masked dancers began to throw placards onto the fire. White boards with "George Bush," "Genetically Modified Food," "Plague," and "Fear" written on them ignited to whoops and hollers. The dancers coiled around themselves, around the fire, beckoning; "Death," the fear I most wanted to burn, was pitched into the fire. As flame devoured our words I did, to my surprise, feel released from something, became unnaturally light on my tired feet.

It would have seemed right to Mama, this circle gathered to acknowledge the thinning of the veil between the two worlds, as she would say. To let slip a little our death-grip on existence, our white-knuckled hold on these self-contained bodies. She would have welcomed the ever-present spirits that this season bids us to recognize, would have closed her eyes and let time blur. But she was at home. It would have been too much walking for her, too much *hekdish* before and after this beguiling ceremony. Yet I was happy. This group of people, to whom I in some way belonged, was together in the cold night, faces an archaic yellow in the flames, naming and erasing our fears. For this moment bound together by our slow, insistent beat, by the fire, by images of death and the supernatural that must yet stir something in our ancient brains, by the cold air promising winter, the sureness of change.

After that there was food, and somewhere, a fiddle. Lining up for squash soup sweaty and ravenous at the long wood table I felt as though the city beyond the park had ceased to exist and life was all mud and steam and children dodging through clusters of adults. The only sad thing was Michael wasn't there. He had met us before the parade and wandered off; I had looked for him as we marched but he was nowhere to be found. He was at home, I learned later; he felt out of sorts, and had fallen asleep on a bench for a while, then left. These communal revels often put him in a bad mood.

I went back to Ty's. Michelle was there, bent elegantly over her schoolwork at the kitchen table; in the warm light she was a portrait of girlish concentration with her bowed, exposed neck and lifted torso, long fingers extended over the pages. As we came in she smiled at us, closed her books saying, That's enough for tonight. Ty kissed the back of her neck then unlaced his shoes, grunting slightly as he bent down, as is his wont. Michelle lit a smoke, walked toward me asking How was the gig?

I extended my arms and blistered, swollen hands and did a monster walk toward the couch. Gaaaaahhhhh.

Augh, babe, exhausting, groaned smiling Ty, taking Michelle's cigarette. But really fun, he exhaled, dropping onto the couch. There was a good crowd. We burned our fears. The kids were cute. It was good.

We put on the Baba Maal and Mansour Seck album that I always want to listen to these days; Ty rolled a joint and Michelle folded laundry. Sometimes I envy Ty and Michelle the domesticity they've got worked out. Even the fighting is, in a way, enviable; they can fight because they know they'll make up. They have agreed to a long-term arrangement. They'll fight, but then in the morning they'll go to the St. Lawrence Market; and in this they seem more grown-up than me, Michelle knows something about being a woman that I don't.

It was agreeable to be there in the dim light on the big beige couch with Ty, Baba Maal's perfectly-pitched vibrato sliding through my tired body, relaxing it like desert heat. Ty found the cd in the library – he's wonderful for that; because of him I have a stash of tiny pieces of worlds beyond my knowledge, the collection of music he's burned for me, things he's learned about it and told me. Too bad the portion I can keep in my disorderly brain is infinitely small compared with what I'm given; but it is delicious to be handed these gems, these pretty stories he pulls slowly from his memory like a canny tradesman producing his wares in good time, letting us take in each sentence, looking unhurriedly for the best word.

It was hot in the loft and we reclined like sultans. Michelle changed into the lab coat that is her loungewear, and dangled her legs over the arm of her chair. You're beautiful, babe, Ty said, grabbing her solid, well-formed foot, gazing at her sleepily, lovingly. Michelle rolled her eyes at him, but smiled. You're my favorite girls, he said, looking over at me, The prettiest, smartest girls in the world.

Right, Ty, said Michelle, clearly happy.

Oh, now, I said, The very best ones, eh? I cocked an eyebrow at him and grinned.

The best ones, he said.

Driving up the misty Bayview Extension I couldn't help casting a regretful glance as I passed Pottery Road, thinking of Michael up that hill in his pretty neighborhood, asleep, alone in his childhood bed. That stern, slightly pouty look of self-reliance he sometimes has in sleep. A half-eaten package of Stoned Wheat Thins sitting by his computer, the cats on his bed. I got in and kissed Mom lightly, not wanting to wake her, but she woke anyway, startling me. She laughed a muffled sleep-laugh and said Sorry, honey, squinted at me, saying You alright? as though she expected me to be otherwise. As she always sounds.

Yes, I said, feeling like Michael, slightly quizzical, detached.

Okay, give me a hug.

And I was folded into her sleepy warmth, her soft, heavy body full of need and love. As always after a moment I wanted to stand up, and as always when I did felt bereaved. Sweet dreams, Mama, I said.

Sweet dreams, my honey girl. I love you.

These are the words I've been hearing my whole life, I thought. And some day I won't hear them any more, not like this.

Fighting a tightness in my chest I went into my own room, packed a bowl and lay in bed smoking it, scribbling a few things down. Spike came and crawled into my lap, trilling contentment. I felt very alone, but happy, as though I was accomplishing something just being awake, turning feelings into sentences. You, self-contained creature, have helped to teach me; I think of you and can suddenly perceive myself, my surroundings, unseen by anyone else, and find a coherent whole, a pleasing picture.

So, my dear Joe, blessings for November. Light a fire in that lovely, lonely old hostel and think of me, write and tell me what you're reading these days.

Much love, Sam.

DOMESTICITY AND DESCRIPTIONS
11/07/2002

Eshe. I loved your Paris villanelle. It's the only poem I've ever been in – like, me as a person who does stuff in the world, not me the zygote or newborn. And yes, I knew you used "fink" for the rhyme....

I wrote my first poem for class. I didn't want to because I always feel like I don't know what a poem is, but then I was at Mike's and he was on the computer and I started writing. It goes like this:

industrial evolution

the sun was a honey-spill,
spreading across floorboards
you recently finished.
i slept right there, you said,
pointing to the bare wood
beneath the window, with willow trees
and Toshiba neon sign outside
where silent highway overpasses
curling like thick grey smoke,

> enfold the fragile sky above
> abandoned factory lots.
> four days with no furniture, you said,
> i loved it.
> the open space made me feel at home.
> one grizzled beige suede chair now
> rests where you slept,
> the whole space swept clean
> of silent huge machinery,
> and damp nights with lightless squatters.
> you say at dusk, flower-smells drift up from the Valley.

Mom helped me edit it, delighted, as she said, to be part of a creative process again. It made me happy to make her happy, and she really did help the poem along ("grizzled," for instance, is a much better word than "old").

Mike is on a weirdly depressive sort of a kick. On Halloween he kept me up until two talking about everything that's wrong with the world but why a revolution would be a disaster – a lot of which I got on tape or wrote down afterward. It's funny though. He can have such hope for the world, and yet can be so scathing. But it does help me pry open my ignorant mind.

Jesse Rock – Mike's oldest, dearest friend – is getting married. I found out from J.R., who's in the same class as Jesse at UVic,. So I say to Mike, Hey, spoken to Jesse lately? and he says Yeah. I need to get out there and see him to meet his fiancé. Mmmhmmm. Oh, I never mentioned that to you, gee, I really thought I did.

Then he talks about how Jesse is ready to get married, has sown his wild oats and all that and now maybe because he's been looking for the one he's found her. (Isn't it astounding that a person can speak like this and not be aware of how much he's revealing?) Yesterday Mike said he might be in B.C. for New Year's, but we'll see.

I'm still waiting on that continuation of your Halloween email. Send it along.

me.

DIARY OF A SIGN JUNKIE

11/20/2002

Oh Joe I can hardly stand thinking about you so unhappy, but thank you for writing to let me know. When I tried to call yesterday the phone just rang and rang. I wish there was something more immediate I could do for you, but if what you want is sketches of my life these days, then here, dear friend, is my best attempt.

A Haphazard Entrance to a Building:

Bri met me at York one evening last week, as an old friend of hers was having an art show up there. I love how whatever Bri does she does completely; as she got off the bus I smiled at her British schoolgirl tweed jacket, vintage satchel hanging at her hipbone – a better look for her I'd say than the suspenders and spiky hair of her gayborhood days. On a bench in the quiet twilight we talked about social cohesion and if we had any, and whether there was more in the sixties, and about discourse versus activism. The IMF, she said, Or the World Bank could be seen as activism without discourse.

Possibly also the hippies, I said, Though not all of them. Or maybe they just had the wrong discourse. And then academics is often discourse without activism.

Yeah, and Latin American labour movements might be seen as a progressive combination of the two.

Well that solves that then.

As we walked toward Vanier's beige tower, she kept looking at me to talk to me and so pushing me into the grass, and I looked up at her dimpled, shining face thinking, lovely. Twenty-one years old, books in our bags, employing all our newly-learned language so enthusiastically, decked out and proud like in new clothes we'd put on all at once after buying them. Admiring each other in them, seeing our familiar selves transformed yet continuous.

Then, disoriented by the fluorescent lights and busy halls after the dark empty outside, we walked laughing, awkward into the building.

You Know You're Right:

I believe I'm doing the right thing with Mike because I am happy. Even when he does things that should make me unhappy (I sit on his lap and he's unreceptive; he talks about the many places he wants to go), afterwards when I think of how I behaved and how we were, I am pleased.

Of course no matter how much careful consideration I give the matter, it's still the same I that wants a certain outcome. But I must have some ability to be objective – or, if not objective, at least to get beyond my own interests. So it goes in my brain, morning and night. Interspersed with accusatory monologues about how If he doesn't want to be with me I should just leave him alone, and Why can't he see that what he's expecting of the world is unreasonable and what I'm offering is not? Things of course I'll never say, and feel bad even thinking, because what right have I to demand that he want what I want?

The other night as I was leaving his place he said, Sam, you're not, uh, having trouble with the way things are, uh, with us, are you?

In the dark of the living room he was a silhouette against the yellow kitchen light and at it I directed who knows what nonsense. Stunned in the glaring simplicity of this question I consider all the time, the answer to which I base everything upon.

I just got this vibe, he said, moving toward me.

I met his eyes, those beautiful blue-green eyes with their heavy Irish lids and slightly Asiatic tilt; looked firmly into their penetrating curiosity, his desire to understand. But he cannot understand, not yet. I felt so good to be leaving it surprised me. For the first time maybe ever I really wanted to go, and I was going, not waiting, not wanting to be stopped, just babbling about everything being perfectly fine with us and trying to seem engaged with getting out the door.

If it's about calling a spade a spade, he said, You know, you can. I mean I never really cared.

For a second I didn't know what he was talking about, then I realized we had talked a while back about owning up to the fact that this is a relationship, that I had said we may as well. Sure, I thought, never really cared my ass. But all I said was, I don't call anything anything, man, I just go about my business and occasionally come by here and enjoy your company. Hoping I sounded more Rosalind Russell than flustered girl that I was.

And my heart constricted because I saw his open, genial manner snap shut, become guarded in the face of my defensiveness. But I don't want him coming to me with concessions, a spit polish for my scuffed pride. *You can say I'm your boyfriend if that will make you happy.* Fuck that shit. Such a distance as there was between us just then I could not take, it was too unnatural so I said, You know what it is? Since you asked, I'll tell you. It's that I can feel when you're getting standoffish, and what you see is me reacting to that. But it's okay. Does that make sense?

He asked me if he should not have asked and I said he should because now I had put something into words. In truth I felt I was wrangling a struggling cat back into the bag. I can only handle our arrangement, only feel that it's fair and not shameful if my feelings and expectations are kept to myself. And basically our situation does suit me fine, because my long-range view keeps me content, and I can bear his actions now because I see he is acting out of blindness and fear. The danger being that perhaps it is me who's acting in blindness and fear – wishing to keep my assessment of the situation to myself to defend indefensible delusions. After all, it is perfectly possible that I am irrationally attached to a man who wants only to be attached to nothing.

But I got in the car and turned on the radio: that newly released Nirvana song was playing, Kurt Cobain growling "You know you're right" over and over from beyond the grave. I thought, Thanks, Kurt.

Then on the oldies station, "Should I stay or should I go" came on and I thought Yup, that's the question. Pondering it as I crawled over the speedbumps up Mike's tree-lined street.

The chorus of the next song to come on was: "I'm free, I'm free, and I'm waiting for you to follow me." Indeed, I thought, that is the case, feeling perfectly free and rational as I sped up the Valley thinking Yes, I have chosen this freely and of my own accord. And in the same spirit you will follow me. But then I thought good lord, Sam. If you took one of those DSM questionnaires asking whether the TV or radio was talking to you, you'd have to say Yes. Yes, I get affirmation of my choices from the songs that come on the radio. Their appearance in a timely moment is important to me. Though I know it's ridiculous I nonetheless feel that the cosmos is just maybe giving me a little bit of encouragement; I piece together random signs to make the meaning I desire. Two steps further along the crazy spectrum I know I'd be put on Thorazine but as it is I still believe myself to be in the realm of the rational. As though there was anything rational in trying to decide who to spend your life with. For such a leap of faith, songs on the radio seem about as good an indicator as anything else.

Write as soon as you can, sweet Joe.

xo, and mad love, Sam.

HAPPY YULE!

12/25/2002

Dearest Joe, it's hard to believe you've been gone more than a year now. I so badly wanted to call you today, but I know you are with your cousins in the wilds of Yorkshire. Your last email was distressing. Your lovely body, Joe, don't harm it. Do you know what is making you so unhappy? Is it the isolation, or running the hostel; are you having doubts about Dave? Isn't there anyone you could see, maybe, like a shrink? I know a lot of times they're idiots, but if you could find someone you were comfortable with it might be helpful. Sort out the Gordian Knot of your insides, as Mike might call it. As though anyone can sort out their insides. Mike likes to point out that the story of the Gordian Knot is irritating because in the end someone just slices through it with his sword; no one undoes it at all. But there is no magical sword for the human soul, though we keep hoping there is – some theory or chemical that will make us masters of ourselves, which serves as a convenient distraction from what we really must do, which is to spend our whole lives sorting through the miraculous, infuriating knot of our own brains, never to be able to hold both ends of the rope in our hands but simply to know, as completely as possible, its twists and turns.

Thank you for the Yule wishes (don't you love time zones?); yes, it has been a pleasant Christmas. Annual dinner last night with Shelagh, my former nanny, her husband and their two kids. And Mike, which was great. After they left Mom flipped through the channels to see what Christmas specials were on. She loves her occasion-specific TV, feels strongly that on major holidays there should be holiday shows. I'm of two minds about it: it is nice that there should be "special days" in the year, days that feel different from the rest because stores are closed and there are different programs on TV; but then it seems cheap to get our sense of "specialness" from offerings on the idiot box. Mom, though, is a child of the fifties, and her feelings about TV are bound to be different from mine. For her it's still a medium of incredible possibility, an entertainment smorgasbord. She realizes that most of what's on is crap, but that doesn't poison the medium for her. She has perpetual hope for the next great show, eternal belief in the well of creativity from which our society draws.

We put on *It's a Wonderful Life*, as we do every year, and Mike took a powder. We watched it the first Christmas we spent together and Mom made a bit too much of Michael's resemblance to Jimmy Stewart. It's true, they do look similar, but more significant is how Michael's peculiar mix of wanderlust and irrepressible decency is rather George Bailey-like.

To bed with me. Work early tomorrow. Time and a half!

I hope you feel better; let's have a phone date soon. xo

EQUIP, EQUIP

01/12/2003

Sweet Joe,

I'm glad your family obligations were not too miserable – that was so cool to talk to you on New Years, I could imagine you staring out at the moors, your ruddy-cheeked cousins behind you getting drunk. Though your description of everyone silent and staring at their plates, when the dinner-table raillery about the various kids' romances turned to you, was like a comically tragic stereotype of Britishness. At least your parents have accepted Dave's presence, and no longer allude to me as your girlfriend.

Don't worry about not calling on the birthday; thank you for the wonderful long email – you know there's no better present than coming home to a page-full of your mind. I'm glad your new job is making you feel hopeful. And though it sounds awful in fact, you gave me a good laugh with your description of your commute in poor frozen William, scraping the ice off the windshield in your fingerless gloves at stoplights, cigarette between your lips, curses on your tongue. Tell me about Newport, and your young charges – what sorts of lives have they had? What do they need, and what can you do for them?

Yes, it was an enjoyable birthday. Mom gave me this cool old card she's had since the 1960s, said she felt now was the right time to give it away. It's very sixties-looking – wavy perpendicular blue and green stripes bisected at the bottom by slanted horizontal stripes and Thoreau's words, in irregular white, "If a man does not keep pace with his companions perhaps it is because he hears a different drummer. Let him step to the music which he hears, however measured or far away." Inside, in perfectly level purple script, Mom wrote that I should consider the message repeatedly, it had always meant a lot to her. Honestly it almost irritated me at first, the card; it's groovy-looking, but reading it I thought oh lord, another reminder to "follow my dreams," a nudge in the direction of that handsome fellah, Greatness. Which it probably is, but then you have to love her for that too. And reading the quote again I thought about how differently it might have been interpreted more than a century ago when it was written – or even what it would have said to Mom when she was my age.

Michael and I went to dinner with Mom and Baba at Le Select, on Queen; it's like an old French bistro, Mom looked right at home with her pink cheeks, hair in a loose chignon. Of course with the family it's always drama and misery: something is always the matter with someone's health, or Baba just wants to sit in despair and recollect when Zaida was alive and Mom gets mad. But with Mike around the whole thing is much more festive: we two babble on and I feel like a kid, indulged and pampered on her special day. So we ate some delicious steaks and tried to keep the conversation off pain of any kind, and Baba told the story about the time she was at a party in her honour and, as she was talking to a journalist, her beads fell off her neck and into her and the journalist's coffee cups. So she went to the bathroom and restrung the beads, wiped the coffee stains off her blouse, came back to resume the conversation, and the same thing happened again. She always ends these stories with, Oh well, those are the kinds of things that were always happening to me. I was always falling out of the car, or going on-stage with chewing gum in my mouth (Mom chiming in with, Yeah, the people in the front seats were hysterical because there was this Diva, beautifully dressed, with these long, kid-skin gloves, and she's got the chewing-gum stuck between her fingers and she's pulling at it while she sings these incredible arias… Mom stretching her fingers out like a jellyfish opening and closing as she talks). Baba saying, But I was a very elegant lady! half-joking and half-serious. Then she'll say, Your grandfather used to get me all sorts of beautiful things, a-ny-thing I wanted, he would get. He would go into a store and say, You look about my wife's size, try that on for me willya, honey? A prince of a man, she'll say, A king. She'll look off into the distance, brows arching toward each other, eyes raised in the universal look of unbearable suffering, and it's absurd, an exaggerated stage pose, and it's completely real.

And Mom will pick at her food, say sharply, Mother, is the drama really necessary?

It's silly to say we try and ward off pain because in a moment any of it, all of it, can become painful. These most familiar faces that will, in all probability, be long disassembled before I leave this world. Some moments it seems each of them, capable of being extinguished at any moment, are themselves as they will be in memory even as they are before me: flickering images; symbols of themselves. I see them as if imprinted on the air around the table, as if all future tables will bear that imprint even when the bodies are gone. And I imagine what those impressions lack – Baba as Zaida's wife; Mom as Irving's, as a defensive young thing; Baba after a performance. What were they like? I have always wondered: even as a kid, when I'd come downstairs sometimes and Mom would be doing the Mashed Potato or, to my horror, the Hitchhiker – licking her thumb and putting it to her bum and everything – I realized this was not just my Mom doing a silly-looking dance, but a person who had been in another time, had been there with rhythm and a mischievous gleam in her eye. Wow, I forgot until now but when I was ten or so I wrote a poem that went, *Thirty years ago men sat in their chairs, watching my Mom wave her long auburn hair, thinking of a long and lusty affair...* Ha! Joe, look at what you make me think of. I remember Baba was horrified at some part of that poem too. But Mom loved it. And it had something in it about her dancing in the living room, heavier, but still light on her toes. Man, I should find that poem.

Speaking of our brains' mysterious ways, Michael had a dream recently where these powerful, priest-like people thought he was a eunuch, although he wasn't, and the priests were chanting at him: "Equip, equip, although you're not equipped." There was more to it than that which I forget, but if that doesn't say it all about his feelings about the future, I don't know what does.

It makes a good little chant really, something you can march around the kitchen to while making eggs.

xo

BODIES V. BOMBS

02/15/2003

Dearest Joe,

today we attended the protest. Yonge St. looked like a fairground, people dragging gap-mouthed children along the crowded sidewalk, eating pizza in the road, everyone heading south in the grey early afternoon. Though it was breakfast Mike stopped at Pizza Pizza for a slice, which he ate drifting down to Dundas, where we were absorbed into the moving mass of demonstrators headed westward. Joe do you know how I love the rabble-rousers with loudspeakers shouting anti-war epithets in rhyme? Loudspeakers get me every time, they just sound like something's going on. Their staticky insistency.

Mike was cagey, darkly assessing the uselessness and beauty of the huge crowd. There will be a war. A million fragile bodies bundled against the cold, their temporary unity through twenty blocks of city streets won't change anything. I know he's thinking, they let us make our noise, why not?

It was a diverse crowd, made the cause seem reasonable and respectable. Happy, frumpy middle-aged couples in Mountain Equipment Co-op gear; burly blue-collar looking dads with kids on their shoulders eating Twizzlers; young couples with babies in hemp slings that I smile at, reflexively, ashamed of wanting their life. Especially in the midst of all those well-intentioned people with their slogans and ideals there in the ashy light telling our government we don't condone the killing they're about to do. And all I can want is to live a good life, envision herbs in kitchen planters, cloth diapers, interesting bean dishes for dinner. I looked over at this boy I seem to love – silent, stern, arguments playing out in his head and barely aware of the thrumming street around him, knowing only that he is not fully in it, that this whole scene asks something of him that he can't give. And this is the man I want, this lonesome, searching creature with his cynicism and resolute morality? Why not someone like that nice sandy-haired goy with the small white teeth, a Robert Redford type in wholesome corduroy pushing his daughter in a stroller, satisfied wife in long cotton scarf and hiking boots smiling at him? I can see their Annex home, colourful and comfortable, see them walking through Kensington in the summers, conscientious, happy in their choices. It must be lovely. But studying their calmness, their sureness, their apparent comfort with themselves and the protest I wondered what my faux Redford would do with my doubts, the bad mornings, the hopeless hours. What would he make of my mom, my family, the rage I sometimes bring to a debate? How much instability can a man like that manage? How much misery would he like to contemplate? Looking at Mike, pale face almost dogged above that massive green coat, long legs striding forward at the edge of the crowd, it was perfectly clear that no-one more sure, more comfortable would be any good. His unease is mine too, only I am there in the street when he is in his head.

The best thing I saw was a group of elderly ladies marching in lively hats and scarves, singing, holding signs, canes, each other.

We didn't talk much, brought no sign, no noisemakers; we didn't chant or answer to call and response. I wondered whether, if this was the '60s, a protest against Vietnam, I would have been the same. Could I have been caught up in the moment more than I am now? Would my belief or the feeling of unity with all these people have been enough to wring shouts from me then? Would I have been here with some organization, more involved with local movements? No way of knowing. We passed a guy with a sign saying "No to War and Globalization," wearing a Nike baseball cap. What do you do with that?

Michael Bobbie and I let ourselves be carried along by the colourful human tide, maybe for no better reason than to say that we did.

xo, Sweet Joe.

TIME TO WONDER WHY

02/18/2003

Dear Joe,

thanks for the email. It's fascinating timing, your writing about how rough the '60s and '70s were in Wales. Michael and I were at his parents' house the day after the protest, telling them about it, and about how powerless we are – even as a crowd of thousands. His dad was leaning against the kitchen counter, smoking pot from a wooden pipe, as the conversation turned to the differences between their generation and ours. Talking with his breath held, as older tokers will do, he said, I dunno. I think you guys are much more, sorta, politically aware than we were.

Janice declined the pipe, passed it to Mike, who said, Well but you guys had the Vietnam war –

Brian interrupted with a conditional, Yeah, but for us it was like, we would hear that some guy we'd worked with at that camp in Vermont was off fighting in the war, and *that's* when we sorta went, whoa – it really made it personal.

I sipped my red wine (the Bobbies make their own), Country Joe in my head going *and it's a one-two-three what're we fightin' for? Don't ask me I don't give a damn...* and admired their solid pine table. I thought of Janice and Brian not a decade older than Mike and I when they bought this house, this then-cheap east-end house not having any idea what it would be worth in twenty years. Lovely old detached brick beauty, nice big tree out front, working fireplace. Bought by a couple of young people with their first kid, a business plan, good senses of humour. That they still have this house and each other is comforting.

Brian was saying, You guys have it hard. You know, when we were in school, tuition for the year was like, uh, three hundred and fifty dollars… rent was maybe fifty dollars a month, you had a part-time job and you could afford to have a car. Brian said all this with incredulous enthusiasm and I churned with jealousy. What sweet ease, what peace and simplicity.

But, said Brian, You guys are gonna be okay. Every generation has its challenges, ya know? The Baby Boom had a serious effect on the world but we're not gonna be running things forever, and you guys are gonna come up with new, creative solutions to a lot of our problems. Yup, from our failing hands we pass the torch…

I've just come home from meeting Michael's Arabic tutor, Mustafa. My professor for Creative Writing (Priscila Uppal, not much older than me and with like four books of poetry and a novel) held a class discussion about Auden's assertion that translation is the only political duty of poets. Our assignment is to translate any poem, and being awful at languages I went to Michael for help, and he suggested we go to see Mustafa. He came here from Syria via the States, where he got his Master's in linguistics. Of course he's been hoping to find some good work – teaching preferably, or translation. But so far, nothing, though Mike says he's an excellent teacher; and I don't know the last time I met anyone who loves poetry so much. His whole face changes when he reads; he looks almost noble – a banished prince thinking of his kingdom. Beneath a harsh overhead light, hands resting on the plastic-tableclothed table, Mustafa said: In Syria, poetry is in the newspapers; it is political commentary. There is a national competition there, where someone recites a poem and the next person must recite another beginning with the same word the last ended on. It is a huge event. Even kids know poetry; well, when I was a kid anyway we'd sit around and recite lines from poems and we'd have to name the poet.

I can see why Mike likes talking to him, and also why, when Mike first met him, he said his tutor struck him as a frustrated intellectual with a bit of a dark side. There is a darkness under his eyes, in the corner of his lovely lips a curl of disappointment, distaste with himself. He distinctly did not intend to come here and be a struggling tutor in an East York apartment building. But then, Mike tells me, he had trouble in Syria, too. He is one of those sharply intelligent, rootless, discontented men that this world seems to produce in such quantity.

I want to get him thinking differently about Israel, Mike said on the way up. There are moments where he'll agree with me when I talk about the problem as one of states and power, and not religion or fundamental attributes. I told him you're Jewish, and he didn't seem to think that was a problem. But he's angry, and it comes out in his politics.

Doesn't it always? But I am glad, sweet Joseph, that some angry young men have you to talk to these days, and that you are doing something that makes you feel useful (so you don't become an angry young man yourself!) I love to think of you smoking at tiny kitchen tables, observant as some rage-filled boy fires off his disgust and despair, leaving him with less to aim at himself and the world around him.

With much love,
Sam.

FAREWELL, NINA, I'LL LOOK FOR YOU EVERYWHERE
02/20/2003

Dear Eshe;

tonight as I was driving home from Ty's I was thinking about how I'd like to climb in through Mike's window but couldn't because he'd be asleep and unimpressed by such shenanigans. Also because he's in BC at the moment visiting Jesse.

Speeding beneath the Danforth Bridge I suddenly thought how I'd feel if I killed Mike in a car accident or something and I couldn't – could not contemplate him being dead. I could ponder N.'s death for an instant, and then I flitted on Mom's and told myself to stop it. Then that old fear that perhaps I have just fooled everyone into thinking I am something I'm not swept over me, followed by the thought that maybe everyone I know isn't what they seem. That was awful for a moment, the thought that inside each of these seemingly together people with their interesting knowledge and skills is an insecure little ball of wants and needs. But then I thought, that's not really the trouble, is it? Thought of Mom saying, To thine own self be true, telling me this throughout my growing up. But also how she and I take as axiomatic Gertrude Stein's assertion that there are only so many types, that after a while everyone you meet starts to fit into one of them; and how crazy it is that both those things must exist at the same time – we can be true to a self that is also a preexisting type of self. Then I remembered and was saddened at the fact of Al Hirschfeld's recent death – no more searching for the NINAS in his perfect caricatures on a Sunday morning with Mom, as I've done since childhood. She always said, Aren't they wonderful? And we must enjoy them because some day there will be no more Hirschfeld. I love how those line drawings distil character – surely drawing on the same archetypes old Gertrude was thinking of, pulling the specific from what we can all recognize. How is it that the arch of an eyebrow, the tilt of a head, can suggest so much about what someone *is*? Fighting tears at the loss of my NINAS, at the whole era going with Hirschfeld, I wondered at how "types" must change too, over time. And yet in our different builds, our movements and predilections, there are repetitions. It was pleasing to think that no matter how much we belong to a particular era, we are always another portrayal of a certain character.

Oh indulged, indulged, smelling the roses atop the shitheap, in Mom's old Saab, whirring into my heated garage. No point in not admitting the roses are lovely. I thought of you and was happy – and wanted to tell you this weird piece of news: Priscila Uppal, my writing teacher, is friends with my half-brother David. There was a show on TV about Irving the other day so I asked if she'd seen it, figured it was an appropriate time to tell her he's my dad; and her big eyes got even bigger – turns out, she lived in the basement apartment of David and his wife's house when she first arrived in

Toronto to go to York. She gave me his number and told me to call him, seemed sure that he would want to hear from me. I don't know, maybe someday....

Write soon.

Love, Sam.

AS LOU SAID: CHOOSE. CHOOSE AGAIN.
        02/22/2003

Joseph,

I'm glad you went to London for the protest – who knows if something of that magnitude will happen again in our lifetimes. Too bad Dave didn't want to go with you, especially as it was on Valentine's day. It could have been very romantic, striding down the street surrounded by a million impassioned people, representing your own bit of British life. But then, how can you help it if Dave wants to ignore this whole question of war?

The other night, I was down at Ty's and he surprised me by asking, in that unbelievably earnest voice of his, how I'm doing without Mikey, who's in British Columbia visiting his oldest friend. We were on the couch in the position Ty sometimes calls "assuming the position," reclining against opposite arms of the couch, legs stretched side by side, a joint burning between us. It was late, Michelle had gone to bed; the fridge was the only sound in the warm, darkened space. Ty was staring dreamily at his drums in the corner, arms over his head, little brown belly peeking out from beneath his faded blue shirt with the happy roller-skating hippopotamus and "wheelies" written on it in peeling bubble letters.

Of course I'm missing Mike terribly, and what's worse, I think he's happy to have gotten away from me. I did a bad thing, and looked in this writing book I got him for Christmas (it's made from recycled book covers, and I got him one that said Codes and Ciphers on it – it seemed appropriate). I know it was stupid, but I couldn't help myself, it was right there, which is no excuse – I'm a nasty snoop and deserved to find what I'd expected to find anyway, which was anxiety. Anxiety that he's doing the wrong thing, that he's going to hurt me again, that he's already hurting me. Fear that his feelings are not what they were when we first were together. So I know he's out there in the BC rainforest ensconced in a life that has nothing to do with me, and loving it.

But there's no point worrying about it.

Sammy, Ty said, Is he the one?

I couldn't believe anyone had actually used that phrase without an ounce of cynicism. He really wanted to know – it sounded exceedingly serious the way he said it. I couldn't even laugh it was so serious.

So I looked for the right words to answer him as my head sped through Yes, unequivocally and No, he doesn't want it and Probably, which is what I eventually said. The random guy we drove home the other night certainly felt we were meant for each other. (To Ty's arched eyebrow and lowered head:) Some people Mike tree planted with were in town for a night, so we were dropping by a party they were having. And there was a guy lying in a bus shelter who wasn't dressed for the cold, and looked like he'd just kind of slumped down... so we said if he was still there when we came out, we'd try and take him someplace. He was still there like an hour later, so we got him into the car – he was super-drunk, but he had a place to go – conveniently, one of those bungalows just north of St. Clair. And he was this kinda sweet guy, who all the way home kept saying, You two lovebirds are meant for each other, I can tell, you gotta get married.

See, Ty said. Everyone can see it. You'd have some dynamite kids.

Hopefully they'd get his long legs.

And your good looks. It would be great if you two could move in here.

Yeah, I told him, But it's not going to happen. He doesn't want to live with me right now. (To Ty's eyebrows drawn pitifully together:) Better that he knows it. (I thought of Mike telling me recently about his repulsion upon seeing a hairbrush of Michelle's on Ty's desk. The intertwining of lives, the casual intimacy – it gives him a stomach pain.)

Ty looked both crestfallen and sorry for me; he was so disappointed I felt worse for him than for myself. He wants a big communal house full of his friends; Mike may move in there, but I can't. Fuck, I told Ty, I'd have to go into so much debt; I'd have to work so many more hours… (and the brain flashed on Mom, alone, in whatever new apartment she would inhabit without me. For what?)

Join the club, he said, adjusting the cushion behind his back. Man, these days Sammy, I feel like a station, not a traveler. Everyone applying for med school has been to fucking Jachunum or wherever, saving the whale-chickens, and they all have a cousin or a brother. They all know somebody, these people. And in the summer, they go give of themselves to the world. How have I given of myself to the world over the past few years? I have to answer that question on the application. I've always just been the urchin on the periphery. It's not like I volunteered in an orphanage in Mali, or collected snails in the rainforest or something. You know? I can't show them receipts for coolant from the bottles I've given away when I stop to help people with their cars.

I'll include it in my letter of reference. That and the time you sutured the butcher's finger.

Which made him smile. Sammy, he said, What if I want to be a doctor for the wrong reasons? What if it's just selfish, just a need to try and fix things?

So? What's so bad about that? Someone's gotta do it. It's a hard job, Ty, hard to train for, especially for you who has no brother, no cousin, no money – and demanding when you practice. You're going to be surrounded by the sick, the families of the sick. You want a selfish job, take writing. Though I can't help but feel there's some use in it.

And will I still have time to play music? I was just getting good with the tabla, and I don't even have time to practice now.

Ty Ty the Gemini, I chided him, blowing smoke into the mellow light. You'll make time. You've always wanted to be a doctor, and you've always been a musician. You can't be a doctor in your spare time. You have to choose it. And you're going to be great at it.

And he turned those dark eyes up to my face, full of that gentle pleading, so vulnerable sometimes it's almost manipulative.

How far we've come, Sammy, how far we've come.

I love how he says this to me with a wistful smile, as if to stop for a moment and look back at our waving selves of four or six or eight years ago. To see how we're the same, maybe a little better.

Indeed, Ty, said I.

Then he surprised me again: Is that going to be in a book someday, he asked me.

You know, Joe, I think it was the first time we ever talked about me writing as though it were really going to be. I assumed he thought I was a bit of a silly dreamer with the whole writing business; perhaps it's only I who think that and he never did. But in any case, the way he said it, it was a foregone conclusion that someday I would write a book, and he only wanted confirmation that something of him might be in it. Which of course it would be. When we were twenty he signed a statement saying that I could use him as a character, if he got to be a rodeo clown.... In fact, that moment in Ty's boss's loft two years ago was perhaps the first moment I really believed I would write a book.

So you see, my sweet Joseph. Even what might seem to be the most straightforward ambitions, the most laudable, practical dreams, even those come with conflict.

Have you looked into the social work programs yet? Perhaps you could study here....

I have to write my first short story. I will write about Morocco, about going to Essaouira with Moukhtar and Mohammed, and my first experience with Berber Love. I think I am excited.

xo Sam.

APRIL IS THE CRUELEST MONTH
   04/04/2003

Dearest Joe;

last night as I drove home from the loft I was listening to Manu Chao, his Spanish and French making me think of you, wanting you there to translate for me; I sang along to the words I knew – *me gusta la guitarra, me gustas tu, me gusta marijuana, me gustas tu...* and it's very much spring now, the dreamy cloudless days where everything seems hazed and soft and slow, nights clear and cold. It was a strange day in a strange week so I decided to write to you, in three parts.

Going to Sleep and Waking Up:

Two nights ago I arrived at Mike's at about 1:30 a.m. to find him wasted and incensed at the kitchen table, reading an article on pharmaceutical companies to his friend Noam, his only remaining geek buddy from high school. I made myself a bagel, waiting for Mike to ask me about the gig I'd just come from (Samba Elegua played at Koolhaus); finally I said, It was great, thank you very much, irritated by my own huffy irritation. I smoked a joint with Mike's brother feeling that Mike just wanted me to leave so he could go to sleep in peace, though he was saying he wanted me there, asking me to stay. It's nice to have another body in the bed, he said, as we climbed the stairs.

Though I know he wouldn't deliberately lie, I was unconvinced, followed him upstairs feeling lonely and lost. Backs to each other he gave me a gentle pat on the rump and fell asleep. Two nights before in my bed in the early morning I felt his arms around my waist and was so peaceful, he hasn't done that in years. Ten a.m. the alarm, kids playing outside, Mike jumped out of bed before I was even fully awake. He was focused on getting out of the house in a half-hour; friends from work were coming to take him to a house in the country for a night. I dragged myself from bed, he went to buy cheese. I thought about the diary on his night-table shelf, full of his restlessness and regret that he can't feel more love for me; his discomfort with our situation. But I carried his cheese to the car and he said, Thanks Sam, in that adorably sincere voice that I know means he's sorry about the distance between us. I kissed him quickly, pulled away before he did and walked to my car, awkward and cold. I am so bad at the "feminine games" Mom believes we should play, the clever ruses and well-timed smiles or coolness. I'm far too obvious; I've got no game, no knack for the beguiling of men.

I drove home shivering in the gorgeous sun and came upstairs, watched the end of *The Black Stallion* in Mom's darkened bedroom which made me miss horses, childhood and Morocco. Mom had to have an emergency tooth extraction so she was in bed, puffy and in pain and frustrated at the hundreds of dollars she had to pay for the privilege of feeling that way.

When the movie was over I went into my bedroom and opened the curtains. The room was bright and pretty, the metropolis in full swing down below. I stood in my unkempt clothes staring at the still-made bed, unable to decide between taking off my jeans and getting into the clean sheets or grabbing "The Soul of Man Under Socialism" and having a smoke on the balcony. I ended up curled on top of the covers, eyes closed in the sun, mind a silent film of thwarted lives and mundane mistakes; I saw Mike peaceful and distant and wanted to hurt him, saw my mother's drowning brown eyes and started to cry.

When I woke an hour later Mom was making tea; she mentioned a headline that got me onto the no-good politicians in this world – I think she could see I needed a good rant and lord knows she knows what to say. She brought out the human nature card (people need leaders) so of course I said, No one's qualified to say what human nature is considering the continuous re-shaping of our environment.

That's right, she said; We are always reshaping our environment. And (as if I didn't know what she was going to say) that's why your generation has to get out there, get involved. You have all these visions of how you want things to be, go make them be.

Later I went to a party at an old high school friend's: one of those hippie girls from a comfortable family in Forest Hill, a house bought when it was not as super-expensive as it would be now, carpets threadbare in places, un-renovated bathrooms. My friend is going to be a lawyer, do something useful in environmental law. One of her friends told us of seeing black kids get beaten by police at Bathurst subway station recently and we were all shocked – thought this city was free of that, but apparently not. I told my old friend my fears that I am doing nothing useful and she said, Writing is useful, but I thought of her and her specific, worldly knowledge and didn't believe her. You just have to pick something, she said, Anything, whatever issue interests you, find an organization that deals with that issue and join it.

My Grandmother and a Hamburger:
On the weekend we went to a diner in Yorkville for milkshakes and burgers, Mom sad and quiet, Baba reminiscing about the childhood shame

of ill-fitting shoes. Mom asking her how she liked her hamburger and Baba saying, It's okay, nothing fantastic.

Afterward sitting on a bench in the last sunshine I sang "Mercedes Benz" and Baba to my great surprise liked it (this is a woman who, when I was singing the Seder's Four Questions at seven years old, covered her ears if I went slightly off-key.) She said, In retrospect, the hamburger was good.

That made Mom laugh. Sure, she said, That's always the way with you. Nothing is good enough at the time, only afterward do you realize how good you had it.

Crocuses and Coffee:

Today I had to do a shift at the Annex store, before which Mike and I had a greasy-spoon brunch and then sat in the car listening to the new Radiohead album as the windshield blurred with rain. They're the defining music of our generation, Mike said. It's like distilled alienation, their sound.

But not just alienation, I said. It's so, so sad. Thom York was intoning *Walk into the jaws of hell* over tragic keyboards, and I was struck still and heavy with the thought of us middle-class white kids, a world at our fingertips and when we play it, these are the sounds it makes. No more "I am the Walrus" and "Sunny Goodge Street," the song's electronic scratching was like frantic rats scrambling beneath an increasingly urgent, painfully human chant, a reminder that because we are animals and programmed to live we will stake our claims on this world of vanishing but indestructible history, crush the bones of our ancestors with SUVs full of fake-breasted Moms and anorexic teens, heads swarming with celebrities and action movies, car accidents, car bombs and greenhouse gasses; starving people on this continent and every other, we will stick with our reality shows, Visa debt racked up on Veterans Day specials, all of it grown in the ashes of the A-bomb, fertilized with stories of the gas chambers and right now guided missiles are seeking out flesh and bone, destroying them. It can never be reversed; this is what we are.

Middle-aged Annex ladies entered and exited the frame of my windows, holding umbrellas above tidy bodies which probably execute camping trips in Algonquin Park and exploratory journeys through South Asia – their well-meaning, insular lives what I suppose I should aspire to having one day. They strode purposefully past with their multi-coloured scarves and funky handbags, impervious to the crocuses just today piercing neighbourhood lawns. They weren't pretty, these comfortable women; not nearly as pretty as my mom, who with her aching body would be stooping to finger the flowers' valiant shoots, exclaiming, Isn't it marvelous!

A song came on with the lyrics Just 'cause you feel it, doesn't mean it's there, and Mike said, I hope that's not about his wife. Mike's interpretation an unconscious message, perhaps. It was time to go to work; I emerged from the car almost surprised to find the day was not the silent, distorted movie I had been watching through the windshield. Mike walked off into the rain as I entered the hot, busy store, disoriented by the unfamiliar setup of the too-familiar Starbucks chattels. I tied my apron and started pulling shots, which made me think of you, sweet Joseph, your grace and adaptability; I allowed myself to simply be a body through which orders flowed. Commands: arms extend hands toward espresso, two pulls, hands to the machine, push the button.

Sealed by the steamed-up windows into the gleaming glossed shell of the shop, the caramel floors and peanut-coloured walls, I stood over my hissing milk pitcher as though that was all I was here to do on earth; my only purpose was filling the empty cups with whatever drink was marked on them in black grease-pencil. It'll take some kind of cataclysm to shatter the powerful inertia we're caught up in, I thought; the inertia of my habitualized body performing its barista routine multiplied to an unknowable power.

Then, strangely, the animal blindness in which we mostly exist was alright with me – wonderful, even. I don't want to find humanity disgusting: I remembered saying that to you once on the phone, apropos something or other, and the phone going silent between gasps of your pained laughter. And I smiled to myself, too, calling a leather-jacketed hipster to her soy Tazo Chai, thinking alright, we can and should laugh at this ridiculous world, its mass of us weird hairless monkeys embroiled in existence, trying to fill it up, understand how it matters – but it has to be a tender laugh, doesn't it?

And off the brain spun into whether or not knock-off music can still really mean something to people, and if it does then what does that say, and what effect does it have, and so on and so forth, until it was time to clean the floors.

x

KIDS IN AMERICA
        05/16/2003

Dearest Joseph,

I've just returned from New York, where Michael and I went for Eshe's graduation. We had a bit of difficulty getting down – we took Baba's 1991 Lincoln, and just outside Rochester I put my foot on the gas pedal and nothing happened. Forty thousand kilometers on the car and the transmission is dead. We spent the night in Henrietta, took a stroll across a swathe of immaculate business-park lawn to the multiplex, where we drank vodka behind a shrubbery behind a parking lot, then saw Matrix Reloaded. We figured, you know, when in Rome and all that.

Riding in a tow truck back to Toronto was frustrating but rather entertaining, and the next day we started again, in a rental car. My favorite conversation on the way down: in upstate New York, we saw a pro-Israeli bumper sticker; to my stream of invective about God and His appalling influence, Michael responded with, Words are a kind of religion for you.

Which made me laugh; No wonder I have such a contentious relationship with them!

Israel, Mike said, Is a state like any other, a product of violence; it's legitimate because it has the force to say it's legitimate. Sure it would have been better if Israel could have actually embodied the new ideals about democracy and human rights that were being kicked around at the time it was created. But there's no year zero, and Israel wasn't conceived by a past capable of producing the kind of state we might dream of.

Fine, I said, ever reasonable and insightful, Get everyone out and nuke the fucking place. Let the End Times come for them that want it, and wipe the whole goddamned region off the map. The Men in Charge must get an itchy finger now and again; they love to see things blow. So do it there – no more holy sites granted by God, no more problem.

Straight-man Mike quietly observed that that is a terrible idea, and I was sad a moment, thinking of the awful reality of the stupid thing I'd said. I looked at Michael, be-flagged colonial-looking houses whizzing by his head, and thought I want this wise, kindly countenance to look on me and see a person who can accept the world with some grace.

Soon enough we had arrived at Broadway & 107th, where Eshe's been living with her closest Columbia friend, whose parents have bought a walk-up apartment from the 1890s, with red and blue glass panes above the wooden doors, and an intimidating granite and stainless-steel kitchen. The next day was the Big Day! Michael and I put on our Sunday best and walked the nine blocks to the school gate, where we met Eshe's Mom. (Her Dad – a doctor who teaches at Columbia – did not come to the ceremony, though he took us all out for lunch later. So strange to see my other single-mother friend with two parents, and such a paternal, generous sort of father! She seemed very young, and small, at the big table after the ceremony.) Erica has always been a sort of fascination to me – her self-contained calm and almost girlish movements, her habit of immaculate housekeeping which Eshe has inherited. Their reserved closeness, the deep personal similarities that bind mother and daughter in the absence of physical expressions of love. And their family stories that Eshe tells me, so different from mine, about Erica's childhood in Dominica, and her arrival in Toronto in 1960, witnessing the burgeoning Black activism scene at Bathurst and Bloor. Through them I've been exposed to a whole other Toronto, more political, more downtown than anything my family could have shown me. Erica works in public health; her stories are full of committees and meetings, organizing workshops for immigrant woman or underprivileged youth – yet she's not the hyper-energetic, join-for-the-sake-of-joining woman one might imagine when thinking of the socially active. She likes to talk, but not to many people – from her, Eshe got her aversion to making plans, waiting instead for others to call her; and also the scan-and-avoid technique she has employed so diligently at school when walking in places she might be forced to have unwanted conversation. But Eshe and I are planning to get our moms together, because they like each other and need us to arrange a play date for them.

Anyway, waiting for us with a bemused smile at nine a.m. was Erica. We found some seats and then Michael and I got coffee and bagels. We returned and sat around in the bright humidity for five thousand rounds of Pomp and Circumstance. Seriously, we waited for at least an hour and a half before the graduates even came out, and that song was dribbling out of the loudspeakers the whole time. Miles from us, it seemed, the stage drapery hung in limp splendor. All around us Ivy League mothers milled in respectable sundresses and wide-brimmed hats, or fanned themselves in their Jackie O. suits squinting at the stage. The bulging stomachs of hundreds of fathers spilled contentedly over black patent belts; folding chairs were sweated into, grass was trodden upon, children dirtied their special clothes, teenagers with still-wet hair looked unimpressed, walked around to flaunt their skimpy dresses. Erica sat still, hands in her lap, a smile on her lips, watching the people. And on and on it droned *da na na na na na, na na na na naaaaa...* slowly, like parade music performed by sleepwalkers.

Finally the graduates came out. We saw a couple hundred tiny figures fill some seats at the front. We saw suited figures step to the mic. We faintly heard some words like Achievement, Pride and Tradition, Challenges Ahead and Opportunities; they speckled the damp air like drops of rain. We waited for the burst of meaning that would refresh the day, for the speaker who would bring to life the struggling bud of excitement wilting under the hazy sun and arid sentiment, shriveling in the breasts of undergraduates and audience alike. But that never came. It was just another undergraduate class, after all, just a bunch of kids pushing off to their next phase. I eventually had to submit to my bladder, thus missing Eshe's three-second walk across the stage, and when I returned, Erica whispered, laughing, that she was so surprised when they finally called Eshe that she was halfway across the stage before Erica realized she should clap.

And that was that. Eshe came and found us, momentarily, so Erica could get a picture of her in her cap and gown before they had to be returned (no throwing of caps anymore, man, they're sixty dollars a rental and have to be returned immediately after the ceremony). So we found an unclaimed patch of grass and Eshe grinned, my singular friend at twenty-two in all her sweetness and beauty, captured for posterity on the teeming Columbia lawn before running off to beat the huge line to return her ceremonial garments.

Even though the ceremony was all Pomp and Circumstance and meaningless tripe the afternoon was nonetheless very sweet, and seemed important. My friend has a degree from Columbia University. Seeing Eshe an official graduate of this Ivy League institution, I thought of the day she found out she'd been accepted – it was on our way down to New Orleans, we'd stopped at a McDonald's in St. Louis. Erica called my cellphone but I was in the washroom, so asked her to call back in five minutes. Which she did, and I gave the phone to Eshe as we stood in the sunny parking lot, and I watched her face light up like floodlights on a football field, her mouth and eyes wide open. I got in? I got in! She hung up and leaped onto a table, did a little happy dance and we hugged and danced around together.

Heading for the highway, Eshe waved goodbye to her beloved NYC without a tear. We headed northward belting out Oh Darlin' with the Beatles, which had come on the radio to remind us of doing the same thing four years ago, on our way to New Orleans.

I must go. It's Mom's birthday, and time to dress for dinner.

x

THE TRUTH OF BEAUTY

06/05/2003

Dear Joe,

Hooray for New Beginnings! I think social work is going to be perfect for you; you'll be mired in all the hard-living stories you could ask for while trying to do some good in the world. Though I understand your concern that it could all be aesthetics – how you're drawn toward people on the skids, desire to enter into their troubles and tragedies. I've always wondered about the same thing in myself – why on earth did I love to watch World Vision ads when I was four years old? What drew me to those swollen bellies and tin shacks? I remember trying to explain to Mom when I was about seven, saying, It helps me remember how fortunate I am, but even then I knew it wasn't the whole truth, was aware of something unsettling in my interest that I couldn't pin to words. It's a kind of voyeurism, of course, and guilt at having the luxury of wanting to look in. But also a sense of being something I could not understand, part of a world I didn't understand. What can we do? That was where my first instincts, my childhood desires took me, and ultimately there's no way to say why I found poor people interesting and not rich ones, no more for me than for you. Of course there are reasons – you can and should analyze your desire to help the underprivileged – but in the end it will still boil down to the fact that you and I and people like us are compelled by the powerless, the people getting gored by the bull of life rather than doing the goring.

What makes it disquieting is that we're not alone in our curiosity; lots of people want to know how dirty life can get. I remember when *Trainspotting* came out, watching fascinated as those emaciated, sexy junkies revealed the scummy lives of poor Scottish kids – that's when I first noticed people's fascination with the poverty and violence we're supposed to fear. Is there a dividing line that separates the moral and the immoral aspects of our impulse to look?

Surely, knowing which forms to file in which offices to procure basic necessities like food and shelter – being able to convince people to fill out those forms – must be a good and true use of the interest in others' pain. I have no such certainty about my ability to justify my early compulsion toward Ethiopian famine victims. How does it help the Iraqis for me to envision their bombed-out homes, their dead children? And yet I'd rather do that than see Paris Hilton's titties, or take a TV tour around some rapper's mansion; those images are not compelling, but a shot of an Afghani man drinking from a shit-encrusted puddle is. It feels like looking is an amulet against blindness – like if I stare hard at what threatens my tidy white middle-class life, I'll ward off the cataract of righteous self-interest.

Speaking of aesthetics, and of having no fucking idea why we do the things we do, I've been accepted into the Creative Writing program! (Part Two of the process: there's an introductory year, then you apply for the full-on program.) At first I was very sure I'd be accepted – there can't be that many people all that serious about writing anyway. But then I started thinking, only twenty-five people out of more than a hundred get in; there might be people in the other classes that are way better than me. But now my worries are over; I got the letter yesterday. Priscila, my instructor from this year, will be teaching both the poetry and fiction workshops, which is fabulous. I'm glad she seemed to like me even before she knew about my father. We had chatted a few times out in the hall after class about the week's readings; as the year progressed, she'd tell me about her administrative burdens and occasionally the difficulties of dealing with the young *artistes* who show up in her office demanding recognition of their genius. She is a weird sort of genius – not even thirty and so many books published, her PHD almost completed, already a tenure track professor. She must have known very early on what she wanted to do and gone about pursuing it with great acuity. And, most remarkably, she's a genuinely nice person – makes time for everyone, takes pleasure in her students' development. So it looks like Mom was right, and York is the place for me. Why study creative writing? Who knows. Possibly very silly, possibly a familial tic, possibly all sorts of things. Nonetheless I'm very excited.

Indicating other forms of progress, good old Chrétien, that savvy crook, has allowed some law to lapse because of a medical marijuana case, so at the moment, pot is in legal limbo. Not that this affects in my behavior at all, but it does make me smile to know, when I walk down the street with my joint, that there's nothing anyone can say about it. Mom is very funny; she still believes I'll get busted. She cannot get past the fear that if the cops see you with some dope, they'll throw you in the paddy-wagon like they used to do in her Yorkville days. We were discussing this walking through Yorkville in fact, headed to Baba's apartment earlier today. Watching the Porsche parade, the Botoxed and bejeweled passengers glistening in the sunshine.

Every Saturday night! she said. Every Saturday night there they'd be at the corner of Hazelton and Yorkville, herding the hippies into the paddy-wagon.

Oh the times they are a-changing.

Maybe so, she said, But I still think it's best to be careful.

I blew smoke toward a tanned middle-aged man with a thick gold bracelet, who caught a whiff and walked past us with a twinkle in his eye.

What irony, Mom said, That I've always loved this neighborhood, and your grandmother who never gave two shits about it is the one living here.

Well, I reminded her, It was an excellent deal for what she needed, this apartment.

Yeah well, remind your grandmother of that when she starts going on about wanting to move. This place isn't *fancy* enough for her, she has to be at the Renaissance. She can't afford to live there, those are like million and some dollar apartments. But I constantly have to hear about how this place, this Yorkville apartment, isn't good enough. As *if* I were going to move her again, after what I went through getting her out of the house. I don't even want to think about it. Look what a pretty day. This is where the Mynah Bird used to be (pointing at a brick structure probably built in the eighties). There used to be girls, go-go dancers, in cages outside. Can you believe it?

I thought of Mom on this street thirty years ago, wearing sandals and panhandling. (Panhandling! she said to me recently. You see, I wanted out of my parents' house so badly I was prepared to panhandle in the street. I asked her why she didn't get a job. I got a job, she said, My father fired me for being late. No, I said, A real job, like a shit job, any job. I don't know, she said, That's a very logical question.)

What fascinates me, I told her, happy to turn the conversation away from Baba, Is that a lot of the same people are here now as then. The same people who were here forty years ago barefoot and stoned are in these cars now.

Maybe so, said Mom vaguely. I hadn't changed the topic as well as I might have. I knew she was contemplating the wealth by which we were surrounded, wondering how she'd missed out on her piece of the pie; wondering, too, what happened to her generation, that this is what it became.

And I flicked my roach into the gutter wishing I could defile this whole carnival, sink it like a tent.

xo

A JOYOUS CHIP IN THE LIVING MOSAIC
06/30/2003

Dearest Joe,

I was thinking of you last night as I sat on the concrete steps outside the Anglican church next to Flo's parents' house. We were reclining on one of Mrs. Shaw's innumerable wool tartans, drinking juice from pretty blue glasses, and discussing the church. Flo was christened, and like most romantic young girls loved the ceremony of it, her white dress, the hushed church dressed up in white flowers. From these recollections we got on to the Puritans that founded America, what their lives were like, the rituals we've lost as a society, and the morals. And then Flo looked at me with her bright eyes and said, Right now you look to me like some kind of Industrial Revolution waif, all pale, with your hair flowing down your back like that. So far it's my favorite character for you.

This particular vision is likely the product of all the Victorian fiction she's been reading for her summer course, but Flo's head is always harkening to other times. Eshe with her calm bearing has been a Nubian Princess, a Tribal Priestess powerful and mysterious; Mike of course is a Monk, sometimes a Wise Turtle; Flo's usual favorite for me is Milk-Maid, especially when I'm in cleavage-revealing shirts and my hair is curling nicely (there's also the Mermaid and the Dame with the Rings). But tonight on the Church steps in a loose shirt with a wide neck I was a Waif – pretty funny for someone with my build, but okay – with nobility in my blood but cast out into the world to become fun-loving and gritty among the common folk. A sort of 1930s movie-storyline, I said.

And Florence, on her back toeing the church wall said, I am of the nobility but I just like people.

You're a democratic aristocrat, said I. Which seems rather a good description for her generally. Her family is such an old Canadian family, so well-heeled and well-established; I don't know anybody else with a history like that, who's been here that long. Lots of artists among them, some not so well in the head but all very interesting, and Flo so very like them, traipsing the city, talking to everyone, indiscriminate in her fascination.

My grandfather, she replied, Used to say that an artist should be classless, that they should be able to mingle with nobility or drink in a pub with working men. I could really see that in him. Especially when he took me to Italy when I was fifteen, I saw how he liked to talk to everyone and anyone would talk to him.

Mom and I were talking about art and class last week, too. She took me to Neil Young's Greendale concert, and afterwards we got to discussing rock and roll, and how it transcended all these racial and class lines. We had a lovely night, though there were moments I had to work at it. The great, and also the occasionally problematic thing about going out with Mom is how you never have to guess how she's feeling. Well, you know Mom, her face tells all before she opens her mouth, which she inevitably will; it's a wonderful trait in many ways, her honesty. And how she's right there, experiencing everything to the fullest, uninhibited about expressing that experience to those around her – but sometimes I want just to be absorbed by my environment. Standing in the dark, almost permeated by the sound and light and heat, almost aware of myself as one body in several thousand all being acted upon by the same chords, the same rhythm at the same moment, but there Mom was with her arm around me, a barrier between us and everything else. I knew she was looking to me to be in the moment with her, knew she was full up with love, with the joy of sharing this experience, mother and daughter listening to the new music of an old head she was digging at my age. She wanted to be united with me in enjoyment and I was reticent, wanting some experience beyond the one entwined with our shared life. Ashamed and saddened at my reticence, and fighting annoyance at how she has to mark every exceptional moment – to name it, make it tangible, acknowledge it very deliberately. Sammy, I said to myself, don't ruin this with petty grievances, adolescent individuation problems or whatever. I put my arm around her and turned to her, accepted her brimful sense of this moment, let her see and feel that I was indeed happy before turning back to the stage, swaying in time with Mom, with Neil Young and Crazy Horse and the whole, packed arena. Not engrossed entirely, but close enough.

Idling below the Front St. bridge in the post-concert traffic, our dark little bubble like the inside of one bead in the neon necklace strung up Bay Street, we got to talking about how amazing it is that the music of her generation spans her generation and mine. It's like, a connecting point, Mom said. My parents were just baffled by what we called music. Although your grandfather got a kick out of the Beatles. We saw them on Ed Sullivan when I was maybe fifteen, and after that he would sometimes sing *I wanna hold your haaaaaaaand* – she imitated it, the inflection this very Jewish sort of loving mockery, the "aaa" very nasal, "d" with the tongue between the teeth. I could see Zaida singing like that to Mom, all defiant in her hippie attire but loving her father, too, and glad to be gently kidded by him. Finding a moment of commonality in five minutes of a variety show they had watched together.

In other news, Ty has launched a lawsuit against the U of T before the Human Rights' Commission. This is because he went through all these hoops to get the University to test him for learning disabilities, which they found, and then failed to accommodate him. As a result his grades are way shittier than they should be, and he wants them stricken; U of T doesn't want to do it, and Ty is nervous about his med school application, because his GPA is just above the cut-off mark even though this year he got all A's and A+'s. And of course it's not like he can afford a lawyer, so he's figuring out the whole legal process himself. Which he doesn't seem to mind. As he always likes to say, The bureaucracy is permeable.

U of T is good for one thing, though: last weekend Samba played in the Pride Parade for U of T's Queer Alliance. My brain is now emblazoned with the image of Ty shirtless in the searing sunshine balancing on the back of a pickup truck, strutting in time and wailing on his repenique, the light obliterating the drum, making it another small sun. In a beaded black bikini top – a wonderful burlesque thing Michelle lent me – I was harnessed to my surdo and wedged into the truck's bed with four other surdos and players, bottles of water and knapsacks, Ty conducting the rest of the band from the edge. On the pavement Michael in an undershirt and Michelle in leather short shorts and knee-high platform boots, collar around her neck where later Ty would lead her on a leash, shook their shakers valiantly in the mid-day heat, the crowds behind the barrier cheering and squirting water guns. Bare-assed, bare-titted, draped in beads, in uniform, in wedding attire, on stilts, in bondage gear, on elaborate floats on flat-bed trucks flailing multi-coloured sweat from their painted bodies the revelers flooded Yonge St., while around us a million bodies – straight, gay, young, old, every race and creed – strained to cheer us on; all of downtown pulsing Madonna, Bollywood pop, every club beat imaginable, and buried within it all, the tenacious boom-clack of Samba Elegua. Only through Ty, man, only through Ty would Mike, or Jamie or Michelle or I, or most of the people in this band, find ourselves in the middle of a mile-long parade.

At the end Ty said it looked like people were dripping off the buildings, and really it did: people were leaning over the roofs of the brick apartments above the stores on Yonge, they were perched on window-sills, legs dangling from the ledges, there were faces in every window. And everywhere rainbow flags fluttering against the buildings, draped off balconies, Yonge St. itself like a disorganized rainbow, a bright mosaic of bodies and floats stretching up the city's longest artery and spilling through half of downtown. So much skin, hair and cloth amid the bricks, concrete and asphalt, changing everything. It made me immensely glad to have been born in this city at this time. To think what Toronto was forty years ago! A parade like this seems a kind of proof that consciousness does change, that, under the right circumstances, humans improve.

Missing you, and with much love, Sam.

GET IN, IT'S WARM
07/07/2003

Hullo Sweet Joe.

Tonight is one of those nights I really wonder about my brain chemistry. In the past twenty-four hours I've been catapulted from a foggy misery to a thrumming calm bliss. Two days ago I was mired in misery, overwhelmed by everything, guilty and exhausted. Irresponsible; not helping Mom enough. Bri leaving for the summer, Samba gigs to arrange, Flo kind of manic and Mom totally depressed. It was the whole tightly-wound, ready-to-cry-at-everything, hyper-self-critical shitty shebang.

But then last night Florence and I went down to Ariel's place, where she had a hot tub planted on her front lawn. She had rented it for an event she called Telematic Tubs of Terror, which, I believe, was designed to reinstate public bathing and investigate the breakdown of public and private space. Bathers were hooked up to EEG and ECG machines – Ariel had designed bathing suits with places for electrodes to be attached – and another hot tub party happening simultaneously somewhere else in the city was projected on the wall behind the tub, as Ariel's tub was broadcast to them. I spent the next five hours topless on College St., jammed between nine other people, posing for pictures with plastic apples in our mouths, Ariel tossing carrots and potatoes and oranges into the tub and taking pictures of the human stew as passers-by laughed incredulously. Heading home from the bars they yelled their enthusiasm, nearly crashed their bikes; street-sweepers pulled up to stare. Dave Arcus played Obla Di Obla Da on a broken-necked guitar and everyone sang along which was impossibly cute. We hollered our praise at each new bucket of hot water – we were boiling water on the stove in saucepans and pots, Ariel in self-designed black-and-white bikini bending in a determined stance over steaming buckets in her meshugene kitchen, floored with Astroturf for the occasion.

Pruned and peering through potato-starch bubbles I watched the sun rise over College St., the graffiti becoming visible on the side of the old Latvian House, streetcars gliding past with staring drivers or oblivious ones. Six of us stuck it out until about seven a.m., then I drove home and slept for a bit, cleansed and quiet.

Woke with a splitting headache but accomplished some of what I needed to – organizing last year's school assignments, dealing with administrative crap. Mom came home in a surprisingly good mood and we talked about religion and visions of the world and freedom; Ty dropped by and soon after

Mike arrived and it was a thoroughly satisfying evening. All the conversation lively and so much love in the room, me wearing hospital pants and that orange cut-off Travelodge T-shirt J.R. gave me, but feeling foxy, the ragged neck slipping over my shoulder. It's all inexplicable, but I don't want to question happiness.

I've been writing this as Mike was in the can, lost, I think, in a Rolling Stone article about the war. He's out now, so I should go – but write me soon.

IN THE SUMMERTIME OF OUR YOUTHS
07/16/2003

Dearest Joe,

isn't it strange how relationships progress? Michael and I have been to a wedding, I've met his cousins in Ottawa, he's met Irving – and this week I feel we are more of a couple than last week. It was very interesting at the wedding. The groom was Michael's friend and neighbor when kids, and though they have not remained close, I saw a tear in Mike's eye during the ceremony. Which made me happy, as it suggests that the real, momentary happenings of our existence aren't slipping by him. Perhaps not, certainly not, if he can squeeze my hand like he did between his strong, slender brown fingers and look at me quickly, look back to the altar like at something truly sacred. As he beamed toward the couple I could see where his crow's feet will come in.

And then there was another old friend from the neighborhood, who we ended up hanging out with after the ceremony and before the dinner. To my pleased surprise, I found Michael always standing close to me, resting his arm casually around me (oh casually, casually, as though I weren't noticing it in every nerve-ending); he mentioned that we were on our way to Montreal, the city where our relationship began. It would be, he said, Like a romantic little getaway.

Indeed, I thought. This is unusual language for someone as guarded as him. Mostly he is so contained; the depth of his interest, his engagement with life is communicated though ideas, his clear enjoyment of enunciating words like "spurious" and "fungible," and the pin-point of light in his eyes as he talks. He's not one for personal theatre, for giving form to his feelings in anything other than words – no pierced lips or stretched ears to display his dissatisfaction with society; no polyamorous love dramas, E-induced massage sessions to proclaim his radical freedom from society's codes. He will talk about himself, though, offer up his psyche as conversation – recently, to my absolute astonishment, he told some people: Sam is the only lifeline saving me from a perpetual, awful ennui.

I was delighted and dismayed when he said it: delighted that I was so important, and deeply unhappy to think of his being capable of a perpetual ennui. What a crime that is, ennui; I can understand anything else besides that – Mom disallowed, never understood, and deeply reviles the idea of boredom. And yet, I think he is right: I do stand between him and a meaningless boredom, a kind of dissatisfaction with the world as it is, or with his responses to it.

Mostly however he feels no compulsion to act out our intimacy for others. He lets his eyes rest on me with a certain recognition, but we have always stood apart when out in the world. (It's like the vision I had of us on our first mushroom trip – I saw us walking side by side, and had the strongest sense of his benevolence and protection, but understood implicitly our separateness.) In the beginning he was baffled even by hand-holding, it made him awkward, though in bed nothing embarrassed him; but to displays of affection in public he would submit briefly, to please me, and then disengage. This is a boy who, after all, hardly even hugged anyone before he knew me. As a baby, his mom has told me, he generally preferred not to be held, would be happy left to himself for hours. But here he was outside some hotel in Ottawa on a muggy July night, all spiffy in his bright blue shirt and with his arm on my shoulder, looking at me with a strange intensity I might even be tempted to call pride. I have seen this look before; I remember a poem I wrote when we were first together – it was terrible, but it had a line in it, like, "the pride and pleasure of no father I ever knew" – well, it's telling if nothing else. So I have seen this look, but it was something new for it to be so out in the open, him standing before another young man talking about our *romantic getaway*.

Same deal with the cousins, too. Though we hardly had any time with them – we arrived, had some lunch, then had to get ourselves ready to go. But Michael was very attentive, solicitous about getting me food, standing near me. As we were getting dressed, he even seemed happy to give me the opinion I asked for on whether to wear my hair partly back or all down. He chose down, beaming at me and playing with my hair. Calendula, he said lovingly, nonsensically, while fingering my locks; for some reason years ago the word tickled his fancy, came to his mind as he let the hair flow through his fingers, and so this is one of his strange ways of praising me.

The next day we left early for Montreal. He seemed to grow rather serious as we drove; I thought perhaps he was unhappy with me or something about the situation. He was quiet as we entered the city; the sun burned through the grey haze, dappled the old streets beneath luxurious midsummer foliage. We drove to the bed and breakfast where we stayed the first time we were here together, for Irving's tribute. When, of course, nothing was consummated – Mike doesn't do anything that fast. He took twelve days to think. And that was why this time, after we had put our bags on the floor of the lace-curtained, shadowy room, all soft creams and old wood, he came to me and said, Time to finish what I started….

Afterwards he kissed me and we lay for a long time with our mouths joined, almost asleep, together in the hot womb of the July day. The room had a pulse; in my semi-consciousness I was suspended within, held apart from the world by our pulsating stillness, the city bright beyond the open window.

We had a day like proper lovers do in books – walked through the streets hand in hand and talked about the future, the past, each other; we stopped in a little park and watched a string quartet play in a gazebo; Michael bought us ice cream and smiled at the children dodging around the trees. The air was light and soft; the streets were full of people making the most of their weekends. In the evening we met some Moroccan men drinking wine in a park and Mike got to talking about the oud with one of them, who played also. We left them at St. Laurent and meandered back to the B&B. After our long, pleasant day I felt like a kid home from the fair, muscles spent, slightly sticky with heat and ice cream but completely sated, crawling into soft sheets, night air drifting in through the window. In the white glow of the old-fashioned lamp it seemed very correct that Michael should be in his undershirt, sitting on the white wrought-iron bed taking off his socks, that I should be tucked in, pink and freckled, in a cotton nightie. We could be farmers, I thought, in the last century. Outside the cows are sleeping and the corn is growing. Or immigrants in this house in the 1920s; this could be our one sweet moment together before sleep, before the next day's storm of factory-work, washing, babies, insults, the confusion of making a life in a new country. But no, we are just us, two kids in a B&B learning to be adults as people do now, taking little vacations, meeting family. A more serious version of playing house.

The next day we drove out to Maimonides, where Irving now lives. Or, I presume, waits to die, since I cannot call what he's doing living. From the moment I saw the huge, institutional building rising from the flat, barren suburb surrounding, I wished I hadn't come. In the lobby, women no more substantial than a wisp of smoke lingered in slippers assisted by conscientious but distant caregivers. You could see the look of shift-workers in their eyes, doing what they are paid to do before it's time to clock out: solicitousness for ten dollars an hour. Liver-spotted men in wheelchairs held cigarettes in trembling fingers. I took a few desperate drags of mine before stubbing it out and heading to the elevator. I knew I should be calmer. This is age, I thought, this is what happens. These people are comfortable, well looked-after; they have some pleasures still within their grasp. But in my head was a line of Irving's, from the poem he wrote for his mother after she died: *the inescapable lousiness of growing old*. This is a line my mother has always repeated to me; now it would not stop. Inescapable as I looked at the women's sunken mouths; lousiness as I watched their fragile bodies huddled around the television.

Stepping off the elevator into the pale pink halls of the fifth floor, I smiled into the expectant faces of my father's neighbors. As I passed, one of the men said, Hello Darling, in his raspy Jewish voice and I nearly lost it. How dare I come here in my youth, my glory, with my love steady and quiet beside me. I felt unbearably strong, as though I might harm them;

dangerous, the powerful, undeniable pulse in my veins. We were taking up all the air, the sanitized air was ringing with our blood. What right had we to disturb the residents' routine? The audacity of me to come in here full of the city streets, the hot night, the bright morning, and traipse memory down the halls of these old men. These men whose lovely brides are now bones beneath the earth, or who come visit them, step tentative steps across their husband's rooms bearing food or pictures of grandchildren. And most impossibly, most incredibly they looked at us with interest, with delight even. Whatever whisper of irretrievable lives, of wedding nights and Sunday brunches, of the strength in their hands when they first held their children, whatever we were to them they wanted it. As their dimmed eyes followed us, bare-shouldered twenty-first century girl with her scruffy fellah in army pants, they seemed to be trying to conjure the life we might make together; they wanted us to breach their bloodless corridors with the tidal force, the taste, the scent of the world they are leaving and cannot know.

Passing an "activity room" with construction paper flowers pasted to the windows I focused very hard on putting one foot in front of the other. Couldn't we just leave? I asked Mike; There's no real point in our being here.

Yes there is, he said gently.

Each of the rooms had a picture of its inhabitant on the door. On Irving's door was one I remembered from his books, a head of unruly dark hair, pugnacious smile playing around the lips. Inside the darkened room Irving was sitting on the bed, a nurse and a personal assistant bent over him. I watched them expertly help Irving to his wheelchair. His assistant, Diana, who's been with him for years, told me he'd just gotten up from a nap, he'd be a moment getting ready. I managed to say I'll just go to the washroom a minute, get into a stall and close the latch before I started howling, howling. I couldn't stop. Appalled by the thought someone would come in and hear me wailing, I had to stop. I buried my face in a bouquet of toilet paper and wailed, thinking of nothing. Sam, I said aloud, Stop this now. I blew my nose; my lip started to wobble. Just go I said, splashed water on my face, smeared some gloss on my lips and went.

Michael looked at me tenderly as I returned to the room. Irving was in his wheelchair; his white hair, still impressive, was neatly combed. He was wearing black track pants that looked slightly dirty, were deeply horrible for their unapologetic practicality. I thought of all the hands that had touched him throughout his life, and of the hands and hands that touch him now; the competent professional hands tending to him, keeping him clean, ministering to the body over which he has so little control. Diana suggested we go sit in a room down the hall, so we set off, Diana pushing Irving, Michael and I walking uselessly beside the chair. She parked him in a pale blue room with no sun but big windows providing a nice view of the surrounding brown suburban grid. She told us he might be a little more disoriented, having just woken up, and that he'd been very tired lately, but she bent over him and yelled into his ear *Irving, Samantha's* here. You know *Samantha? Your daughter?* He made no reply. So she smoothed down a wayward tuft of hair and said Okay, smiled slightly guiltily, as if it were her fault she couldn't rouse him, and left.

And I looked at him a moment then ran off again, at the mercy of myself and ashamed of my weakness.

When I returned Michael was sitting close by Irving, telling him how he first came upon Irving's work. After we'd come home from Montreal and found out Mike had gotten the part in the play, he took himself to the library to read up on the man who'd suddenly become such a presence in his life. This was what Michael was relating, his benevolent face eager and open, resting without pain on the silent, white face of my father. For an instant I hated him, Michael, for being so calm, for beaming so peacefully. *Sir Mortimer doesn't shake you* I thought bitterly; for you this is only another part of life.

Then I heard him saying Mr. Layton, I know you don't know me, but I just want to tell you… you have a very beautiful daughter. Samantha is an amazing – a really special person. I'm glad I met her, and so I guess I should thank you.

It seemed absurd, this little speech – who ever heard Michael say *special*? – it seemed a shining moment for an actor in a TV special, until I realized, knew all through me that it only seemed absurd because this moment was so removed from ordinary life. We have no proper speech for these occasions; what could he say, other than that? With the formality one would use in meeting a girlfriend's father for the first time, and the bluntness reserved for special occasions or children, Michael was saying perhaps the only reasonable thing to say: Old Man, I love your daughter. You have never known her, will never know her, but I do and before you die, know you've done a good thing in this world because you created her.

Michael looked up at me, pulled a chair around and said, Talk to him. Tell him about yourself.

And I loved Michael beyond all reason, felt myself delivered up to him and into his care. I wanted to do as he told me, knew that he was wiser and more admirable than I.

I've been writing, I said, looking at my father's downcast eyes. Their magnificent blue was dimmed, had become clouded. I saw a tear roll down his cheek. Was he crying? Did he know me? Was it pain at this situation, the words he couldn't quite grasp that caused that tear, or was it simply bewilderment? Was he crying at all, or were his old eyes simply leaking, knowing nothing?

I got into the Creative Writing course at York, so, um, I start in the fall, taking workshops, and... I traveled last summer. Around Europe, Morocco. Didn't get to Greece, though, that's the next trip. And Mom's okay... stressed, you know, working, looking after my grandmother, I'm sure you remember her, ha.

And I sat there trying to keep my lips steady as the tears coursed down my face. Why, why oh why did I not give him my number when he asked for it? When he walked with me to the door of his home on Monkland, no taller than me and shuffling but beside me nonetheless, and he asked me, Can I call you? His mind already failing but still able to hold a conversation, to be pleased by the stash of poems I so shyly presented to him, delighted by the songs I played for him on my guitar, there in my braids and heavy eye make-up at sixteen. Eager to get back to Bri in her uncle's empty house, put this strange interlude of day behind me, I said No, I said No; I was frightened of upsetting the established order of my life. What if he called and

Mom answered? What would he and I say to each other anyway, with my young self so unknown to him, so new and fascinating to me, and his world already shrinking, becoming a cocoon of sustenance, a shroud of routine around him.

He did call me once. It was a few months after Mike and I had returned from our trip to Montreal. One afternoon I had flung myself around Michael on the couch in the sunlight, warmly thrilling with the warmth of his body but peaceful as a tired child, arms clasped behind her father's neck. I remember so vividly because of how new the feeling was, that stillness and comfort. I remember feeling that I was delivered into Michael's hands there in the hushed apartment in the golden afternoon and then how strange it was that at that moment, with my face buried in his smooth, boy-smelling neck, the phone rang, and it was Irving. But that's all. I don't know what was said.

Back in the car outside Maimonides the water-works started up again. I lay my head in Michael's lap, the car muggy and smelling of stale coffee and Smartfood. Holy Jesus Motherfuck that sucked, I eventually managed, sniffing and hiccupping. Michael unpasted the tendrils of wet hair from my cheek, smoothed them back on my head. I told him, I'm never living in a place like that. If I get Alzheimer's, I'm leaving instructions to be put down before that happens. Fuck that, man. Same goes for you. (And I was suddenly struck almost hysterical with the thought of his paternal grandmother dying of Alzheimer's at fifty; his maternal grandfather died of the same, although he was ninety-three. It was inescapable and I could not bear it, Michael would forget me, he would look with that bewildered tragic delight at this world we have known together and how would I stand it?) You don't know me, I said, It's heroin overdoses for us both. Ride some horse off into the sunset and adios, world.

Michael waited until I had lit a smoke, a tremendous, wondrous, glorious smoke which I also resented deeply and with every fibre of my body but inhaled with defiant gusto; he waited until we were moving safely toward the highway to say Don't say that. Don't say you'd choose to end my life, if I were senile.

I'm not talking senile, dude, I'm talking like, practically vegetative. Did you see him, man, did it seem like he was having a lot of fun? Was he getting a lot out of life?

I don't know, Sammy. That's the problem, we can't know. What if I can't communicate anything, what if – I mean who knows what the brain is doing at that point, what it feels like to be living that way? But I might just be grateful for one more day with the trees and the sky. I might still get pleasure from that. You can't decide to take that away from someone else. And for yourself, too, how can you know, now, how you'll feel about life when you're that old?

You're right, I said, eyes trained very carefully on the traffic, knowing utterly that he was right but overcome by the thought, the image of Mike old, dying; saying goodbye to the trees and the sky, loving them as he leaves them. I knew it should all be – as he sees it – experience; but it was too terrifying. All the little deaths, faces changing beyond recognition, mouths a black hole rent in the universe – that's another line from Irving's poem. I look at my mother's mouth sometimes, in sleep, and am taken down by the undertow of that line sucking beneath my consciousness. It seems impossible, this leave-taking, yet that is of course what people do.

And so, the privilege I most desire: to know Michael Bobbie another seventy odd years, to watch his skin crease and his beautiful lips wither, run my gnarled hands through his thinning hair. All the way home from Montreal I imagined it, the different stages of our lives, the woman I might become if he stays with me. And you know, he might.

Goodnight, sweet Joe; write and tell of your midsummer.

x

The Winter of my Grandmother's Discontent
07/17/2003

Joseph, as a postscript to my last email, I must relate to you the conversation I've had three times now with my grandmother. Earlier today I was on the phone with her, and she said, So your mother tells me you were very glad Michael was with you when you went to see your father.

Yes, I was very glad, I said, thinking, I just told you all about this two days ago.

Well was it so horrible?

Yeah, it was pretty horrible. And I briefly revisited the conversation we'd already had, resenting what I believe to be her fascination with all things painful. Thinking, if I told her I'd just won the Pulitzer it wouldn't garner half the attention she gives to one difficult hour. It would have been a lot more horrible if I'd been alone, I said.

Oh really? Well what did he do that was so good?

Oh, you know, he was just supportive and, uh, talked to Irving a bit. I was just kinda sitting there not saying anything.

So what did he say?

I told her what he'd said.

Oh well that's very sweet. Mike is a nice boy.

Yes, he's the nicest person I've ever come across.

Mmm. Too bad he doesn't want to marry you.

Maybe he does but just not now.

Not now, you always say that, not now. So then when? I don't think he's gonna do it.

Look, I said, trying to secrete reasonable sounds, Now would be an unreasonable time to get married. He has two more years on his degree, I have at least that. He wants to travel, live other places. I want to travel –

He wants to live somewhere else so maybe he'll meet some other girl while he's away there and then what?

Then he meets another girl. Nothing I can do about it. I'm twenty-two years old ferchrissakes. No one gets married at twenty-two.

Well Mike's friends are all getting married you tell me.

One friend. One friend who is Mike's age and isn't in school. And the other one is just engaged, but who knows when they'll actually get married. It's expensive you know.

Oh, she said. If he wants to marry you, I'll pay for the wedding.

She said this slightly mockingly, teasing me with what she believes to be the impossible. But I think she was serious about footing the wedding bill.

Poor Baba, living without her husband for fourteen years – her worst fear, day after day. I think she would like to see me married before she goes, and I would like that, too.

This morning Michael and I had breakfast in Kensington, in the little shack of a café I used to play gigs at when I was sixteen. It has changed owners, and the menu now encourages patrons to "Share a True Market Experience." I rolled my eyes. Well, you're in the Market, said Mike.

Yeah, but now that they've marketed my Market Experience, it's a little less marketful, you know? It's not just the thing anymore, it's the thing and what people are trying to get out of it.

But you were trying to get something out of it, when you first started coming down here. Me, too. There's a particular culture this place offers, so it's to be expected that the local businesses will try to profit from that.

We went on talking about the neighbourhood, what it would be like to live there, how it might be possible to keep it from changing too much for the worse. What it will mean for the housing market if the economy is truly headed for the "disastrous course" which Michael has lately been predicting and which the Dow Jones now, according to Reuters, also predicts, as a result of Bush's new tax cuts.

Companies and governments need to be hedging against decline, Michael said. 'Cuz it's coming.

It struck me as funny, Michael's foreboding prophecy, delivered beneath the lush foliage and bright blue sky, a forkful of French Toast suspended in his hand. Knowing what's coming doesn't change much about what we do, does it? To my soft laugh he looked up with eyebrows raised, and smiled; said, We'll be fine around here, though. People like us. Things can get worse, but they're unlikely to get too bad.

As Mike left me on the steps of Starbucks in the white afternoon light I thanked him for the lovely morning. It seemed right and appropriate to be that way with him, slightly formal, appreciative that he is still himself, with his separate world. These days are like a second courtship, a proper one, and I like our old-fashioned formalities.

Much love, Sweet Joe, Sam.

OFF THE GRID

    08/17/2003

Dear Joe,
 what a summer it's been for catastrophes! First SARS – poor Mom's been going around in a surgical mask, because it's been advised that those with poor immune systems should take extra precautions. Did you hear about SARS-stock? Like a hundred thousand people in Downsview Park for a free concert headlined by the Rolling Stones, because the whole communicable disease thing has really screwed the city for tourism. I didn't go – too many people crammed into a concrete yard in the sun for too many hours – but Florence did. She went with this guy Paul and a bunch of his friends, took 'shrooms and had a grand old time, apparently. Florence, man. She has no fear of that kind of mayhem, and I love her for it.

 And now this crazy blackout, like sixty million people across Ontario and the States without power. Most of Toronto came back within a day, but I think even yesterday some places were still out. I was working when it happened. Deanna and I had cups lining the bar, I was about to start making an iced Americano when suddenly – black cash screens, silent espresso machine, blender stopped mid-frap, back room encased in darkness, daylight checkering the floor.

 A breathless pause, waiting for the store to click back on, expecting it to happen any moment. But it didn't. We apologized to the customers, still standing looking at us as though we could make their drinks appear, electricity or no. Someone went out and came back in saying all the streetlights were out, and the stores dark up and down the block. I went out to look and College St. was vaguely apocalyptic: there was a peculiar deadness to the yellow-grey sky, to the air, the lack of electricity a frequency deleted from our sensory equation.

 Reports started to filter in that it might be city-wide, then regional. We gave away what coffee was in the urns to those who wanted it, and pretty soon people stopped coming in, though the sidewalks were crowded. We had heard, but were not yet certain, that the grid was down along the entire eastern seaboard; it was a strange sensation, this darkness uniting millions of people – all our days suddenly halted in unison by the split-second failure of something we take for granted. Good god, I wondered, what's going on at the stock exchange?

I called Mike and was happy to find he had not gotten stuck in the subway as I feared he might. After a couple of hours even mighty Starbucks accepted that the juice wasn't coming back so we closed up best we could, stumbling around the back room with flashlights. At about six Mom called from the airport in North Carolina – she'd been visiting her cousin Bonnie and was, of course, supposed to fly home that day. Which obviously was not happening, but she sounded alright, a bit worried and harassed but caught up like everybody in the strange excitement of something so unprecedented happening.

When we finally left, traffic was moving remarkably well. There weren't many cops on the road, but at various major intersections random people were directing cars; I heard on the CBC today that volunteers had been keeping the roads orderly – apparently it's a thing people have a deep desire to do, direct traffic, and are just waiting for the opportunity. Which seems very psychologically logical somehow. I drove east into the bright, darkening sky, the buildings silhouetted against it like comic-book art. Inside the sweltering loft, Michelle and I rolled ice cubes on ourselves and our boys as the room was swallowed by Valley darkness, and we speculated, as one might expect, on why this had happened and what would come of it. Mike told us that our water reservoirs are run on electricity, with about a three-day supply in the tanks. This of course led to all kinds of Mad Max speculations – I find many boys take a certain enjoyment in envisioning the worst kind of social breakdowns. I think they get some kind of primordial jollies from the idea of being forced to contend with physical hardship, having to exert their masculine will on a world in upheaval. Thus Mike and Ty amused themselves with talk of where to store canisters of gas if it were necessary to flee to Mike's parents' cottage, or of creating community groups who could prepare for shortages or other such disruptions. The conversation strung me between irritation and excitement. On the one hand, fuck that shit, I don't want some major plague or fuel shortage or whatever to come decimate my life, and I found their readiness to envision such scenarios a little unseemly. On the other hand, I too occasionally find myself lost in daydreams of destruction – wouldn't it be great if the stock market just crashed? It'd be the Great Depression all over again, and then a new New Deal, labour movements revived, people united against the robber barons. And then a huge war, probably. So really not all that great.

Later I held a flashlight for Ty while he barbecued in the alley in his faded red-checkered boxers, and then Mike and I decided to see what the city was doing. It was nearly ten o'clock when we set out, and the sidestreets were mostly quiet, though by the time we reached the Danforth about an hour later it felt like a street festival. Restaurants were cooking on hot-plates, eager to sell what would go bad otherwise; Alexandro's, an old-school Greek take-out at the foot of Mike's parents' street, was cooking kebabs on the sidewalk for grateful hordes. People lolled about on the rim of the fountain; there was a buzz of charged energy, as at a concert or a high school lunch hour. Kids up late flitted between the adults, little bodies tingling with the strange darkness. No AC units hummed, no TVs flickered. I felt like we were in a factory that had suddenly ground to a halt, had the roof popped off like a lid, and there we all were amidst the lifeless machinery with the vast sky above.

All went quickly back to normal, however. Mom returned the next day, happy to have seen Bonnie but as usual wishing she could have had a real holiday, where she wasn't staying at someone's house and thus required to make her own bed and go grocery shopping and help cook dinner. Also, I think Mom has recently become more acutely aware of Bonnie's political conservatism. (For example: they were shopping, and Mom saw a sequined purse in the stars and stripes. Oh, she said, picking it up with a chortle, I should get this for Samantha! A flag-bag! We don't find that funny, said Bonnie, walking on.) For the third time in her life, Mom is taking an interest in politics: the first time was during the election of JFK, the second because of Pierre Trudeau, but this time it seems more than just aesthetics – she's thinking about, like, the economy and imperialism and shit. I think it started with 9/11, when I was freaking out constantly and Mom couldn't understand why. I guess I've spent so much time haranguing about the miserable world over the past few years that she's been forced into questioning things, and being concerned about things that simply didn't register with her before. Possibly, it occurs to me, in large part because she loves me and wants to care about what I care about, to be able to enter into the world I'm experiencing.

So she sometimes watches *The Daily Show* with me (introduced to us, of course, by Eshe) – Mom especially adores Lewis Black – and she brings up the *NYT Magazine's* articles on Al Qaeda or health care reform at the dinner table, along with her longings for Broadway plays reviewed in the A&E section. Frank Rich is her new favorite, she circles his article for me every week. It's kind of fascinating that it's *now* Mom develops a political conscience. This is a woman who got gassed in the 1968 Paris Riots accidentally. She was just taking a walk, seeing what was up with all the ferment, and then all she remembers is her eyes stinging and some nice guy with a bandanna on his face taking her back to his apartment where she washed her eyes and hung out with him and his friends.

But when I asked her, years ago, what it was all about, she said, Who knows?

This past Sunday was the first legitimate car-free day – remember how those Kensington folk closed the streets to cars one day last summer? So they got permits this time, closed a few streets in the Annex and Kensington. Ty borrowed a van from a friend, which I got to drive (fun blue 1980s creature), and we shuttled around from site to site playing Samba in the sunshine. Yes, we discussed the irony of driving around to celebrate car-free day, and the possibility of rigging up bike trailers for the instruments. But empty of cars the streets filled with people, who might otherwise have driven somewhere else to do something with their afternoons. In any case they would likely not have been bouncing their babies and stomping their feet out on the road with their neighbours. It was happy-making, what can I say? For me, at least, it's not so much a protest against cars as a delight in aspects of life that don't require one – perhaps a protest against a life that demands one.

We finished on Augusta, outside La Palette. Dave Arcus – the guy who played on my cd, who studies composition at U of T – was playing guitar with another fellow on bass; a troop of brass players, known, I believe, as the Kensington Horns, emerged from the crowd, and suddenly Ty was conducting Big Band! The players surprised and pleased as the audience that the parts worked together to make a song.

At nine o'clock we had to let the cars through. There were boos at first, but soon people dispersed into groups on the sidewalks and patios, or wandered off to the park, or home to wash their feet and go to bed. All tuckered out from our summer fun and feeling good. Sitting on the curb rolling a joint, I felt like the city and I belonged more to each other, like I was less distant from the people among whom I live.

Mike was supposed to move into the loft yesterday, but unfortunately the place is up for one of its inspections so he had to wait. Instead of moving Mike in, we spent the day toting shit out into a moving van that will remain parked inconspicuously in the back lot until tomorrow night. For now the place is some kind of computer fix-it place. Ty has a stash of defunct but respectable-looking computers which he set up, and we removed all obvious signs of habitation. There's nothing to do about the shower, really, but take everything out of it and put stuff in front of it to make it look unused. In the past the inspections haven't been too thorough – just some city person who comes to hastily check that the zoning laws are being respected. You show them your permit – Ty owns Obelus Unlimited, didn't you know? – and away they go. And hopefully Tuesday or Wednesday night, we'll move Mike in! So hooray, and onward into tomorrow, when I'll be hauling Ty and Michelle's life back up the crooked stairs I hauled it down yesterday.

Yours, Sam. x

YESTERDAY, TODAY AND TOMORROW
09/06/2003

Oh my dear Joseph, I'm so sorry to hear about Dave. It is a miracle that he's alright. Too bad about his darling little car, though I suppose that's the least of his worries. But you must listen to me when I tell you not to blame yourself – I know that sounds trite, but it's true. One has very little control over whether or not someone is going to tear madly around the country in the dark and the rain. We have limited powers over ourselves, never mind anyone else. Perhaps it will be better not living together, and with you hopefully learning some interesting things. Anyway send him my love, and also best of luck to you on your first day of school.

I came back yesterday from Mike's parents' cottage, which is forty minutes down a logging road outside of Timmins. North Ontario, man, it's a whole other deal. I'd never been past Bracebridge and had no idea how the province changes. But about four hours north of Toronto the sandy, weedy lushness, the stately deciduous trees of south Ontario are replaced by darker woods, massive granite boulders and hardier-looking vegetation; the pines close in around the road and birches rise like smoke between them. About two hours from the cottage we passed into the Arctic Watershed which, Mike informed me, is where water starts flowing north into the Arctic Sea rather than south into the Atlantic. Crazy, eh? There's a wooden sign that tells you when you've passed it and when we did I really felt I was entering a whole other part of the planet. I couldn't believe this was the same province in which I was born and raised, at the base of Highway 11, the spine connecting hundreds of kilometers of near-wilderness.

The drive was fun; Mike's parents rented us a car (extremely nice of them!) and we had Mike's younger brother, Grant, passing us cds with filthy but hilarious rap songs to play until he fell decisively asleep, mouth open, body sprawled across the backseat. I felt simultaneously like exactly what we were – three young adults enjoying a mildly raucous ride on our way to a family gathering – and like two parents with a youngster in the back entertaining us and needing entertaining, making Mike and I allies in our adultness (even though I'm only a year older than Grant and three younger than Mike). Mike and Grant have been making this trip since earliest childhood – Janice and Brian only bought the cottage a few years back, but Brian's cousin Gary and his wife own the lot next to it, so Mike and his family have been up there at all times of year staying with them. Mike told me some stories about past cottage vacations, and it was all very new and beyond my ken, this felling of trees and erecting of buildings, bit by bit over decades. As I drove through Timmins itself I liked the idea that Mike had grown up knowing this landscape. The low, flat, unadorned houses and buildings stark against the immense sky reminded me of frontier towns in old movies, or of the desert – the living things all had the same utilitarian hardiness I'd felt in parts of Southern California or Nevada. I asked Mike if he saw the similarity, and he said Yes, it's because the North is a winter desert seven months of the year. In both places it feels like the environment doesn't want you there, like you can eke out survival but the natural world can swallow you up in a heartbeat.

Stepping out of the car felt like being thrown back a century, entering a frontier. For hundreds of kilometers there were no buildings above five stories tall, though there were pits extending hundreds of metres beneath the earth. We had no phone or cellphone service, no electricity (I had to drive halfway back to town to call Mom from a high point in the road). A few hours north we'd be above the tree-line. My lungs filled with the cleanest air I've ever felt; nine hours smoking and eating junk food in the car were swept from me by the high, sweet wind rushing through the endless trees. We were only a temporary encampment within the vast boreal forest, three little upright figures in a clearing of wilderness. I caught a whiff of wood smoke that made me shiver with delight. Transported a moment, I was a child ambling down the long stone steps, blue-white in the dusk; I was a lady in a hat gathering the purple and white wildflowers lit by the last of the sun; I was a sun-browned woman in an apron emerging from the screen door with a freshly-baked pie in my hands…. But no, that was Janice, hands empty but open toward us, head to one side, smiling warmly. I was in green cotton pants and a tank top emerging from a well-inhabited rented Mitsubishi, slightly disoriented from our bumpy drive through the dense forest in the deepening twilight, in need of a sweater and reeking of cigarettes, kissing the sweetly proffered lips of my boyfriend's father. With great pleasure Janice and Brian greeted us, ushered us inside the squat brown cottage.

When I walked through the door it was as though I'd seen that kitchen a hundred times, though I'd never seen so much as a picture. It all made perfect sense: the hanging propane lamp, the stocky black and white wood-burning stove beside the 1950s gas oven on the stone wall between the kitchen and the living room. The sink beneath the light fir cupboards and the window full of the lake beyond. I knew what I would see before I walked out to the screened-in porch. When I beheld the white wicker couch and chair with their blue cushions, the round pine table, the thin brown frames on the screens, I had this flash like I would be looking at it my whole life. All was weirdly familiar.

But I tried to put such thoughts out of my head. No sense picturing the mornings to come that I might spend sipping coffee on that porch, or how I might rearrange the furniture in the living room. Though helping Janice wash the dishes after dinner – they pump water from the lake with a generator and put a drop of bleach in the basin to avoid getting "beaver fever" – I couldn't help envisioning doing the same thing in ten years, a kid or two scampering around outside, Janice and I having come to know each other through the ancient ministry of household duties, child-bearing and rearing, eye-rolling at and admiration of our menfolk. It all seemed within my grasp that night.

But who knows? I washed the dishes and felt my own youth, hands smooth and cautious beside Janice's veined, confident ones. Once she was the newcomer to this family; almost three decades ago, when she was younger than me, she would have first met the people I was about to meet; it occurred to me that, like me, she came to the Bobbies from more overprotective parents, from a smaller, more tempestuous family than that of her future husband. In the intense quiet palpitating with life, with the full, inexorable generation of the ecosystem around us, I felt our city-lives thrown into sharp relief; our young, bustling university lives seemed frenetic and slightly absurd in the flickering white kitchen light surrounded by darkness. To be loved and make love and make children and some kind of good life, that was all. Why all the doubts and fears? Why stay in the city, even?

As we followed our flashlight's beam to the little outbuilding where we were staying – what Brian calls "the bunky" – Michael was attentive and kind; he made sure I didn't fall in the "swale" (a ditch around the cottage, I learned, to prevent flooding when the snow melts), and stopped with his arm around me to point out planets and constellations. This was my dreamy, indignant, theory-loving Michael Bobbie, at ease with a place and way of life totally foreign to me. I was being granted access to his family life, parts of his childhood separate from the city life in which I'd come to know him. It was my responsibility to appreciate that gift for itself and not desire anything more, if I could help it.

In the morning light I found myself wrapped in his arms, sun flecking the bed through the old bamboo shades. The bunky is all windows nestled amongst a grove of pines; our prone bodies were a canvas for their swaying shadows. I silently rejoiced at Mike's rare closeness, tried not to get too excited, thought perhaps he was only cold in the night. But he woke and looked at me very sweetly, face rumpled and rosy from our long sleep in the clear, highly-oxygenated air, and didn't let me go.

So we passed six lovely days. I swam every day in Scott Lake – sometimes many times a day. It is like no lake I've seen in Southern Ontario; there the water is usually brackish, a clear, caramel colour near the surface, darker brown below. Scott Lake water is blue-green, "spring-fed" as Brian informed me, which means it's very deep in the middle, and the water is especially clean – it's the headwater of a system servicing a few small lakes, apparently great for fishing. And there's only one motorboat on the whole lake, another thing you can't find in Southern Ontario. I think swimming is the closest I come to meditation, and it only works in lakes. In the mornings my skin was cobwebbed with golden light, in the evenings tinted a mossy green. Mike is not much of a swimmer, but would sit on the dock reading de las Casas (on the Spanish arrival in South America, given to him by Eshe for his birthday), looking up regularly to make sure I was alright, smiling as I breast-stroked toward him.

We took to going out on the paddleboat after dinner each night to watch the sunset. It doesn't get fully dark until after ten o'clock out there this time of year, so in the clear, indigo light we'd drift in the middle of the lake smoking a joint, laugh at the dragonflies that hummed around our heads, seeming to play with us and each other as they munched on the mosquitoes come to munch on us. Legs peddling in unison through reflections of trees and sky Mike and I would return in the last light, cottage windows two yellow cubes glowing against the black trees behind, wood-smoke skimming low across the water. It was utter peace, those quiet approaches to the cottage at nightfall. Mom would say my contentment had something to do with past lives and who knows, maybe she's right. It would be good to know that was the case, to know there was some reason for the tranquility I experienced.

On our third last day all the adults went into Timmins to make final preparations for the wedding on the morrow. Michael, Grant and I decided to do some hallucinogens – mushrooms for me, acid for the boys. I was nervous, as I always get nervous before a trip. And, as usual, I spent the first hour curled in a chair, half asleep. When I opened my eyes it was to cry. Grant was worried but Michael looked down at me without fear, green eyes shining around their swelled pupils, and said It's okay, she always cries at first. The tears coursed down my face, I thought of nothing, was not even unhappy, simply obliterated, the levee of my will washed into a relentless, primordial tide. Though powerless to stop it, I came to the knowledge that it would pass; I let myself be turned to salt water. Michael and Grant were on the porch; I could sense their immediate, hyper-real reality unfolding some feet away from me, pulling me back toward the day. Michael came and looked in on me, a moss-green presence, something live and resilient as pine needles in him. In a flash of wonder and gratitude I sat up to him; the room was light, suffused and green-gold as a forest. I had to pee, of course, and did, babbling Yiddish phrases I didn't know I knew and now cannot remember. I babbled to the cream-coloured walls and rounded door-frame, thinking of my grandmother's grandmother who spoke only in rhyme.

On the porch I sat on the green floor, wrapped in my blue and red Moroccan blanket. The boys were glances of light and heat to my left; I was suspended, reverential, between sky and lake, at eye level with the trees opposite. For an instant the continent was young and I knew all its secrets, could hew a life from its rock and forest and expanses of water. I was a celebrant in the temple of the world, had ingested a substance, as people have always done, to bring me closer to its mysteries. Yet there I was on a screened-in porch in a red 1960s caftan that had been my mother's and a blanket woven by a Moroccan woman I'll never meet, my rental car waiting out front, my true home grey and bustling a mere nine hours south.

I looked at Michael and at the pines across the lake. We can only be from the time we're from, I thought, yet everything that has been comes through us. Inaccessible wisdom illuminated the edge of my vision, made it light and ghostly as an overexposed photograph; my veins were a root system, ancient and endless, burrowing blindly, unstoppably through fecund darkness. My breath came full and steady. And someday I'll write it all down, I thought. But then, as always, it seemed so ignominious, and impossible that I should ever do anything justice.

Then I was on the wicker sofa and Michael was there next to me; he seemed to be wearing a suit vest, a light-grey suit vest and black bow-tie, sort of 1920s-like. All around us was light; I had the feeling we were at a wedding, the air was bells and chimes and light. His eyes were a complicated green, hooded and intimate; I felt very pink and new under his gaze, so sweetly, suggestively male on our secluded sofa with the woods all around. I knew that centuries of ancestors, and each definitive moment of my own two decades was visible to him then, his green eyes like my own in the mirror, alien yet utterly familiar. Whatever singular expression of unknowable histories I am, he wanted it. I began to laugh, and every time I looked at him I laughed. Every atom of my being sang with love for him, and their song emerged as laughter. I laughed until I cried, and then I cried because I loved him too much. It was absurd, it was shameful, it was futile and deadly to love anyone so much.

I stopped crying and went inside. The light in the cottage was a stony blue-grey. Michael began to irritate me. He was weak and undefined, almost amorphous, a non-entity. I couldn't understand it, was terrified. Swallowed by a poisonous loathing like I'd never known, everything he did and said was further proof of his irrelevance, his wrongness. I could hardly breathe. For some time I stayed pinned to the chair in which I'd begun the trip, staring out the window at the deepening blue of the lake. Gradually I saw that this hatred was only a warning: there would be times, I knew then, that I would hate him. I had placed too much significance on one person; it required too much faith to sustain. I would falter in that faith sometimes and doubt it all utterly. But I saw too that it was only part of love, that this evil loathing was only the brain's fear cutting down what is too large to comprehend. It had latched on to small details – his hair, his laugh, the memory of an almost-cruel stubbornness suggested by the set of his lips when he sleeps – and manipulated them to signify every bit of the doubt and fear that love inevitably creates. This fear insisted on a reckoning; how could I even know I loved him without testing it against this all-consuming doubt?

Down at the dock Grant told us to get married. He wants Something to Happen. He wants life to be moving forward, tangibly. This is something, I know, that haunts Michael, to whom Grant turns looking for life-altering Grand Plans. He wants to get rich quick, he wants to distinguish himself; he knows he and Michael are fated to distinguish themselves somehow, he just doesn't know through what medium. Michael doesn't know either. Not wanting to be responsible for his brother he also does not want to fail him. He said, Give things time. We have time to figure out what we want to do.

My mind wheeled a moment and I wanted to scream I was so sick of thinking, of thinking and thinking and pondering and questioning and naming and discussing and trying to find the right tool with which to chisel our names into the thick bark of existence. The roots go down so far, why this desperate, prideful desire to carve my name into the trunk? All of us, all undeveloped and searching for our two inches of bark and the right tool with which to etch I WUZ HERE. There are always, have always been more new lives, more new minds.

The boys went silent as Grant saw a muskrat stopped behind us on the dock. I turned around just in time to see its dark form scurry into the tall weeds.

I said something to Michael like, Language is terribly inadequate isn't it?

It's like going up to a waterfall and trying to catch it in cups, he replied.

What a fool's errand, I laughed, delighted by the image of myself standing drenched on a promontory in a deep gorge, water surging down the rocks, a chalice and a tin cup brimming in my two hands. Thousands, millions of others have stood on the same rock, in the same foolish act of devotion, and I drank to them in gratitude.

...Ha, Joseph! I started this email three days ago, saved it to look over, and haven't had a chance to come back to it 'til now.... Getting ready for school, etc. You must be, too! How is Cardiff and your new apartment? I can't wait to hear all about it. But I wanted to tell you about the wedding – such a perfect ending to our time up north...

The ceremony was held in a small brick Catholic church. I had a moment of sorrow that I was distracted wondering what this church, or the vows, meant to the couple, and if they knew the minister; if Shelley was comfortable in her dress; if it was possible, as a bride or groom, to fully experience the ceremony as it was going on – if it felt profound at the time, or if they were going through motions whose meanings would only become clear later, if at all. I was strung between the ordinariness and extra-ordinariness of the day. I felt that all the trappings of tradition – the church, flowers, white dress, the ceremony itself – purveyed the day's uniqueness to me, and also kept me from it. As they said their vows Michael took my hand; all at once I saw the very simple truth that the extra-ordinariness of the proceedings had nothing to do with the wedding itself. If the promise was made truthfully and with good intentions, that was beauty. They could be any two people starting a unified life, anywhere and ever, as bells tolled and the new husband and wife floated joyful and unseeing from the church.

Dinner was held in a log hall with long wooden tables and high, sloping ceilings – I liked it immediately. Relatives had made hundreds of perogies; servers and family members rushed in and out of the steaming kitchen carrying foil pans full of them. I thought how wonderful it is that despite the destruction of communal life over the past two hundred years, and notwithstanding that any ritual we observe is filtered through layers of commerce, we still have true celebration. I met Grandfather Bobbie and his wife Esther for the first time. Harry is going deaf and needs a walker, but sat looking very debonair in a red bow-tie, performing for us a little two-fingered dance, poking them into the air in time, face completely deadpan, and ending it with a horizontal finger across the neck. Later Esther, a sweet, thin, sad-eyed lady, came up and asked Mike and me why we weren't dancing. It was very loud and she couldn't really hear our answers; brows knit she said, Well, either you like it or you don't. I always loved dancing. And then she shuffled off to get another Rum and Coke for Harry, and I fought the feeling that we were not doing Youth the way we should.

Then a funny thing happened: Mike started doing this goofy little seated dance; I could see exactly how he was of this family and for the first time I really, really laughed at the silly thing he was doing. I usually enjoy his silliness, it makes me chuckle, but at that wedding he really gave me a gut laugh. It was because all of a sudden he had become a very real identity to me – not just this boy I love, who I want certain things from, am a certain way around. He was himself, a contained, perfect work that existed regardless of me; does that make sense? It was as though I was seeing him from a great height or distance, but very clearly, and he was very beautiful.

He fell asleep on my shoulder as we hurtled home through the cavernous darkness. I looked at Brian silently steering us forward, his wife beside him, and thought of them at our age and now, watching their parents become old; I saw Harry's big frame resting awkwardly on his walker, Esther gingerly heading for the bar. Michael, I realized, was nearly one third of the way through his life. It seemed impossible. I was sick with it; there were only two thirds left and it would go by in an instant. I wanted to slow down, to be there in the car at twenty-two with my palm against Mike's head and the bush invisibly teeming around us, but I could only be growing older, time had been compressed like an accordion, I was being spun through a merciless polka that would reel to its end any moment and I was dizzy with the speed of it, its relentless progression. I nuzzled my cheek against Mike's downy hair, soft and unmanageably swirling from two crowns. I wanted to alight from that car, in the whole world I only wished that Michael would open his eyes, and together we would brush our teeth, wash our faces and climb into bed.

Which, soon enough, we did.

The next day we prepared to come home. Michael and I took a walk in the morning and collected a wonderful assortment of mushrooms, which we later had identified for us by Wilda, Gary's feisty, white-haired mother, whom I adore after hearing her "whisper" to Michael, This one's a keeper, while jabbing her thumb in my direction.

We stopped someplace on the way back and Janice and Brian bought us ice cream, delicious country creamy stuff that we licked on a picnic bench beneath a vast grey-white sky. This is what a family vacation feels like, I thought. We got back in our respective cars and Mike, Grant and Brian amused themselves with the walkie-talkies Brian had recently acquired, testing range and different channels, enjoying themselves immensely.

You are very sweet to ask about Mom. No, she's unfortunately not returning to school this semester. Maybe next. She has too much work, is feeling too crappy. It was a hard decision, after going through so much to get enrolled, and struggling through the brutal, mandatory Bibliography course. She wanted so badly to get to the point she could do her Gertrude Stein thesis, but she still has another course or two to take, and "doesn't have the koyekh" as she said. Of course Mom hates to feel she's giving up on anything, especially that she's incapable of it due to health and finances, but what can she do? She'll write that thesis someday, even if it's after she retires.

My word, this is probably the longest email ever written! Monday, my first poetry class....

Much love; write soon, Sam.

DIVING IN

09/30/2003

Hello Dearest Joe,

thanks for the email, it made me laugh out loud even as I was feeling bad for you in your classroom full of idiots. It is a bit frightening though, that these people are supposed to help other people get their lives together.

My first classes tasted of the usual: anticipation, pleasure and abysmal terror. In my first Fiction class everyone seemed like a genius, an organized well-read disciplined genius. I knew this was impossible, that it was unlikely that they were *all* more talented and knowledgeable than me, but I couldn't stop feeling that they were. And then hating myself for that, of course. But I could see their willingness to participate, sitting comfortably in their cramped desks happy to gulp down Priscila's words. And I could see myself slumped in a back chair, tired from my weird schedule, capsized by the word "presentation."

One lovely, apple-cheeked blond girl said, And we're not here to be competitive, but to urge each other on with our successes.

Guilt. Shame. A gleam of rage at her suggestion. How can we not be competitive in a Creative Writing class? Yes urge each other on; no, don't be a pretentious asswipe. But those rules apply to everything. What does that have to do with wanting to be the best? I'm rationalizing. More shame.

One guy I knew from last year said, In the movies there's always that one special one. The one kid who's far better than the mass of mediocrity that is his peers. They do it so we can identify.

And the tall guy with a stated crush on Priscila said, But I thought I was that guy, and everyone laughed.

Why can't I at least, like my classmates, have an imagination, an eye for quirky circumstances, a knack for allegory? On that first day my terrible obsession with "real life" put me into a cold sweat in the windowless basement bunker of a classroom. Of everyone here, I thought, I must be the most narcissistic and the least educated.

The first poetry class was equally mortifying. Priscila wrote "Poets are the _____ of the world" on the board. My first thought is, of course, to the embarrassingly literal – poets aren't the anything of the world. They're fathers, daughters, assholes, caregivers, pencil-pushers, citizens of the world just like anybody. What decides whether you're a poet or not anyway? Half the "poetry" out there is just literary psychotherapy supported by arts grants and venerable old Tradition. While I was having a cantankerous seizure in the corner, some blue-eyed boy called Matechuk says, They're water to the small spongy dinosaurs.

Gah, my lousy brain. Why didn't I think of that? Yes, those little capsules you drop in the bath and they turn into sponges, cherished image from my childhood. A lovelier and more evocative way of saying what I'd been thinking a moment before, which was Microscopes, or Telescopes.

Someone else said "scapegoats/subverters" which I liked, if nothing else as a nod to the artists jailed or killed throughout history for writing what they thought. Also it's an argument against poets being the "unheard musicians" most people in the class seemed to feel they are. Generally the responses tended to veer toward "crazies" and "visionaries" – a class of people set apart from, and mostly ignored by, society. I suppose that's a kind of liberty. They get to be Misunderstood Artists from the first. Misunderstanding being an inevitability, and an Artistic Nature being the hat you happen to have chosen from the Great Haberdashery of Modern Life.

So passed the first two weeks of school. In Fiction class, Priscila read us a short story by Barry Callaghan, about taking his famous father, Morley, to the doctor. On the board she had written an Aristotle quote, something like "chronological detail is a low level of awareness." The story was from a collection called *True Stories*, and it dealt with how "true stories" are written, what imagination is, what genes mean. All pertinent things to me, of course, and listening there I suddenly emerged from the chaos of the previous week into the blue calm I find sometimes when driving, or lying in bed with Mike.

To my inestimable gratitude, Priscila then told us to write the histories of our births. This was to be our class exercise, the telling of how we came to be. Oh sweet bliss to have a class exercise I could do; I can never think of a goddamned thing for the cue-card exercises. But that day was my day, man. Write about my own family, my own history? It was nice to not have to worry, for a moment, about the narcissism of it, to accept as my job for fifteen minutes the documentation of my mother in her hospital room with the birds of paradise her father gave her and me in her belly, the hours ticking down until I was taken out; my grandmother reverting to Yiddish, forgetting all English in her labour-madness; and my one great-grandmother with 16 children. The weird mythology of Irving's birth – a circumcised child. If there's one thing my family has never lacked, it's stories about themselves; it surprised me how effortlessly they tumbled to my pen, easy as 4'9" Annie brought forth her five children, even my Zaida, her thirteen-pound first. The stories came as though they'd been waiting for me to transcribe what has been told so many times.

On the one day I have two classes, I usually retreat to my car, eat some lunch, maybe have a sleep. Then I'm all refreshed for Modern Canadian Fiction, which I love. It's taught by this crazy, rather awesome person named Christian Bök, experimental poet of some renown – his lectures seem both laconic and excited, they're fast and full of things that make sense to me. I haven't taken an English class since the appalling one I had at U of T; and Mom's insistence throughout my life that studying literature is magnificent because you can say whatever you want about it was always an argument against it rather than otherwise. So this is my first time reading criticism – which I'm finding kind of difficult – my first time, I guess, learning about literature as connected to its society. I never knew, for instance, that Irving was involved with starting a literary magazine called *First Statement*, and that that magazine was influential in shaping Canada's literary scene in the '50s. Well, there are lots of things I don't know, almost everything in fact. But there shall be a few less things....

So has gone September. Mom and I hung our Indian corn on the door; our patio flowers are beginning to die. We changed the dishes from the flowered Villeroy and Boch to the solid brown Denby set, as we do every fall. Mom admiring the pattern of pansies and bluebells on the plates and bowls as she wiped them down; handing them to me to put away until spring, saying They're so pretty aren't they? It's such a nice tradition, a little way to mark the seasons.

Sending you everything good for autumn.

xo Sam

A DIFFERENT KIND OF TYRANNY
10/15/2003

Hello Dear Joe.

Well, the needs of the body do indeed trump the life of the mind. Two weeks ago it seemed life was going to click along smoothly for awhile. I'd written two poems I was happy with, and had enjoyed writing. For our first assignment we had to write a poem based on an encyclopedia entry. I had never checked to see if Irving was in my old *World Book Encyclopedia*, so couldn't resist looking, and there he was. And out the poem came, simple as breathing. It went down really well in class, too. Except there was this kind of funny moment where that Matechuk kid was like, It kind of sounds like the speaker is imagining the poet as her lover, which is cool…. And Priscila goes, I should probably tell you now that Layton is Sam's father, which had Matechuk blushing very prettily. It was useful, though, his comment; I saw I needed to change "buttock" to "thigh" – what I'd really seen when I wrote the phrase, but somehow buttock got in there…. Anyway, I guess that's what writing workshops are useful for. That and Praise, oh sweet Praise; it's such a relief. The Irving poem I just knew was good (it made Mom cry, of course), but this other one, I liked it but didn't know if it had merit. But people enjoyed it, and I got an A, so hurrah!

Then Mom got pancreatitis. I came in one evening to find her white as the walls, in bed hugging a pillow and talking on the phone to Franceszka. She was saying, Well it's been hurting for a few hours now. It's not the worst pain I've ever felt, but it's not too great. I don't know, do you think I should go?

I hung at her doorframe for a moment as she observed me with her tired, loving eyes. I so badly don't want to go back to the hospital, she said. After the anaphylaxis, you know, just the thought of going there makes me very anxious.

But she was wincing, having to stop talking because of the pain.

And this has been going on for several hours?

So down we drove to Toronto General. We waited to be seen until about four in the morning. I watched the nurses in their pastel scrubs and running shoes, fascinated by how they can seem so vulnerable and so effective at the same time. The vulnerability, I decided, comes in part from the fact that we end up physically closer to nurses than to most other people whose expertise we require: their skin is right there, with only those thin cotton pajamas between them and the complicated world of the hospital. That fragile membrane of skin, freckled, wrinkled or smooth, makes them seem so delicately human in their institutional environments: their veins visible as they bend to take a patient's pulse or stretch to change a saline bag. I watched them joking around with each other at the nurses' station, like workers at any job, putting in their hours; coming back from breaks with coffees and take-out food, at home in their workplace with all its daily grievances, dramas and rewards. To be able to live so calmly among all this mortality – I envied them.

It was a Sunday night; Mom's bags had actually been packed to leave for ShowEast the next day. I had a Fiction workshop, the first round of stories to be edited in class. At three, four, even five, I still thought I would make it to York for 11:30. But in the wan seven a.m. light, on a bench outside the hospital clutching coffee, cigarette and cellphone, lungs and mouth ashy as I called Bonnie to tell her what was happening, I gave it up. Mom was being admitted; if she hadn't come to the hospital her pancreas might have ruptured; she could have died. Why had this happened? No one knew. I called Pat, Mom's boss in L.A., to inform her. The most extraordinarily decent person in that Biblically corrupt city, Pat was all concern and kindness. I fought back resentment then tears as she said, Well it's a good thing your Mom has you there to look after her.

I had to agree. But why, why did it have to be just me? Any time anything goes wrong, it's me who has to witness it. If only there were some man around to chase down doctors and ask them questions, some man to look lovingly into Mom's face and comfort her when she's frightened. I know it's wrong and petty but I wanted to be like everyone else I know, a child. A child of parents who look after one another, a child who has not yet been required to put on the mantle of responsibility for her parents' well-being. I thought of Florence when her grandfather had his final stroke and was dying. She called from the hospital, where she'd been with her whole family for several hours. I have to get out of here, she said; I can't stand it. For the first time, literally the first time, at twenty-one years old, she realized her parents too would fail and die. She realized it but very abstractly, as she realized also that her grandfather's decline was difficult for her parents, and that she should be there to comfort them. I consoled her, I empathized with her, but in my heart I berated her for her weakness. What do you expect, I thought. You think it's all going to be joints and contemplation of ourselves and pretty cups full of ginger-ale, forever? In fact, of course, I resented that she had the freedom to leave, and I never would. But then that passed and

I felt sorry. Seeing her parents distraught, her beloved grandfather come to the end of his long, interesting life, is awful; and nothing in her upbringing had required the selflessness needed to deal with these things, or the acceptance of circumstances beyond her control. She had been protected. It is a tremendous privilege, such an extended childhood, and one that often comes with wealth – like wealth is lovely and freeing, yet leaves one unequipped for many things.

I tried to draw strength from the knowledge of my experiences, but really didn't feel equipped for shit. As I smoked my second cigarette stalling going in and seeing Mom in her hospital bed, hooked up to her IV, I was only bitter and ashamed.

Mom was in the hospital for a week. One night when I went to visit her after school and before going to work, my car window was smashed and my discman stolen. Michael had stopped by the hospital with me and so was there to see me lose my shit when I saw my broken window, and the discman he'd gotten me for my birthday gone. What the fucking fuck, I yelled into the brittle autumn air; What the fucking fuck. I'm parked in front of a fucking hospital. Who steals from someone who's obviously visiting someone in the fucking hospital?

Someone who really needed that discman, said Mike very reasonably. This isn't the greatest area.

I knew that was perfectly true, and cursed myself for not listening to Mom and putting all valuables in the trunk, always. I was feeling very hard-done-by, and mortified about it. I knew comparatively my life is a bed of ease. Even if a new window cost me a couple hundred bucks I wouldn't have to go hungry, just further in debt on my Visa. And Mom would be out of the hospital before long. Though I knew these things and tried to concentrate on them, that night I had no power to focus; there was a film, a grime smearing my vision of the life I sometimes believe I can have, making it a distant shimmer, unreachable from where I stood.

Of course it all worked out – ridiculously well, in fact. Yesterday I took the car to Mom's long-time body mechanic and he replaced the window for free, because he's an incredibly nice person (and maybe because over the years Mom has given him a lot of movie tickets and swag for his daughters). And Jory, Franceszka's son who I've grown up with, gave me a new discman because some job he was working had provided him with several.

Now if I could only quell my constant fear of everything – or, more specifically, of my mother's tyrannical body and my treacherous mind – life would be a dream.

xo

P.S. Here are my first two poems:

Layton, Irving

I

Out of hubris I pursue you
in the glossy pages of the World Book
Encyclopedia we've had since I was six.

There, below laxative and above
Lazarus, are your three paragraphs:
your life, glossed.

"(...), is a Canadian poet.
He writes forceful poems that praise creativity and energy."
(I see your rounded thigh raised in dance like Pan, your moist
closed lids on a face upturned with praise; see the form of your
great grey mane flaming against the sky)
I stand below

my cluttered bookshelves, Post-Structuralism
for Beginners crushed by Childcraft Books, beneath
Hemingway, tattered Kerouac, Austen and your Freud;
there, the L book – number 12 – tells me many of your poems
"express the idea
that human beings and nature are identical."
(Do they? I never knew. And you will never see

me on the couch, hair everywhere, agreeing with you)
I realize

I never knew the name
of the town where you were born,
and that now reading it,
I cannot pronounce it.

       II

You seem smarter than me.
Then again, when you first published,
you were thirty-three,
the same age my mother was
when she had me.
But how did you acquire your ten trillion words?
How did this knack
for allusion occur?
When did you learn Sagittarius
has 800,000 billion stars?
Or the particulars of so many wars?
I cannot ask you. So,
I read four poems and look up six words.
Two of them are not in my dictionary.

The Encyclopedia does not say
né Israel Lazarovitch, and does not say when
irritated, his eyebrows twitched,
and with gusto he pissed people off.
You influenced verse. You won the Governor-General's.
You were a teacher. The World Book does not
say he tapped fingers counting syllables,
and the perfect mouth kept him awake nights;
nor how some mornings,
tickled with delight
just to be awake
you would do a little dance,

a sweet absurd bounce, like a child who has to pee,
and you'd sing a little song for the new day.

capitalism i praise you

for your neverending ability
to convert yourself

for the peace of mind
you've provided rich and poor alike

for the sense of hope
you bestow upon hungry adolescent nations

whose most shining
aspiration is the attainment of your virtues

i salute you
for so valiantly defending inequality

for upholding
aristotelian ideals and making modern

social darwinism
in all its astounding convenience

i praise you
for deliverance from the gates

of communist
delusion and for freedom from expression

as my best
wishes can be bought for $2.95 from the drugstore

i thank you
for adidas in addis ababa and the assurance

that my wealth
was earned and deserved, and also

for the knowledge
that my life demands lysol

i thank you
for secular kings and disinfected serfs

for cleverly
doing things with my money i'd never think of

and also for
multiplex movietheaters and the dream

that some day
i too will purchase the beautiful housecarbaby

and own my very own life.

ME ME ME ME

10/28/2003

Dear Joseph,
    thank you again for calling last week; it was so good to hear you, and Mom really enjoyed it too. Yes, the gall bladder removal has been successfully completed, and it totally sucked. It's now out-patient surgery, and they tell you it's no big deal, but that, my friend, is a crock of shit. When I went to Mom in the recovery room she looked worse than I'd ever seen her. She, with her excellent pain tolerance, was in agony. They ask you to rate the pain on a scale of one to ten, and she said nine. I sat with her and handed her the little plastic cup of juice they provide, and petted her head, and tried not to be horrified. She put on a brave face, and eventually I took her home,

every bump jolting her disrupted insides. Incredibly, a young man she befriended several years ago through work – this charming self-starting Jew whose company supplies some of the promotional doo-dads Mom always needs – had come from Montreal to be there for her. He was waiting when we arrived, helped to get Mom comfortable and to cheer her; and a little while later Eshe came by, as always restoring to me a sense that life continues with a degree of stability. More: that it is and shall be sweet and full of promise.

I wish, when these situations arise with Mom, that there was no thought to how I wouldn't be able to stay at Mike's for a while, or how maybe if Mom had made different choices she'd be healthier. But then, maybe not; she's had a hard life, whatever way you slice it, and she's been valiant. Although I'm often, in the moment, glad to be there, pleased to be able to bring her tea and sit with her as she recovers, I will find myself thinking, what would she do if I'd gone away to school? Of course she would say that I should and must pursue anything I have the desire to. But how can I even desire it? It would hurt her to know I think this way, and I don't want to be thinking these things as my mother hobbles, breathing very deliberately, to the bathroom, or as I boil a bouillon cube for her to drink. I don't want to think that I'm going to hurl if I ever smell vegetable bouillon again. All I can hope is that she doesn't sense my reticence, that there is something useful and good in acting the person I want to be but am not.

Eshe came to my Canadian Fiction class because she's missing school, and I thought she'd enjoy Professor Bök's lecturing. We're reading *By Grand Central Station I Sat Down and Wept*, which I'm kind of hating, because the narrator/author seems rather crazed; but having Eshe there made it more fun because we could mock the book's excesses, and still take a moment to thank her and women like her for putting their shit on the line. Maybe now, Eshe said, The emotional tumult and narcissism and, like, bodily obsession is less necessary because it's been done already. I mean, she's bananas – both the author and the narrator – but considering it was 1945 or whatever, it's a pretty brave book.

But weren't there always women willing to sacrifice everything for love? Yes. But they weren't always willing to publish it.

Hm. Maybe I just instinctively hate everything that's not realism – lord, Professor Bök would ridicule me if he heard that. He was very vocal about his hate-on for *The Tin Flute*, and I felt like an imbecile, because I loved it.

But of course. That's what you want to write.

I wrote my story about Ty coming to Mom for help on his med school application; about his dark curls against our white couch as we conjured the future, like children in a basement with their secret plans; Ty channeling Tom Waits growling What's he building in there?

It felt like a start, at least.

We had to skip our Thanksgiving festivities, but put up our Halloween decorations the other day. Mom was disappointed it was so late; she likes to have these things up for the whole month. It's always comforting, taking the familiar things from their box each year – the little ghost candle we've had since I was small, and the witch lamp, the spiders and cobwebs and disembodied arm. Some of the things I unreservedly love; others I sometimes feel would be more appropriate if there were children around. But Mom loves her seasonal decorations, and doesn't mind if it's a little kitschy. I so look forward to giving her grandchildren.

xx
Sam

CLUMSY NEW

11/19/2003

Dearest Joe,

well, once again, Canada fails to live up to its own self-image. The beginning of this month the Globe reported that the Kyoto Protocol will likely not be ratified. If this fucking country can't bring itself to sign on to this one miserable little accord, this tepid commitment to the barest minimum of environmental progress, we're doomed. I mean, as it is Kyoto's not going to halt the damage we've already set in motion, but to think of ourselves as this benign, enlightened country, this moral counter-weight to the Behemoth Below, and not even ratify the stupid pissing Kyoto Protocol? We're just, as Mike said, A particle on the back of the larger beast.

He and I were having breakfast at the Canary, this wonderful old red brick diner on Cherry St.; Michael was reading the paper to me while we waited for our eggs, and I rolled dust off the plants on the windowsill. He pushed the ashtray aside and spread the paper on the table in the ashy light, said, Look at this shit. The Made in Canada Solution; what the fuck is that? "Kyoto isn't right for us; we need something that works for us, as a country." I don't know, dickweeds, I thought the point of an *accord between countries* was that it's an accord between countries. Gee, I wonder who financed this ad, the oil companies maybe? Hydro companies? Yup, there they all are, down at the bottom.

The waitress came then, saying as she placed our greasy breakfasts in front of us, Oh that whole thing is so stupid. Why don't they just sign on to the damn Protocol? Politics… and she ambled off for the coffee pot.

I was down at the loft last weekend, helping Ty with his application, and met his new roommate, Jake: an old friend of Ty's, back from years working for human rights organizations in Nigeria and Israel. I remember the first winter I knew Ty, he used to read me emails Jake was sending him from India, where he was riding a motorcycle from north to south. After preliminaries, my first conversation with Jake was an argument over the tragic fate of Rachel Corrie, that girl recently killed by an Israeli bulldozer as she tried to prevent a Palestinian home from being razed. Jake said, She's a hero.

I said, Sacrificing her life will do nothing. Protesting, yes, but get the fuck out of the way before they kill you.

But what if it's an accident? (His blue eyes were bright and hard on my face; I thought of everything he's seen, and felt very stupid, yet the very idea of martyrdom put me in a kind of frenzy. In a world with so much death and calculated suffering, the thought of adding another body to the pile of corpses for yet another idea was abhorrent.) Jake was saying in his rapid but unflustered way, They don't know the full circumstances. She might have tried to get out of the way and been unable. And there were other people in the organization she was working with who were also killed shortly after her, one trying to get kids out of the way of Israeli bullets. Or actually, he's still in a coma, I think. Is that also foolish?

I don't know, I said. I felt suddenly that I was only outraged at Corrie and her comrades' deaths because I am not imbued with similar selflessness. How could I leave Mom to go die for strangers? I am impotent and useless, if that is what the world demands. But I thought of Jake, or Ty, or Michael getting shot trying to save some kid in a war zone and couldn't bear it. Why should they destroy themselves for a conflict that won't be affected one iota by their deaths? But perhaps that is only a kind of nihilism, or despair to cover cowardice. To Jake I said, Isn't there some other less dramatic way to help change things? I mean, you're right, she is a kind of hero; she stands for the kind of sacrifice humans are capable of making for one another, and I don't mean to devalue that. But ultimately, to the people making the decisions that keep this conflict running, she's just another dead body. So all that happens is you get a few more conversations about how terrible the whole situation is, but the issue itself still seems totally removed and much too large for people to understand.

The issue *is* too large, Jake countered. But all change starts in people's minds. So if, like you said, people are talking about the Palestinians now, are thinking about their situation more critically than before, then that's a step toward change.

Well that's true. But I think it's wrong that the only way that happens is through more death. What about people like you? Shouldn't the fact that day in, day out, people like you are trying to work within the system to benefit people's lives matter to someone? I mean, I know there's little symbolic value in the image of a guy sitting at a desk, but maybe there should be.

I see what you're saying, said Jake, And yes, Adalah was doing good work, they really did get compensation for people who'd been badly fucked around. But there's ego involved in that too, don't forget. Lots. And it doesn't help to change the course of events, it's more like crisis management. I don't know. It's not the only way to engage with the world's problems.

All the while Ty, an Israeli himself, was sitting on the couch staring at the computer screen, typing, oblivious to everything but McMaster's forms. I stayed up half the night with him, trying not to get caught up in reminiscences as we attempted to wrangle his irregularly-shaped life into the five one-hundred-word boxes the school required. For one question, he had to describe a situation that had not gone as intended, and what he had learned; he said, Yeah that time I tried to fix that guy's bike, and couldn't, that taught me something. I nearly destroyed his whole engine, I felt terrible. I learned you should only fuck around with your own shit when you don't know what you're doing.... And then he laughed briefly over himself and Mike, when they were first becoming friends, trying to rebuild the engine on Ty's 1979 Suzuki bike, making monkey noises and laughing at themselves. I had to pay someone eventually, Ty said with that goofy chesty laugh, mouth open. But we learned a lot. Turning as he does suddenly earnest and humble, the counterweight position to all his slipperiness and bombast.

It feels very serious, that Ty has made the application. It's like how our lives are going to go is beginning to be determined. Even Mike seems to be feeling it – he's more serious about school this year, trying harder to get things in on time, do all the readings. Though he never can read everything that's assigned, because his notes are so detailed – but he remembers everything he reads. Yesterday he was telling me things about nanotechnology that he learned in Grade Four.

He's doing well with the Arabic, still tutored by Mustafa, who brought Mike's grade up twenty percent last year. Mike says he knows tutoring is the best way to learn a language, and anyway the Arabic program at U of T is small, underfunded, and poorly structured. It's fucking stupid, says Mike; The Middle East is everyone's biggest problem these days and no one can even speak the fucking language. The Near Middle Eastern Studies department is in a building that's been swallowed by another building, and there's a rogues' gallery of hundred year old Egyptologists on the walls. It's pretty wild.

Almost everyone else that's not a native speaker has already dropped out, but Mike is enjoying himself. It amazes me how willing he is to sit over a book translating, conjugating, getting his hand around that delicate, intricate cursive. I wish I had his tenacity with it. I started a poem, actually, about watching him study Arabic:

> The strange syllables fell from your mouth raw
> as tendrils peeling from a bud. They curled
> away from you, clumsy, new, and my awe
> was absurd, complete, watching you unfurl.

I can't get any further. But I loved him very much as he was bent over his books at my kitchen table, trying to master the *kh* sound, feeling his adam's apple as he tried to get it right. He seemed so young and separate from me, somehow very male; like young men throughout history preparing themselves to take their places in society. My own studies seem to have so little to do with the world – something, but not the same as Mike learning about political theories that have shaped societies, or a language that will enable him to interact with millions of people. Or Ty, learning how to fix bodies. They're taking in concrete information – anatomy, language – that will change the way they act on the world.

Like you, sweet Joe, learning to change how others act on themselves. And you shall tell me all about it on the 15th! Tell me what terminal to be at, and I'll be there with bells on.

Much love, Sam.

WRIGGLING MY LITTLE TADPOLE TAIL

12/27/2003

Dear Joe,

first the bad news. The Saab is no more. She was on her last legs anyway, and the engine is too damaged to fix. Mom is being really kind about it – she knows about ice, skidded out once on a country road when I was a kid. Still, this was the first and only car she bought for herself; she loved it for seventeen years, and I am responsible for its demise.

The day after you left I went to a reading at The Pilot, a historic bar on Cumberland. When I asked Mom if she wanted to come, she said, Sure, the Pilot, that's been there forever – it's a landmark. The reading was put on by some students who had just graduated from York's Creative Writing program, and Priscila also read from her new book of poems, *Live Coverage*. I loved how earnestly Priscila read, and everyone was beautiful, and the whole scene made me miserable. Mom and Bri and I were sitting at a table near the stage. Around us people were talking, holding beers; we were simply observers, our table like a small void in the full, noisy room. I felt like a half-formed thing, deficient in the face of these students, only a little older than me and seemingly so purposeful. How do they know where to begin? Every few months or so I find myself hyperventilating in a bookstore, goggle-eyed at the array of literary journals – even just Canadian journals…. At moments I'll think it's splendid, this bounty, it's our parents' legacy; think, thanks Dennis Lee, thanks Queen Mags you paved the way! But sitting in this old bar, where they've been having poetry readings for decades, it seemed that my generation doing what my mother's and father's had done could not possibly be as meaningful.

Mom surveyed the place dispassionately, as though waiting for something to entertain her. It's all old hat to her – she's been to the epicentre of the Canadian literary world, seen so many eager creatures striving and asserting themselves on its periphery, piercing the membrane of success with the narrowness of their self-confidence. This little display by the young and ambitious was nothing but more of the same, the would-be writers only so many tadpoles wriggling in their muddy little pond.

After the readings were done that Matechuk kid came over and we got to chatting. Suddenly, almost embarrassingly, I was all animation and ideas. We were talking about parents.

Matechuk said, My Dad got married at twenty-three, you know? Right after the wedding he went off to the Northwest Territories and built houses. They've been married for twenty-five years. I just feel like they must think I'm kind of crazy, you know, going to school to learn writing. Like maybe I should be doing something a bit more practical.

Well, I said to him, There are so many ways to disappoint one's parents. But I think often we think we're disappointing them when really they're just worried about us. And they can't help that.

As if on cue Mom came up and I introduced them. She didn't like him, smiled scornfully as she shook his hand. Perhaps she was upset that I had hardly spoken at the table with her and Bri, and now was babbling happily away. I felt bad about my sudden garrulousness, but somehow Matechuk had attached me to the rest of the room; vague bodies that had seemed miles away had texture, expressions I could understand: their noise was conversation. What I had been seeing as stereotype cloaked itself in tradition, and I felt young, supple enough to learn.

Soon afterwards we all left, Mom to go home, Bri and I to have a little walk. And it was lovely, Rosedale Valley road all gleaming after the rain – Bri saying the city is hideous and me convincing her otherwise: You see, I said, The rain coming down the hill makes waterfalls for us, and the streetlamps are many small moons. We were striding upwards in the bright darkness, arms linked, yelling about art – We compare mountains to movies! Make all beauty over in our image, as if it existed for us! *Being beautiful just for youuuu...but that might not be quite true...* Howling just because we were excited and it was raining and our breath was dragon's breath in the cold night.

But when I went home Mom was up and unhappy. *Zorba the Greek* was playing on TV but she was only half-watching – she watches it every time it's on but this time it didn't seem to be working its usual magic on her. Are you in a better mood, she asked, and I literally envisioned the word "mood" with little icicles dripping off it.

Yes, I said, and laughed, hoping she would be glad because I was.

Good, she said, and was silent.

You were unimpressed with Matechuk, I said, thinking perhaps I could lead her into a nice vituperative rant about the whole scene and then she'd feel better.

I just came away with this feeling. I'm tired. I'm ready for change in my life.

Well that's good, I said, 'Cuz that's about the one thing you can count on. She didn't even crack a smile.

I think she was angered by my intimidation at the reading. Whenever I get despondent about how many people are publishing, how little I've done, she thinks it's absurd. It must seem an affront, my combination of reticence to actively "put myself out there" as she would say, and my readiness to assume I'm a deluded slob unworthy to study the poetry of my peers. As though I'm rejecting the talisman of my birthright, which she won for me with great sacrifice.

I went from her room and ate a quarter tub of ice cream, some nuts, some chocolate, then felt ill. I read over some of my poetry and wanted to say things, but it was so clear the pressure in my brain would never create the diamonds my mother is sure are in there; it would only crush me and any possibility of a normal, decent life. I was doomed to chip away in this stifling pit of a consciousness, fated to seek the nonexistent treasure that would redeem my existence.

All I wrote was How do I atone for growing up?

Then I went to bed.

But I woke thinking I might have gotten a story out of the night, something to use for my next Fiction assignment. In the early afternoon I met Michael at work; a few of the homeless guys whose money he keeps for them (so they won't get robbed) had bought him a present. One of them had been a tailor before his life went to shit, and he always ribs Mike about his threadbare shirts, so he and two others chipped in and bought him a shirt and tie. Can you believe it? It made me happy, this gesture, and also to be loved by someone who inspires such goodwill. He and I bumbled our ways through the Christmas Eve LCBO crowds to procure a bottle of Scotch for his parents, bewildered and slightly childish-feeling amid the purposeful flurry of liquor-literate shoppers, Mike in his fingerless gloves making the check-out girl laugh as I fumbled for my wallet in the army satchel you gave me. I thought, it's alright. If this man will love me, if we can make a life, everything will work out fine.

I ate Christmas dinner with Michael's family for the first time: the table set with Christmas colours, Janice's mother looking like a grandma out of a story book with her curly white hair and blue eyes, brooch – a cardinal, for the season – pinned to her white cardigan. I like Mike's family, and how he seems different from them, yet theirs. Sitting drowsily on the carpet by the fireplace, I watched Michael goofing around with his brother, imagining their long, muscular bodies as the soft, uncoordinated ones I have seen on home videos of them as children in that same living room.

It was good to have you here for a holiday, and Chanukah at Franceszka's is an excellent one. She has that same sensibility as Mom, of wanting to mark special occasions, and create traditions, and her family is also small and mostly not in Toronto. It feels very much of the modern age, doesn't it? These two divorced women and their kids gathering each year in one rental apartment building or another, both women's homes furnished with family heirlooms and beautiful things from the women's younger days. I am so grateful for Franceszka and her children, family made by circumstance – like any I suppose, but more recently, and without the obligation of shared genes.

I hope your Christmas was not unreasonably horrible, and thanks again for having come to visit. Give my regards to your folks, and have the happiest of new years, Sweet Joe.

ROLLIN' ON THE RIVER
01/19/2004

Joseph!

these bright cold days have me thinking you'd approve of my life at the moment: the hours spent striding through the east end in Mom's old sheepskin, admiring the skyline as Michael and I cross the Queen St. bridge, hollering over traffic sounds rising from the DVP below.

Names, Mike's breath puffed into yesterday's grey-gold afternoon, We give things names out of necessity but we should never think that the names for things actually correlate to what they are. That's the danger of language – it makes us cocky. Like "freedom." What the fuck does that *mean*, actually. It's a logocyte, that word, an empty vessel that can be filled with whatever you want.

That's a good word, logocyte, I said. It should be in the dictionary.

Oh, I'm sure there's another word for what I mean, but anyway it'll serve my purpose for the moment. So in this society freedom means a certain thing; somewhere else it means something else. But it's used to instigate all kinds of actions. It has tangible, material effects, that word. Human Rights; there's another logocyte. Two World Wars in half a century, man, the Great Powers gazing into the maw of modernity and seeing total war, economic collapse. They were terrified! The Universal Declaration was a response to a visceral terror that the rational, technological world was in fact totally irrational and apt to destroy itself. So Human Rights were born from very authentic intentions, or feelings, but legally, they're in the same domain as NAFTA and the IMF. By the nature of the system they're in, Human Rights are something to be exported. But at least it's a standard we're not meeting.

Yeah, but isn't it tragic that our species finally looks into the fucking maw, and *expresses* its horror at it, and yet perpetuates it, *using the very idea that was supposed to redeem us*, as a species, to legitimate the same bullshit humans have always been doing?

I still say it's better expressed than if it never had been. Ideas create the conditions for their perpetuation. People are always working on changing things for the better.

Thusly we keep ourselves warm as we traipse around Leslieville, admiring its old trees and crooked row houses, thinking of his grandmother as a little girl running around on Booth Street. I love the neighborhood but feel conspicuous there – we are so very much the young leftie students, with our woolen scarves and serious talk, come to ogle the working class. Or so it sometimes seems as we pass the men outside the Good Shepherd, the women congregating with their broods at the donut shop on Gerard. To them we must be aligned with this new spattering of hip young things striding the streets with their headphones, cellphones and fashionable boots, here for the cheap rents and retro appeal.

I always hope that by chatting with the homeless men, by becoming friendly with the Eritreans who run the place we get breakfast, I can prove myself apart from these other impostors, who will surely raise the rents and have a Starbucks in there within three years. So Mike and I discuss that too, Mike saying, But we can try to use our privilege in the best possible ways; we don't have to be, like, Ivory Tower academics who preach leftist bullshit and then complain about squeegee kids or whatever. There are ways to make a life that doesn't involve stepping on other people's heads. And it starts with being the kind of person who gets to know, and tries to get involved with, the people in their immediate environment. Then you're not atomized into these little adult worlds where it's easy to start prioritizing the wrong kind of things.

And agreeing on everything about caring for aging parents, or extra-curricular activities for children to supplement our increasingly shitty educational system, we'll stomp into the loft with ruddy faces and snowy shoes. Yesterday evening we came in to find Michelle and Ty on the couch, studying; they looked up at us with so much love it halted our talk mid-sentence.

You guys never run out of conversation, Ty said. It's great. Every time I see you it's some interesting discussion.

Of course for Michael it's all just talk; an interesting way to spend an afternoon, making stories for his political ideals, hashing out what might be, in theory at least, an acceptable life.

How are your days, my friend? Are you loving the winter as much as I expect? Write and tell me.

x

THE YEAR THUS FAR
    02/06/2004

Dear Joe,

it is good to hear that things with Dave have finally come to a kind of rest. Your email sounded liberated, and gave me a smile, glimpsing you nailing Pollock to the wall – mounting your figure of controlled chaos, possibility.

Thank you thank you for the beautiful writing book, I love it. And your timing is wonderful; I'm almost through this nutty brown thing that I've been writing in from both sides. It'll be a nice business extracting anything from that; but I'll be better with this new one.

For the birthday a Samba friend and I did a joint party in the middle of the month, at the house she shares with two vegan yoga instructors. Mostly I stood in the backyard, smoking with other people who pollute themselves and talk about things besides meditation or mountain climbing. For awhile I listened as Ty held court talking about playing music for patients in the psych ward at McMaster. People who hadn't moved for weeks got up and danced!, he said, before playing a recording on which we could hear patients clapping in time.

A little later in the crush of the kitchen, tea-lights sputtering in their holders as I munched on the remains of cake (vegan chocolate, made by Bri and shockingly good), I got this feeling about a birthday present. People were saying mysterious things; conversations would mischievously cease when I approached. Waiting for the streetcar home, the snow shifting drifting like sand dunes as we huddled in the shelter, I told Mike I thought I knew what he was getting me. Other couples held each other as they stooped into the wind, tramping across the whispering street.

Oh you do, do you? Do you want to guess?

Maybe, I said. I won't be disappointed if I'm wrong. But I think you're getting me a laptop.

And indeed he is! He and Ty collected a lot of money from all my friends, including some of Mom's old friends and Mom herself, and have ordered me a new computer. It's such a massive undertaking, I am shocked he orchestrated it. So much planning and calling of people. I felt very loved and looked-after as I wrapped my arms around him, beneath the rough, heavy wool of his greatcoat. Such a singular gem he is; just when I think I have the whole of him in my hand, always some new facet comes winking at me.

You really need your own computer, he said. You can't be doing your writing in the living room, with your Mom around distracting you, and then you only end up writing in the wee hours of morning. You need your own space. And this way you can work down at the loft, too. Anyway that old Mac is a piece of shit by now.

This. Is. Not. My. Fault.: I quoted the Mac experiencing some incomprehensible fuck-up.

The bad news is that Mom has finally decided we have to move. Ever since they renovated the rent has gone up and up, and now, even with me contributing a little bit, it's too high. Mom is understandably unhappy; she's liked it here. She loves the view, walking into the apartment at night like finding a perch in a forest of concrete and light. And she won't have the pool, which she's been swimming in fairly faithfully to try and help her arthritis and fibromyalgia. Though it doesn't seem to help, really. Nothing does but Fiorenol and sometimes lots of sleep. Anyway it sucks, but what can you do? It seems like everywhere we live the same thing happens: months of renovations, which usually make the place less cool (they replaced the lobby's '70's shag carpet and coke-snorting coffee table with a floral carpet and staid wood tables, very respectably boring); then the landlords can raise the rent more than the standard three percent, and we have to leave. It was the same thing in Walmer. Mom finds it demoralizing. I find it infuriating. So go advocate for rent control, Sammy….

Be well, my dearest Joe. xo

MAKING HISTORY

02/25/2004

Dear Joe.

I'm glad today is done, and I'm home, writing to you. This morning in Fiction class I sat staring dumbly, strangled by terror. As I walked from the classroom at the beginning of the break, Priscila, sweet woman that she is, asked me if I was alright. And my stupid face just crumpled, I tried to regain the composure to at least answer an honest No, but
I'd barely gotten it out when I had to dash to the washroom, where I stood with my streaming face against a stall door, thinking What the fuck.

Just yesterday, Priscila told me I've been given a major award. The biggest award for poetry in our program, enough to pay more than half next year's tuition. This happened on Mike's birthday, after Poetry class. Priscila said she wanted to talk to me in her office. Uh-oh, I said, The lateness? But she smiled and said No, a mysterious benevolence in her lovely dark eyes. And then that's what she told me, that she'd nominated me for the award, me and one other guy, but there are two awards. I don't have to tell you the blissful relief of validation it was, how possible everything suddenly seemed as I rode the train in the afternoon sunshine, down to meet Mike in Kensington. Calling to him across the snowy park on Augusta, I couldn't have been happier. I gave him the T-shirt I'd had made – it says "A guy named Arkhipov saved the world" – homage to the Cold War-era Russian submarine captain who, while being bombarded by American fire, decided to follow protocol to the letter and refused to fire the nuclear missiles that the other captain was ready to let loose. Mike read the story in a Chomsky book somewhere, and we marveled at this person whose name no one knows but who literally did prevent nuclear war. Mike loved the shirt; he put his arm around me and off we went for coffee at Moonbean, young students at the start of everything, bound to distinguish ourselves, heads full of important thoughts.

Then today there I was crumbling in the hallway of Founders College. I suppose it's the upcoming move and all. The dismantling. A vase we've always had, formerly my great-grandmother's, broke. Mom took it down to clean it and the handle which had been previously glued came off, the rest smashed to pieces on the parquet. Now the twilight blue, the red and pink peonies Mom and I have admired all my life are in a little heap. We used to lie in her bed when I was younger and talk about how someday I'd have that vase in my home, a little piece of Zaida's mother Annie's love of pretty things. Mom says someday she'll try and glue it together again. Every time something breaks Mom says she just doesn't care about things anymore, that everything keeps breaking so what does it matter. But every time she cries. If it didn't matter, our home wouldn't be full of cracked, re-glued things (to which I too am attached) – the sunbathing frogs from Florida, an old pewter picture frame that won't stand up. Sometimes I feel we are living collage – Past and Present of the Middle Class. Those are the best moments, when I can make bricolage of our belongings: Waterford crystal glasses Mom bought when first making big money as General Manager of Buena Vista crammed into the ancient Ikea hutch with our daily plates, my great-grandmother's serving platters. I scrape cat hair from the throne-like chair that was my grandparents', heaping piles of swag Mom brings home from work – movie t-shirts, bags, DVDs contained between the chair's ornate wooden arms.

At my worst, I lurch around the apartment as though in the grip of some dull possession, lining things up on the coffee table, putting bills and unread newspapers into piles, trying to bring some unity and order to the infelicitous mash-up of our domestic existence.

More awful even than the vase is that all our Halloween and Christmas things are gone. The box is just gone. It had been in Mom's parking space – we didn't want to take it down to the filthy, horror-movie-creepy storage space. Other people had sports equipment and all kinds of things in their parking spaces; we thought it would be fine. But one day I said Where's the box? And we haven't been able to turn it up. I can barely think about it. The little ghost with his too-close-together eyes; the witch crystal ball; the elf on a swing Mom and I bought in Kleinberg on a day-trip. It's ridiculous, I know, to mourn such things, but they were things I had known my whole life. I envy people whose childhood possessions are safely in some attic or basement; they don't realize what a luxury it is, but to me that is the symbol of middle-class comfort. Any time something like this happens, it's the same feeling of deprivation and consequent self-loathing. Ah yes, the meta-hate, as Mike always jokes.

And thank heavens for him, his jokes, and for how well he understands me. Although sometimes, this vision of life we're always conjuring in conversation is like a cruel trick of the eye. The downloaded TV shows, no commercials for the kids, farmers' markets in the summer – oh yes, it's all mapped out; only the two of us, together as a family, has not yet been identified as the destination. Ezekiel Bobbie. Methuselah Bobbie. Candi with an i. Icabod Bobbie. We joke all the time, we have litanies of bad names. You should name your first-born that. Cornelius. Beulah, ha ha ha.

Twice last week Mike referred to us as being married. You married a monk, he said, and I made a joke about monks thinking, did I miss the ceremony?

Get some for me and the missus, he said to Ty later that week as he was off for burritos, and I said nothing. I figure he tries these things on for size. I am afraid to draw attention to it.

Then last night in bed joking about names again he said, Our firstborn, but then he said, Maybe we won't get married or have kids, you never know.

Fury! Does he consciously want to keep me off-balance? Does he need to say that to remind himself he's still free? Or did the phrase just fall from his mouth, psychology spillage, mood-killing and unbidden as a burp?

Lying around, still smiling, still joking about on his twenty-sixth birthday I thought, Well, I'll have to know sometime. Never is a logical impossibility.

But this morning everything seemed a logical impossibility.

I was chatting with Ariel about the laptop thing, and she said, You guys are getting married. When he starts buying you major appliances that's the sign. I've known three other people whose guys bought them major things, a washing machine one of them, I think another was another computer, and they all got married.

She seemed pleased. Sitting in her shoe-box of a store with her computer on her lap, a garment in one hand, bits of material everywhere as usual she seemed worldly, knowledgeable and calm. Creative and unflappable in her anarchic, hyper-coloured domain. Still I found myself thinking maybe he just didn't know what else to get me. He knows I need a computer, he knows about computers, he fixed it up so I could have one.

Oh well – may as well see it like Ariel does, as some kind of meaningful choice.

The lady Mike gets his bagels from at work said in Chinese that we have what roughly translates as "coupleface."

xo, Sweet Joe.

LIFE ON THE BERNSTEIN CARAVAN
     03/15/2004

Dear Joe,

sorry I didn't reply to your email sooner. I tried, the night I got it, the second night after the move, but I couldn't clear my mind of the boxes everywhere, or of the feeling that my life would always be boxes everywhere: boxes I would never fully unpack but haul, ever more tattered and burdensome, wherever I go. I thought, you know, I would describe it; lit a smoke to try – and Mom yelled at me from her bedroom, so I hit Save draft and stayed up until four putting things in reasonable places.

The new apartment is cozy, though, and the furniture fits well; I like that the street is only three flights of stairs away. Mom hates looking out the window at another apartment, and misses our old view. Our last night on Jackes Ave., those city lights turned on us, seemed hostile glaring in on the exposed walls of the dismantled apartment. The concrete boxes that had sheltered us ready to be painted, become someone else's home. Mike wasn't there and I was angry. He had schoolwork to do. I resented the thought of him at the loft, all warm and easy in his computer chair, Ty on the couch, dishes in the sink, everyone going about their business. Well, this is our business, I thought, going through my closet again to see if there was anything I could bear to part with. All these Celine shirts I've dragged from home to home; Baba's hand-me-downs and things bought for Mom – I keep thinking someday I'll want fancy blouses, a suede skirt, a linen pants set. That I'll grow into them, be old enough for them someday; that if I give them away just to make more closet-space, I'll be sorry. But then I think, I don't want this stuff to fit me; it's mostly too big and should stay that way. Nevertheless when it comes time to cram them into the movers' wardrobe or a new tiny closet I think how stupid, and do it anyway.

And then there's shit like the ceramic musical Mickey Mouse we've schlepped along forever. Why, I don't know, since Mom has nothing good to say about Disney and god knows neither do I. She says it might be worth something; if it is, then why don't we sell it? But somehow it always manages to sit on the floor of wherever, mostly hidden, until the next move when it gets packed up again.

Four years, though. Four years on Jackes Avenue, that's pretty good. Madison, of the permaflood and hostile landlords, we were in for one year. That was the first move Mike helped us with, Walmer to Madison. Walmer was six years but in two different units. Before that two years on Relmar after Mom sold the house in 1994. Oh that house. I know Mom thinks about it all the time, but especially whenever we move again (or when the subject of real estate in Toronto comes up. I'm the only person ever to lose money on a house in this city, it seems, is what she says, and it might be true. Bought at the end of the eighties, sold in the beginning of the '90s…). It was a nice house built in probably the '60s or '70s and I loved it because it was ours and because I could easily imagine I was living in "the olden days." There was a round fireplace of rough pinkish brick and I could sit "before the hearth" as it delighted me to think, on my little sheepskin rug in my flannel nightie sipping cocoa and knitting, and believe I was one of the Little Women or Five Little Peppers.

It fascinates me that when Mom bought a house she bought it in Forest Hill. Having grown up there hating it intensely, having defined so much of herself as apart from that whole world of "conventional Jewish girls" – that she would return to the very heart of it! I asked her about this recently and she said, It was a safe area, I was a single mother, I felt comfortable with you walking around there, or being alone at home with you there.

Which seems batshit insane to me, because it's not as though her beloved Annex was crime ridden; it was crawling with kids, largely spawned by the hippie home-owners of her generation. But she chose Thelma, a cul-de-sac hidden in the heart of the village, though bizarre: a lower-middle-class street in a rich area. It had two low-rise apartment buildings, several hideous early-'80s brick bunker-style houses, and a row of crooked wooden semi-detached houses for rent which, most weirdly, were rotting away empty so far as we could tell. Except one, which was inhabited by a spirited old German woman I loved; I used to fetch her smokes when I walked my dog. Hilda had only one leg and spent most of her days on a pink-covered daybed in her front room, surrounded by photographs of her departed husband and white bisson frissé. The automated lift she had put in when she got her scooter is still there, and whenever I step onto Thelma Ave. for a peek at old times I can conjure Hilda, in a black shirt with small white polka dots, riding down the street calling, I'm off to the races! Two doors down is the recessed Tudor house beneath dark old trees, where the twenty-three year old dominatrix lived with her menagerie of cats and dogs, taxidermy on the walls. Not that anyone but Mom knew about her profession. To everyone else she was just the unusually pretty girl in rags with two scary dogs on a chain. But Mom befriended her of course.

I guess it all makes sense, as everything does in its way. No point speculating on whether or not Mom would have been able to afford to keep a house in the Annex, either, after she quit her job and the recession hit. And, come to think of it, her decision to live in Forest Hill was not as illogical as I'm painting it. She was General Manager of Buena Vista then – the first woman in Canada to hold that job – and so when the landlord of our house on Vesta said she wanted her place back, Mom wouldn't have had a lot of time to run around looking for houses or researching schools. And Zaida had just died. Mom was getting phone calls at all hours from Baba; then Mom got walking pneumonia. No wonder she gravitated toward what was familiar.

So here we are installed in Heath St., between Yonge and Avenue Rd., around the corner from Bregmans, a restaurant my family has been going to for thirty years. We're in the last of three identical low-rises built in the fifties; it's laid out pretty much like every other Toronto apartment built at that time, a good-sized living-dining area, strip kitchen, parquet floors. The bathroom is a fabulous post-war mint green tile, we fell in love with that immediately. And the light fixtures are sweet little copper jobs with holes in them that make a pretty pattern of light on the ceiling. It was the first place we saw and we just said Okay, we can live here. Mom even decided to try living without air conditioning. After the endless search that was the last move, neither of us had the *koyekh* for a long apartment hunt.

Mom's bedroom is massive, that was one of the best things, no measuring for the bedroom set. The collage Mom made back in the sixties will be hung above the bed, as it has always done, and this place will be home. Andy Warhol eternally drowning in his tomato soup beside a guy who (as Mom said) looks like a million guys at that time, emerging from a flower; that quote, Mom's motto, "We should behave to friends as we would wish them to behave to us" beneath a naked Roman statue positioned between huge crossed eyes.

I think I sort of swore that my last move with Mom would be my last move with Mom, but I guess it wasn't time. It's hard to justify moving out:

there are so many pragmatic reasons not to, that really the only reason to do it is to not live with Mom. Which seems irrational and kind of cruel. I'm down at the loft usually three nights a week, anyway. It's all end-of-school bustle these days, but taking my first hazy pee as Ty emerges from the shower, or as I walk dripping shivering across the wooden floors in a towel toward the bedroom, I know that in forty years I'll still be grateful for these mornings. Mike and I are compulsively listening to a Modest Mouse song called "Dramamine" – I shall make you a mix cd with it on; you'll love it. When I think back on twenty-three, I'll hear its guitar line and see myself mouthing "if I said what I meant would you know what I mean" as I pull on red corduroy pants in the pale sunshine, take my rings off Mike's dusty black desk as he runs down the stairs, greatcoat flapping open at his chest.

A pretty particle for our attics... x

MEMORIES OF THINGS I DID AND DIDN'T DO
04/09/2004

Hello Dear Joe.

I've just come back from North Carolina, where Mom and I celebrated Pesach with cousin Bonnie and her family. We flew down, then drove back in the Volvo that Bonnie and Thor have donated to us; it was Cari's car, and they just bought her a new SUV so she doesn't need it anymore. Mom is understandably conflicted about accepting this hand-me-down, however, not having to take the TTC and borrow Baba's Lincoln to grocery-shop (Baba decided she wanted her car back, despite not being able to drive) wins out over embarrassment at not being able to buy herself a new car.

The night of the first Seder, Bonnie and Mom came in together from shopping, all big brown shining eyes and wisps of frizz escaping from hair-clips, looking strangely similar despite how different their features are. People used to ask them, as children, if they were twins. Watching them bustle around the kitchen together, I thought how good it was to see Mom with someone who knows her so well.

As we ate our macaroons, the talk turned to family lore. I asked Rose, my Baba's older sister, if they had ever done Seders as children.

Oh no, she said. Mom and Dad didn't have any time for religion. Well you know, Dad was an atheist, and Mom – she laughed what seemed a slightly bitter laugh – she was just interested in keeping us fed and clothed, kicking out the stray dogs Dad was always bringing home. We didn't really do family things like that.

Baba told me about a birthday party for you, when she stood at the door and asked each kid that came if they had a present.

Rose laughed. That's right, she was like a bouncer, she wouldn't let them in without one.

She feels bad about it now. She remembers this one kid, a poor girl who'd come without anything. And she went home and washed some handkerchiefs and came back with them as a present. Baba always says, That was bad of me.

Well, Mom chimed in, Who was watching her? She didn't know any better, she was just a little kid.

Rose said, No one disciplined Mary anyway. She got away with everything. It was always Mary doesn't wash dishes, Mary has to practice the violin. Rose will wash the dishes, Rose will watch the store. But she was a good sister. If Mom was going to hit me for something, Mary would stand in front of me because she knew no one would hit her. She looked out for me.

But she'd eat all the icing off the cupcakes, I said, remembering another of Baba's rueful-humorous childhood stories.

That's true, laughed Rose. My cousin Cari smiled at me, her dark eyes like her grandmother's, comforting in their familiarity – a familiarity made strange by how little time we've spent together. To the table I said, Yeah, Baba still eats the icing off everything! Oh well, here's to the three Cohen sisters – *Rosa da Gita, Bubie de Schlechte, and Mary de Meshugena* (Rose the Good, Bubie the Wicked and Mary the Crazy).

The next night we had what is commonly known as a one-two-ten Seder. Thor was on call; Rose and Mickey were having their Seder with friends at their retirement community. After dinner we were listening to the radio, an oldies' station, and the host was taking requests. Mom decided to call, and after some time, got through.

It's a special night, she said into the phone. My daughter and I have come down from Toronto to see my cousin, who we don't get to see that often. And we'd really like to hear "So Glad We Made It."

The announcer said he didn't know what song that was.

Oh shoot, said Mom, Is that not what it's called? You know – and she started to sing.

Oh! The deep radio voice said, laughing. Great! You mean "Gimme Some Lovin'"!

And on it came. Mom, standing in the high, white hall, began to dance. Radiant with pleasure she shook her ample rump, put her hands over her head and danced. In a moment Bonnie got up and joined her. Shimmying, shaking and stomping in the elegant hall Mom and Bonnie sang *And I'm so glad we made it*, so glad we made it into each other's beaming faces.

I sat next to Cari at the napkin and crumb-strewn table, her face a mask of wonder. She leaned over to me and with absolute incredulity said, I've never seen Mom dance before.

She used to, though, back in her wild youth, before she was a respectable doctor's wife. But, as Mom said on our way home, Everything is some kind of trade-off.

Indeed. So let us befriend Compromise, the poorly-sighted beast: if we learn to approach it properly, it won't eat us.

xx

GOOD NEWS, EVERYONE!

04/17/2004

Dear Joe,

I hope this finds you well, or better than well, in fact – in a mood to rejoice! Ty got an interview for McMaster's medical school! The Human Rights court case is dragging on, meanwhile he's had to apply with the shitty grades from U of T still on his record. Only four hundred people out of five thousand applicants get an interview. Seventy-five of those get in. Cross your fingers.

Also, Eshe has hooked up with Dave, the musical wunderkind who kindly played on my (never-distributed) cd. Eshe came to a Samba gig we played (a party Mike's brother had organized, at a bar on College), and Dave was there. A few days earlier Eshe had said to me, in a half-ironical, sing-song girly voice, I like Dave Arcus. She's always had a thing for musicians; when we were younger and used to dream of the different varieties of men we might fall in love with, she always came back to musicians. They left together to go off to another party, and that's that. Now they're a couple, and so well-matched. I'd never noticed it before, but they have the same proportions, and similarly-shaped heads. Also the same laid-back sweetness. I bet you they get married someday, and have couple-face. Meanwhile it's making Eshe's return to the city more cheerful. (In the winter she was doing an internship at *Eye Magazine*, but she hated it and most of the wired, cynical social-climbers who inhabited its offices.) Indeed, I think she is about to learn what it is to be in love.

So my friend be well, and write soon. Tell me about all the beautiful crazy men you're bringing home.

Much love, Sam.

TARRYING WITH THE NEGATIVE
05/06/2004

Hello Dearest Joe,

congratulations on finishing your first year of school. One more to go! Do you think you'll get your Master's as well, or stop with the Social Work degree? I'm glad your professor liked your presentation on the Roddy Doyle book, it sounds very interesting.

I never quite got back into the swing of things after the move. I did the assignments but wasn't particularly pleased with any of the results, although I still did well on the portfolios, thankfully. This semester Michael got almost everything in on time. He's been haranguing with himself about his scholastic diffidence since he was a child: his parents have a home video of him at eight, on New Year's Eve, lisping that his resolution was to Be more organithed. Now, after five years of university – during which he has probably absorbed quintuple the amount of information anyone else has – it has occurred to him to care about grades, and so he has, indeed, gotten organized.

It was helpful that Michael's Arabic tutor was let out on bail in time to help Michael study for his final exam. You remember, when we spoke in February, I told you how Mustafa had just been arrested for disturbing the peace? So, he was let out for that, but then arrested again a few weeks later for writing some hateful shit about America and Israel on a subway platform, and struggling when people tried to stop him. He's been in the Don Jail ever since. Got the shit kicked out of him, of course. Michael, Mustafa's roommate, and a professor friend were finally able to get him bail at the beginning of April.

The craziest thing, Mike told me last week, Is that if he had just not been cut off welfare, this would very likely not have happened. I mean yeah, obviously the guy has an anger problem, but I think that under normal circumstances he might have been able to manage it. Even angry as he was to be on welfare in the first place, I don't think it would have come to outright violent behavior if he hadn't been cut off for missing one appointment with his social worker. Even after he showed her a doctor's note. That shouldn't happen – I mean, he's an educated guy, a guy who wants to be working, but he gets treated like someone trying to cheat the system. So he goes and does shit that he knows is ridiculous; and now he has to live with that. I feel for the guy, man, I really do. I don't in any way condone what he did, and I hope that he gains some insight into why he behaved that way – he's definitely reflecting on it. I like to go up there and see him; I feel… like I can maybe do some good, like he listens to me. I don't mean to sound arrogant, I mean it's weird, he's older than me, he's done a lot of stuff; but when we talk about the different things that have contributed to his life being how it is, it's like, his anger gets less personal.

I had no doubt of it, watching Michael Bobbie's earnest and slightly irascible face, loving the umbrage and goodwill in his voice.

Right after classes ended I went to BC and met Mom at the end of her convention. It was a weird trip. All the way to Tofino, the natural beauty I was staring at through the window might have been television. Listening to Mom's tales of DreamWorks' relentless stupidity, I stared at the incredible forest, and all I could say was Wowie Zowie. Wowie Zowie.

Truly it was stunningly beautiful – we just don't have trees that size in Ontario. We stopped at Cathedral Grove, a famous bit of forest, and briefly walked around grokking the magnificence with a couple other tourists. I thought of Joni Mitchell singing "We cut down the trees, put 'em in a tree museum," dismayed that surrounded by this vibrant, astonishing display of life, that was what I was thinking. On the one hand, it seemed a good and healthy thing that we come to natural wonders looking to appreciate them; on the other hand, it felt forced, this coming to a place to worship its trees. The same way we'd drive up to a monument or any point of man-made interest, we drove up to Cathedral Grove, got out of the car, looked at the trees, said Wowie Zowie, then got back in the car and drove away.

We drove to the Wicaninnish Inn, all stone and huge windows, natural fibres, bronze Haida-looking art and ocean views. Mom was in raptures immediately: the service was impeccable, the food magnificent; her only complaint was that she couldn't stay for three weeks rather than three days.

I thought of Wicaninnish, the great chief whose biography is politely displayed in the lobby, and wondered what sad changes he witnessed before he died.

Hoping to seem peacefully contemplative, rather than null and miserable, I walked along the beach each day as Mom rested. Watching the gulls our first day, I remembered how my grandmother had taught me to draw them when I was a child. I loved how she did it – it seemed so childlike, one stroke of a pencil, like a long, extended M – and such a novel thing for Baba's old, gem-enrobed fingers to be doing. But I'd always thought it an abstract, easy out for really drawing the bird's form, until I saw a whole great gull vanish into a sliver of grey, a pencil-mark in the sky, etched and erased. It occurred to me that disappearing gulls with their desolate cry have probably made Baba sad.

Thinking of Baba, Mary Simmons in her finery singing arias to packed concert halls as her daughter put herself to bed, I thought of Mom singing Donovan to me as a child – "and the gulls are wheeling spinning on Jersey

Thursday." How simply I loved that song when I was little; how simple and peaceful to have it sung to me as I drifted to sleep, or lay warming on a beach towel in Florida. Nothing can be simple like that anymore: not the song, not the gulls, not my mother's love or her singing to me.

And not this vacation where I should be enjoying her generosity and pleasure, rather than judging it all mercilessly. I could not help seeing our activities transposed over my life at home, and it made them seem equally ludicrous. Yet I wanted to be back at the loft, riding the shared high of ideas, the indisputable importance of discussing them. When being raised as I was can be made to make some sense – the Lobster dinners at Park Plaza for my third and fourth birthdays; a Mom who lived there while she finished high school, blocks from the squalid shared house from whence her father plucked her after she ran away – it's all logical at moments. With Michael on Eastern Ave. or Kensington, talking house prices with Eshe on Euclid, at least then I am framing my situation as I choose, with people who think similarly. I can put my history into a context, imagine a life that integrates the best aspects of what my family has offered me, and discards the unnecessary or immoral parts.

But gazing out at the muted Pacific, all my beliefs seemed mere reactionary juvenile nonsense – worse, vengeful spite against my mother's desires. Once again, a sense of my meanness and ingratitude competed with rage that Mom is only happy when swaddled in privileges she can't afford. Perhaps if she were simply rich, it would be less complicated; her expenditures would be frivolous, yes, but at least they wouldn't signify to me her terrible disappointment – this tragic proof of how little we know ourselves when we're young. How can we, when the patterns that will show us our pathologies are so new?

Back in Toronto, the time to choose things is beginning – Bri graduating, Michael going into his last year. How to make something tangible from the things we think we believe? Bri is thinking teacher's college. Jake, having become disgusted with his days spent doing hits of Ty's pot-crumbs from the gravity-bong he rigged up, has moved to Guelph to do communications for another NGO. Jamie, now gunning for grades good enough to get into a Master's degree, is doing an honour's thesis. He's writing about Marx and Hegel, talking about tarrying with the negative.

Which is, I'm thinking, what we all must learn to do.

Write soon. Much love,

Sam.

CONFESSIONS OR, WHAT DIFFERENCE DOES IT MAKE?

06/14/2004

Oh Dear Joe, what a weird night it's been.

I've just come back from serving wine at Priscila's PHD party, which was held at Barry Callaghan's house, because he seems to have sort of adopted Priscila – she told me she still sometimes house-sits when he's away, even though she's like a proper grown-up now, with a house of her own. You remember Mr. Callaghan, he wrote that short story Priscila read us early last year which I liked so well. Also he runs Exile press, which publishes Priscila's poetry, and the *Exile Literary Quarterly*, which has been going for decades. Irving published in it. And I went to hear Callaghan read up at York one night. I thought he was cool. This large, sonorous-voiced man in his sixties, reading with his old friend blowing saxophone behind him. Anyway the party was at his house, or rather, mansion in Rosedale.

So there I arrived, at about five in the afternoon, in a long green dress that was Mom's in the sixties, with a wide neck and drooping sleeves. It was a warm sunny day; Rosedale was humming with kids and landscapers. The opening door yielded two large, wriggling dog bodies; I was glad to have animals to fawn over, to absorb my initial shyness as I took in the artsy woman who had opened the door. Claire, Barry's partner, had interesting jewelry and hair the colour of champagne; she greeted me pleasantly, then ushered me through the high-ceilinged hallway with its ornate wooden fireplace and compelling art, into the massive kitchen. There was Barry, looming over the granite counter in a rumpled white collared shirt, his jowls bespeaking centuries of carousing Irishmen. We stood there a moment in silence.

This is Samantha Bernstein, said Claire.

Hi. He ran a glance down my form.

Do you know who she is? This is Irving Layton's daughter.

Then he looked at me.

Oh hello! he rumbled. Nice to have you here. And he shook my hand, before returning to the piece of paper he was scrutinizing.

The whole place was exactly what you'd imagine a Rosedale mansion to be before a dinner party – fridges stuffed with food, platters and cake boxes on the counter; the hosts still in their day-clothes about to go upstairs and change; an air of accustomed bustle, finery handled and worn casually, rented dinner-ware from vendors with whom they have accounts. The place made sense to me. I could imagine Mr. Callaghan settling himself in a rich-toned study of an afternoon, snifter of Scotch in hand, head back against an arm-chair as he takes in some Charlie Parker, while Claire upstairs paints in her studio. Family dinners beneath the dining room chandelier discussing politics or the next issue of *Exile*.

Before going upstairs to change, Barry took me down a set of wooden stairs to the carpeted basement, where the walls were lined with headshots. There was Gwendolyn MacEwan and Yehuda Amichai, Patrick Lane, Joyce Carol Oates, Queen Mags with those dramatic eyelids; and there was my father. That was what Barry had brought me down to see. The eight-by-ten black-and-white of Irving staring out from the white wall beside the pool table.

This is the gallery of most of the authors that have appeared in *Exile*. I published your father many times, Barry informed me in his rich baritone. He was a fine poet. A fine poet.

He drew my attention to a few more photographs, informed me of the involvement of this or that author in *Exile's* almost thirty-year history. I looked at the white wall with its rows of faces shining beneath the pot-lights, considered the various authorly poses wondering how people decided to tilt their head in such a way or rest it in a hand, what image they were trying to project with their varying expressions. It seemed most of them were going for either serious or mysterious. Irving looked pugnacious and happy beneath his white mane, as I was accustomed to seeing him in photographs. It was his happiness that set him apart, and the sense of vitality that emanated from within that shiny black frame, like even then he might bust out and say, Hello people, in that weird old-school voice I've heard on recordings of him.

How is he these days? Do you see him?

He's in the advanced stages of Alzheimer's so…. Ah, he's well looked after. I saw him last summer.

I had a terrible flash of the emptiness of Irving's days, the sterile world that sustains his decaying body. No Scotch for him; no conversation. Pale Montreal dribbling through the slats of off-white blinds. Orderlies and nurses wiping his ass. Diana reading poetry to him, his and others'. The terrified moans of old women. An occasional young seeker showing up at the door, satchel of Layton books on his back, come to see the man himself before he dies. Who of your old friends comes to sit with you, I wondered; and would you even want them to? And I thought it wasn't many, probably, of all the people he'd entertained, enraged and encouraged, whose presence would be any comfort, and not just a tragic embarrassment.

It seemed to me that Barry's question carried more of a sense of obligation than interest; or perhaps he was just struggling with the muted terror that people must experience when the generation preceding them starts dying off. In any case, it was not the time for me to discuss that strange, sad visit last July, nor the others before it. I kept my answer brief. Yet I wanted to trust this large, solid man. Perhaps later, I thought, he could tell me some stories. Perhaps it's strange for him, too, to have me in his house.

Boxes of wine had to be brought in from the yard. I was set to this task, grateful there was something for me to do. Shortly thereafter Matechuk and another classmate showed up. We finished moving wine and arranging glasses on the table set up at one end of the kitchen, then installed ourselves behind it as people began to arrive. The next few hours were perfectly pleasant. Guests came by; we asked them red or white, and poured. We opened bottles, put empty ones in boxes. Priscilla, who I'm starting to realize loves dressing up, was resplendent in fuchsia silk, her amazing dark hair curling down her shoulders. I was glad to be there, helping her celebrate; she's had, I am learning, a pretty rough time of it – family difficulties – which makes her remarkable accomplishments even more so. The guests were mostly friendly – I suppose drunken people at a swank party are usually affable; why not?

Then I went out to the garden for a smoke. Barry was holding court among a circle of middle-aged men. He put his arm around me and told me he'd loved my father.

I loved your father, he said. So I have to love you. I didn't know your mother well but I recall that she was a very beautiful lady.

I could only smile, feeling young and conspicuously female. I would have liked then for him to tell me a story about Irving; I wanted to know something the two of them did together, a conversation they had. But it didn't seem the time or place. I was a happenstance interlude in a conversation; my smoke was half-done.

Becoming expansive Barry said, You got the best of your mother, and the best of your father!

The men smiled and nodded.

All I could think to do was smile and say, Thank you, like a polite young lady. Thinking, you won't win your way in with wit, you mute wonder.

Minutes later it occurred to me that I should have said, We don't know if I got the best of my father yet; that remains to be seen.

After that the strangeness of my situation became increasingly apparent to me. For the first time in my life, I swear the very first time, I wished to god my father was there with me. Father, Daddy, Dad, Papa, Irving you paternal entity, I thought, I wish you were still walking, even if feebly. You could have walked arm and arm with me through this house and talked to me about the people here. Finding Dad for my breaks and accompanying him outside where he would smoke his pipe, I my cigarette, and people would come over and chat with us. I could have just sat and listened.

Instead, each time I went out for a smoke I found myself at the mercy of whatever middle-aged man I happened to be standing near, tongue-tied as stranger after stranger told me what I should read, talking casually about their first books. I was drowning in a sea of authors whose names I didn't know, as though being punished for my ignorance of contemporary literature. With each of them I could only try and be charming, grateful not to be standing there smoking alone, thankful for the attentions of these authors though constantly horrified that my unfamiliarity with them or their works would become apparent. I was also revolted. Revolted at the assumption that I gave a fuck what they thought I should read, that I was in need of their advice. Do you know who my father is? Who the fuck are you? But then I was disgusted with myself for that, and veered back to thankfulness that I was at this party talking to these people. Authors who spend their days, presumably, writing or being otherwise involved with literature. Culture. And for a moment it would be nice. I'd think I *will* read that book, or thank heavens I seem to be making a good impression on this man; or, this is how one gets her start in this world.

But then they'd be talking and talking at me, some more interesting than others. I wished it were possible to be drawn into a conversation I could participate in rather than simply partake of. To be asked an opinion, or be able to ask one of them. But it wasn't my place, and anyhow I couldn't have thought what to say, I doubt, if I'd been given the chance.

Throughout the whole thing I felt as I had at the tribute to Irving in Montreal, when Max read a poem about each child except me. I was more related to what was going on than the other guests, and more excluded from it.

As I was leaving I got into a conversation with a nice-looking though extremely drunk young man, a friend of Priscila's. There was some small picture with Irving in it on the wall by the door, and this fellow started talking about what a great guy Irving was. Someone informed him that I was his kid, and the drunk young man went on and on in the hallway about how Irving had been so kind to him, had always been encouraging, how they'd gone for a walk and eaten ice cream in Montreal. I was happy at how happy Irving made the guy. He had obviously been really touched by my father, and was delighted to have an opportunity to recount their time together. But I was saddened too; this drunken stranger had more memories of my father than I did. He remembered Irving walking around, holding forth on ideas; he had been buoyed by Irving's belief in him.

Nonetheless, as he flung himself out the huge doors and flailed down the stairs spouting Italian love poetry, his collar open, I was glad to have met him. The scene was too timeless not to be appreciated, the weaving fellow's beautifully pronounced Italian being the crowning touch. And he loved my Dad; he was happy that I existed because he'd loved him. He didn't seem to want anything from me but that I should hear how Irving was a good man.

But when I got in the door at home I was just nothing.

At least I have been able to write to you, my distant friend – my cursor your blinking eye.

Under whose kind scrutiny I will confess to being both frightened and comforted that even tonight, as I come stumbling bewildered out of that acre of literary forest, my first impulse is to write to you. Grasping this amulet of creativity, though I can't yet know if it's a charm or a noose. Only I know that as I have been sitting at this computer, the vaporous entity I was an hour ago has become these solid lines and defined spaces.

So what shall I do with my paternity? I grew up thinking myself my mother's daughter, giving very little thought to Irving Layton; I should remember that, when talking to writers.

xo
Sam

RAGE WITHIN THE MACHINE
06/30/2004

Dearest Joe,

thanks for the email. Your description of Cardiff's gay pride made me laugh – "a celebration of diversity where everyone looks the same" – how marvelous. And the fact that the "celebration" in question was sequestered behind ancient castle walls, decently hidden from the rest of the city…. It's funny that you've been returning to French authors lately – I just polished off *Père Goriot* with relish, and am now on *L'Assommoire*.

Thanks for asking after Mom; I wish I could say she is well. The heat is aggravating her asthma, though thankfully she has gotten an air conditioning unit in her bedroom so now she can sleep. She may have lupus. She definitely has skin lupus, for which she's on drugs that can make you blind, and which means she has to be covered head to toe on sunny days.

She looks at herself ruefully in the mirror in her wide-brimmed sunhat and gauzy scarves, and on better days says, Don't I look like a respectable middle-aged lady? It's very nice, young things in the elevator treat me entirely differently now, you know? They smile, they hold doors. Once upon a time men used to hold doors – I mean, they still do, but it's because I'm an older lady and they're being polite. But the young women, it's very interesting. They used to look with that sort of haughty suspicion, they'd be sizing me up. But it's a whole other world when you get older. It's okay, I feel like I have them all fooled.

And she laughs at the joke that she's pulled on the world with her linen jackets and supportive shoes; her unconventionality now a secret she can chuckle at.

On worse days, she just looks at herself with mild loathing and says, Oh Samanth, Samanth, it's good to be young. Enjoy it. Take all the looks, the hollers, the attention, because it goes fast. And it's nice to be a young, beautiful woman.

The other day she came home with her bag full of expense sheets she didn't have time to sign off on at the office, her twenty-pound daytimer, bills to pay for Baba, leaned on the counter and pushed out a bitter laugh that turned into a sob.

I'm just so tired, she said. It's this constant pain…. Sometimes it's hard to know why I should go on…. I must really want to be here, she said, looking at me, her tragic eyes full of exhaustion and love.

What could I do but say, Things will get easier. Make her some tea; listen to her as she vents about her day. It always amazes me how she'll say I don't even have the energy to talk about it, then go on to recount it with full-scale re-enactment, working herself up to a fury depicting the innumerable stupidities and insults of her job. I wish I knew whether her profound reactions to the world, which never dull, give her strength or drain it from her.

I just want to sit at the dinner table with Mom and rail against Mammon, against the ideologies that have made her life what it is, but she is often too weary for highfalutin' ideas. I'll light into some money-guzzling CEO who just fired three hundred people, or whatever the latest idiocy may be, and sometimes instigate a good conversation. Other times I can tell by her distracted air that it all seems like big empty talk to her. She just wants to rant about her day, hear about mine, then watch some TV.

I don't blame her – my spiels are maybe a way to avoid entering her specific misery, as if by thrashing about in my own abstracted indignation I can prevent myself becoming mired in the heavy mud of her life. But she needs me to be involved, and I know I could do more. So at least I can listen, let her make theatre of her absurd days. It's less deadly that way.

As you do for me.

With much gratitude, Sam.

BIG DREAM BLUES

07/17/2004

Well Dear Joe, the weirdly menacing summer is starting to get its blows in now. Ty did not get into medical school. I don't even know what to say about it; everybody's stunned. Ty said he knew as soon as he saw the envelope in the rusted box at the end of the drive: it was too small, he said, to be an acceptance package. But he opened it standing there beneath the rustling poplar trees, and then ran inside, sick to his stomach.

It must have been his grades – he said the interview went well; or rather, the bizarre new interview process for which Ty and his cohort were guinea pigs. But very few people with his grades get in; his court case against U of T is dragging on interminably. Both in an effort to make him feel better, and because I really believe it, I told Ty that it will just make an even better story when he does become a doctor. And everybody sees Ty's life as a story – J.R. has written about him; this kid last year made a documentary about him and Samba for his film school class. So, I said, Everybody loves best the hero that triumphs over the greatest adversity.

He smiled bitterly. Great, he said. That's great. But meanwhile I've staked everything on this; I have debt – you don't understand. I've wagered everything on getting into medical school this year. Now I have to start again with the scholarship applications and racking up more debt to get what? A B.Sc? Whoop-de-fuckin' do. I'm gonna have to take the fucking MCATs. I can't take the fucking MCATs, it's all multiple choice.

Perhaps I'm just on a weird kick about this, but a part of me thinks this has happened to teach Ty humility. We were all so confident that he'd get in, that he wouldn't be subject to the same rules and setbacks as everybody else because he is who he is. We said, Hey, you were teaching your anatomy class a month after you began at Mac; you hang out with the head professors just because they like you; how can you not get into medical school? We thought that with those things, on top of his unusual life circumstances, how hard he's already had to work, and how passionate he is about medicine, life would reward him.

He and Michelle aren't getting along too well these days, either. They've been having numerous and noisy arguments, one of which involved her dumping all his shit into a pile in the middle of the living room, and Ty having a flashback freakout of his Dad doing the same but on the lawn of his house. Since the rejection she's been trying hard to be kind and patient, but Ty is inconsolable; when she talks to him about his next move, he doesn't say rational things, and they both get frustrated.

He doesn't study as hard as other people, she said to me. He thinks he can work, and teach, and do school, and run Samba, and it just doesn't work that way. Yeah, he has a learning disability, yeah it sucks that U of T is fucking him around. But other people devote their lives to getting into medical school, and he just doesn't. Do you know how much time Samba takes? There's always an email that needs sending or a call that needs to be made about a gig or whatever. So maybe this will show him that he's not exempt from the shit and drudgery everyone else has to do.

There was a hard edge in that last sentence that made me think she's almost a little pleased at his rejection, though if she is I'm sure she feels bad about it. But sometimes I think that Michelle doesn't want to believe Ty is capable of pulling off this great heist on life that everyone else is expecting of him; she's compelled by the character of that Ty, but has been burned and wearied by the practicalities of it. His crazy hours and lack of time; the two alarm clocks required to get his narcoleptic ass (yes, medically) up at the crack of dawn; her nightly fight to get him off Mike's couch, where he'll have passed out watching Futurama or David Attenborough, and from which it takes many tries and repeated gentleness in the face of his whining, Leave me alone, you don't understand….

He says that everything he does he does for both of them. He says, I'm trying to build a life, and I want this woman to share my life. She doesn't want the life I'm trying to make. She hates Samba – or, she doesn't hate it, but she doesn't want to participate, you know, she's intimidated, and so then it's just something that takes time away from her. (We were in the car on a muggy day, and he was gripping his gearshift, voice veering between desolate and bitter.)

Well, we do evict her for three hours a lot of Sundays – a lot of winter afternoons she's over at the Tango Palace studying because we're banging drums in the loft. And you are insanely busy all the time.

I know. She makes a lot of concessions. But I'd like to think the reward is worth something. That the life we have, and the life I'm working toward, is something good and beautiful and worth some amount of sacrifice. I know it's hard! But that's life! You gotta do it with love in your heart. She hates that I'm happy when I'm doing shit, because she feels like I'm always trying to out-class her or something, like everything I do is because I need constant reinforcement of how great I am. But I'm like, whatever! I love you! We can talk about microbiology together. If I want to be berated I just have to pick up the phone when my Dad calls. I tell her Baby, we can do amazing things together but not if you're always trying to cut me down. Why can't she just love me, Sammy? Like you and Mikey. So calm.

Well you know, Itay (I cocked an eyebrow for emphasis), Mikey doesn't lie to me. And anyway, we have different, uh, issues I guess. It's funny you should say that, about him and I being calm, because we just had our first fight. It wasn't really much of a fight, but.

What happened?

Oh, it's these fucking computer games. Literally even for the ten minutes he has in the morning before he leaves for work, I hear the computer – in my sleep, as soon as he gets up, *ping*… and he's clacking away down there. The other night he was up till three playing Civilization, and he looked like fucking death dragging himself into the shower so I, stupidly, suggested that maybe he should cut down on the computer games. And he was like, What's the fucking big deal with the computer games? I do my life, I go to work and see people. He said I was sounding like my mother.

Ty inhaled through his teeth, looking pained.

Like because I'm really jealous of his time, I guess.

So what did you say?

I… I didn't know what to say! He sounded so defensive, and, like, angry, and the shock made me cry because I'm a huge fucking crybaby, and he started apologizing. From the shower. I mean, it was fine, of course. He said he didn't mean it, and he was just testy because he was tired, and it was true he'd been playing them a lot. What really got me was that it was defending this stupid fucking activity.

Well, Sammy, he's a boy, you know, he needs to stimulate that part of his brain, that strategizing and spatial calculation stuff, and there's nothing really wrong with it –

No, fine, not in moderation. But I worry about him, when he seems sort of out of it generally, and then he's wired into the digital crack every free moment of his life.

It's not every free moment. But it is a lot, it's true.

There are just so many more productive things one could be doing. Like, whatever happened to reading as entertainment? He wants action and excitement, there's plenty in literature.

But I shan't get into that now, nor did I with Ty. We had been on the way to Canadian Tire to get something for the Samba trailer (Ty half-bought, half-built a trailer), and had arrived. I tailed him as he strutted through the wide white doors, serene and efficient within the maelstrom of his life.

There is one good thing: some of my poems were accepted for publication in Exile. Priscila offered to show some of my stuff to Mr. Callaghan, and he took "Prelude" – the short story I wrote after the Pilot reading – as well as "Layton, Irving" and "Night Scenes on Jackes Ave." (about writing and thinking of Irving). I met Priscila outside the U of T athletic centre on Harbord and she gave me my poems back, the ones he wanted to take with a few edits on them. I made some comment about the high level of Irving content and she said it was "Prelude" he first wanted, then decided on the poems afterward. He doesn't really do political, apparently, which surprised me given his war reporting years. But what the hell; I'm getting published in a respectable journal. Matechuk and another kid from our class, Matt Shaw, also had some things accepted. It'll come out in the fall; I'll send you a copy.

For now, it's off to see my grandmother. Huzzah! On with the battle, my sweet friend.

ALL YOU NEED (REALLY) IS LOVE
08/30/2004

Dearest Joe,

it was lovely to find your email waiting for me upon my return from Timmins. I'm glad you've made friends to go dancing with. It's interesting about the paranoid anarchists: one wonders if they're unfriendly because afraid of the cops or because they're naturally unfriendly, but either way it seems strange that people committed to social change should be so forbidding to talk to. How do they expect to get anything done if they can only talk to fifteen people?

Our drive to the cottage was prolonged by the fact that at Matheson we misinterpreted Brian's directions, so Michael and I drove to Quebec. He was a little mortified at not having realized earlier that we were on the wrong road; he took it as a sign, I think, of his ambivalence toward adult responsibilities. I suppose with his parents driving, he never paid attention to where he was – though it's not all on him; I might have noticed that we weren't seeing signs for Timmins sometime before hitting the Quebec border. Anyway, we were finally rumbling down the logging road at about 11pm, driving through utter blackness until we saw the high beams of Brian's car aimed at us from the cottage turnoff. His folks laughed at us, and teased Michael about the time he was coming up on the bus and got off in South Porcupine.

The drive was entirely enjoyable except for my new terror of accidents. I don't know when it started, but now, in the middle of having a perfectly lovely time, listening to tunes, talking, I'm suddenly struck with how easily we could just die. A blown tire, a sleepy driver, any one of a million random circumstances and that could be it. Sometimes I almost panic, think I'll have to pull over. We can't do this, I want to say; We can't put ourselves in this situation, let's take a train. I don't want to be responsible. I can almost see the swift shattering of glass, limbs, faces. The sudden, irrefutable violence; seeing Michael's undone body; Mom being told I am dead. But I take a deep breath, concentrate on the road. Keep my eyes moving, take in everything.

And once settled at the lake, I never tired of the view from the screened-in porch, of waking in the morning, percolating coffee and drinking it admiring the blue-green water. I feel at home in the stark landscape, its bushes and hearty purple flowers swaying at the roadside, growing tall as me from its rocky soil. Walking to the gravel pit – which is as it sounds, a natural basin of rock and gravel carved out of the forest – I stared at the leaves and the bugs, the resolute petals of beautiful weeds. Humans survive, I thought, but our survival warps us. Or at least, it is hard to tell adaptation from damage.

I wanted very badly to not interfere with the place. I didn't even mind the bugs. One day sitting by the dock I had a deep desire never to kill another one, to let them feast off me; to have everything in this world live and exist as if I did not.

Mike and I had similar dreams a couple of nights – one of sex, one of water (I've had a few dreams where I'm separated from the water, like by glass. Mike says it's about creativity). Often he says what I am thinking. Also, he described a memory of being on a beach when he was young, and it was exactly how I would have described my memories of Florida; it was like having my four-year-old brain excavated for me. If even as children our brains were forming similarly, processing experiences similarly, that must count for something, right?

Though I promised myself I wouldn't, I marred many moments silently questioning our future. I constantly expected that he would mention it. In the paddleboat looking at the sunset or walking up the dusty road, I would be awaiting the proposal. Or at least a hint that it was on his mind. But when he spoke it would be an observation, or some moral or political question he'd been contemplating.

One evening in the paddleboat I did bring up the Dread Future: and suddenly we were discussing how we probably would get married. He said that, that we would probably get married – our conversation interrupted periodically by greetings and cooings to the playful dragonfly investigating our vessel – but he's terrified. He's terrified because marriage signifies one's commitment to the world and to one's self. To a particular life. I remember, he told me, The first time I felt this awful burden of choice. I was about four years old, and was playing with a neighbor on his front porch. His Mom had to go somewhere and offered to take me with them. And I remember having no idea what I wanted to do – I just wanted to keep playing, I didn't want to have to make a decision. So I said no, I didn't want to go, and I remember the feeling as I watched them walk down the steps – like I'd made the wrong choice –

So why didn't you say you'd changed your mind?

Because I didn't want to do that either – I didn't really want to go. I didn't want to go and I didn't not want to go. I just sat there feeling lonely and bad. I wasn't able to go back to what I was doing – that was the thing – the element of choice destroyed both things for me. If she'd just said, Come on, we're going here, that would probably have been fine. It was that I'd had to decide and couldn't.

But I make him happy, he said later as I chopped mushrooms and he garlic beneath the white propane kitchen light. Before bed he came to me and I put my hand in his hair; he let his head rest on my chest, hand strangely suspended on the water bottle he'd been reaching for on the counter behind me. The flickering white light within the blackness beyond made a stop-motion eternity of our momentary tableau, and I saw all the other doors shutting, the other possible storylines falling to the editing-room floor. How badly I wanted this love story, and not another.

Sometimes it almost makes me shy of him, how well he knows me. He must have known, even before I did, that all my life I had wanted to be kissed on a bit of filigree the pines and afternoon sun had made of a dirt road. But then he must have wanted that too, and I fulfilled whatever ideal of his made him do it, just as he fulfilled the ideal of mine that made me deliriously happy when he did.

xo sweet Joe (and best of luck with your first classes)
Sam.

ROW THAT OAR
                09/30/2004
Dear Joseph,

For some reason the beginning of school this year has been worse than usual, although I was looking forward to it. I'm sure it's partly because I did well last year and so am terrified I won't live up to my own former achievements. You'd think I'd learn that that's just how I am – I remember worrying I'd never again write anything as good as the short story that won the Prism Award, and Mom laughing, But you're eleven years old for heaven's sake.

Our first assignment in Fiction class was to write the first chapter of a novel. Hurrah, I thought, I'll actually begin this book that's been in my head for five years. Fat fucking chance. I paced the apartment, chain-smoked, walked the neighborhood, stared at the computer screen, depressed by the cliché I was enacting. Finally, the day before class, I called Susan, our professor. She's a wonderful six-foot-something blond writer in her fifties who glides into class in a cape and splays her disorganized folders all over the table. I guess there was something about her that made me feel comfortable to call her home, in the middle of the afternoon, to ask her what I should do about the fact that I couldn't seem to complete our assignment. I'd never done anything like that in my life, and was embarrassed about it, but she was extremely understanding. As soon as she heard me speak she said, in her warm, deep voice, as though it were the most natural thing in the world, You're having trouble with the assignment, are you?

At which point, to my deep mortification, I began to cry. I told her I have a novel I've been wanting to write for years, but I don't know where to start, and I'm terrified.

She said my assignment could be to write a Dialogue with Fear, which might help me figure out what's preventing me from writing. As it turned out I quite enjoyed myself, and did manage to articulate some of what's freaking me out. That said, in class the next day, when everyone was handing around copies of their novel openings, I felt like a dope.

Lately I keep finding myself wondering how it is that Irving never seems to have suffered a moment of doubt. I took one of his collections, *A Wild Peculiar Joy*, up to the cottage with me. The joy, as Mom always made sure I knew, being his forthcoming fatherhood of me. The edition I took up to Timmins has on the first page a little man Irving sketched in blue pen, with a flat head and square nose, a scrawl of hair and a crooked tie, and a word bubble emerging from his mouth, "For Samantha, love and all good things." Then it quotes his poem for me: "Grace keep you queenly and kind, a comfort to the ill and poor, your presence a bounty of joy to all. see p. 207." And he signs off, "Daddio…." It's dated March 12, 1991, which must have been the year he tried to call me. The year I took the phone from the wall in the kitchen, and in the familiar brownish light of our north-facing living room told Irving that he'd made a mistake when I was a baby, and he had to live with that mistake. I was thinking of how he kept writing articles about the divorce for the newspapers, because Mom had always told me that was why he lost his right to see me. I remember having no sense that there was a real person on the other end of the line. There was a sort of presence: someone not a stranger exactly but who didn't know me. He wanted something from me, something I felt was unfair to ask. A man, "my father," was on the phone, a man whose face I knew from books in the basement. He wrote about love. He was a troublemaker. My mother had to tell my teachers every year that if he showed up, he was not to take me from the classroom. His poems were forceful and tricky, nothing like the lovely Theodore Roethke I enjoyed while sitting on the can downstairs. The quiet enchanting "Elegy for Jane," the incomprehensible but wonderful "Papa's Waltz." This Irving with his raunchy, menacing poetry was on the phone, and Mom was hovering nearby, concerned. I felt bad for the old man wanting something I couldn't give him; and I surprised myself with my audacity, a child telling an adult he'd done wrong and would have to suffer the consequences.

And that was the last I had to do with him for six years.

Now here I am at twenty-three with his book in my lap, his words in my ears, finding that I love them. There is one about Palm Beach, which he must have written when staying at my grandparents' condo, that I just thought, Yes. That is exactly how I perceived it, when I was too young to know.

Then there are others that infuriate me – some of his politics, for instance, make me wish he were sentient so I could give him a piece of my mind. I suppose if I got in touch with my brother, as Priscila has encouraged me to, he could maybe tell me if Irving meant this shit or if he was just trying to be outrageous, get a rise out of people. I can see what young people like my Mom found so incendiary about his writing – not just the politics (which Mom probably hardly noticed), or even just the sex, but how boldly he claims the world as his.

Reading him, I know there is no way I can experience poetry as Irving did. I don't think, for instance, that I would ever write a love poem – I simply don't believe in extolling mouths or breasts, pleasures given or received. Mike and I discussed this at the cottage. I said there were poems I felt condemned to mock though I want to be moved by them.

He said, Irving didn't have so much advertising making him immune to everything. We're over-stimulated. Love is toothpaste is baby formula is boots. We're bombarded, incessantly, with images trying to make us *feel* something. It's no wonder we've toughened up and become these cynical, alienated creatures, trying to consume ceaselessly to fill the void meaning left when we killed it.

It's true, I laughed. But then, Irving was cynical in his way. About human nature. Or, if not cynical, I mean, he wasn't wearing rose-coloured glasses or anything. He knew the world is fucked up and humans are fucked up; lots of his poems are about that.

Yes, but he was part of the last generation who could believe in these, like, grand myths. He could believe in Greatness and Talent as absolutes, so of course poetry would have a different meaning for him. And he reaped both the good and the bad from that outlook – like, he wrote some great poems, he got his renown as a poet, but he was kind of an egomaniac, which took a serious toll on his personal life.

Indeed. I asked Mom about his ebulliently misanthropic outlook on life the other night. How did he manage not to direct any of that misanthropy at himself, I wanted to know. She laughed. We were getting dinner ready, throwing salmon into the oven, seeding tomatoes, the cats getting underfoot. Oh, he did have self-loathing, she said, About, say, his inability to make a relationship work. I mean you know, we were on and off for years – he was trying to save me from him. He was afraid he'd ruin my life. (She was silent a moment.) He was aware that he was obsessed with writing at the expense of all else – or, rather, he knew his flaws, but he saw them as unavoidable, as the burden that came with his creativity. But he was immensely grateful for that creativity also –

Sure, it meant he could barrel through life doing exactly what he wanted.

Well, he felt it was his calling, and it was the most important thing, that's right. He loved the Romantics, you know – he believed in that sort of destiny, to be a poet, to create great art. And that also gave him great joy. Better than Baba, who for all her immense talent could only be miserable every day for her entire life. Crippled, crippled by misery and fear. No, I can't sing at La Scala, I have to be near my husband – who ever heard of such a thing? All of how she was she excused because she was a genius – her terrible behavior at family dinners, her running through the neighborhood in her nightgown, her constant fears about her health. But Irving, whatever else he was, was immensely happy to be alive. Sure he would rail and rant against this or that tyrant, or a stupid thing the government did, or the small-mindedness of people, but never, *ever*, did that cause him to lose faith in himself, or in art. But he also felt he had to choose between art and love – go read "Letter to a Lost Love" if you want to know about that. I always believed it was a curse, his hamartia, that he was doomed to foul his own nest. But you, she said to me, Want to deny yourself happiness. I don't know why it is, but you're always throwing obstacles in your way with all this what good is art and I don't really have talent. It's like you don't think you deserve to be happy.

Which at first I thought was ridiculous. I'm not one of those pain-mongers, don't believe that pain is profound and happiness frivolous like some emo-kid or something. I'm pro-happiness and have always intended to live a happy life. But then I thought maybe she's right – if no one else in my family is happy, why should I be?

Of course that's ridiculous too. What can children give their parents, other than to show them we are happy? Otherwise this life they've given us is only a burden; the consciousness they've helped us develop only endless toil, a heavy oar to which we are chained. And why would we want them to think that?

After dinner Mom pulled down two old boxes full of Irving's letters and drafts of poems. He was a meticulous craftsman, she told me, He'd write version after version. It might be helpful for you to see how they changed.

I can't read his handwriting, I said.

I'll help you, she said. But she saw my reticence; You don't have to look at this stuff now, she said without disappointment. I just thought you might want to know I have them.

And maybe eventually I will look at them. Certainly he's been on my mind these days, Old Pa. I manned the Exile booth at the Eden Mills Literary Festival last weekend, and George Bowering was there, this old poet, and I knew he'd known Irving. I watched him read and liked him – there was something straightforward and humble about him – and I wanted badly to go say hello, thank him for the reading and tell him who I was, ask him a couple questions about Irving, about writing poetry in Canada forty years ago. Mom would have wanted me to do it. But of course I never got up the gumption. I was glad to be at the festival, though – another little step in the right direction. I bought a picture you'll like, a sketch in black, white, and red of a 1940s-looking typewriter, a chapter just begun on the page.

Write soon,
Love, Sam.

COME AS YOU ARE

10/16/2004

Dear Joe,

Well, I have had my first reading, and seen my name in print for the first time. Satisfying! There were a goodly number of people there to celebrate the issue's launch, and I thankfully wasn't too nervous up on stage. Mom was there of course, beaming, and Mike's parents, Bri, and Ty – it was funny to see him in that environment! In the eight years I've known him, I've never seen him in a bar. But there he was at the Dora Keogh, a cozy, wood-paneled place on the Danforth, full of artsy folk in colourful scarves and cute flat shoes drinking at the low wooden tables. Ty found it all weird and amusing: he surveyed the room with his narrow, Semitic head very straight on his thick brown neck, and clapped and hollered like a madman after I read, the sweetheart.

He's doing okay considering that Michelle has just moved out. They're not broken up, but she needed to get out of the loft, she said, to live a "separate life" – so now she's having a torturous affair with a Professor, going out with her girlfriends, living in a shared house in the Annex. Ty missed a deadline which had been moved, so it looks like he won't be able to apply to medical school this year. Which makes me fear that he has a secret desire to thwart himself – that the decade since his mom's death, during which his father has consistently told Ty he's a worthless worm, has become fertilizer for self-sabotaging instincts. When I try to talk to him about his psychology, suggest he inquire into his mental processes, he inevitably dismisses me with: I know, I'm fucked up 'cuz my Mama died and my Daddy beat me.

But you don't know in what ways you're fucked up.

And that's as far as that ever gets.

Meanwhile he's working on a research project with the head of faculty at Mac. They're studying something to do with eyeballs and brains. It could turn into a Master's project, which would help him get into medical school; all may yet work out well.

And you, mon chère? Tell me about your classes, about Cardiff, about the view from your apartment. x

CLINGING, CLANGING, AND THE CASE OF THE HEADLESS CLOWN
11/01/2004

Well my dear Joe, I now have a flesh-and-blood brother. Two nights ago I was at Priscila's Halloween party; standing in the kitchen with some dead bloody people and a rabbit, waiting for Mike to get a drink from the prodigiously be-liquored table, I felt somebody tap my shoulder and heard, This is your brother. I looked up into the weirdly familiar face of David, who said, Hello!

It might have been the circumstances – in the kitchen at a drunken dress-up party – but he didn't seem the fifteen or sixteen years older than me that he is. Dressed as himself, in a brown suit that I liked, he warmly and with some bewilderment suggested we go outside and chat. Which we did, for the rest of the night. We sat on Priscila's swinging bench on the porch as the party swirled on around us; I smoked compulsively and he pretty much kept up, teasing me about my rolling tobacco and offering me "real smokes" from his pack of DuMauriers. Looking at him it was like I'd always been looking at him, not like looking at a new face. More like filling in the details – the texture of his skin, his smile – of a picture I was already familiar with. Although really I've only ever seen his author photo, and the one picture of him at about fourteen that my mom showed me when I was a kid. At which time we decided there was a resemblance, especially around the eyes and mouth. His skin and hair are much darker than mine, but we do definitely look related – our bodies are proportioned similarly, and the shape of our faces; our eyes are both green though his are light, like young leaves.

But it wasn't just looks, either. There was something in, I don't know, the rhythm of our speech, how animated we both get when we talk. The funny thing was how we didn't talk about our dad at all, really. I'd always figured, you meet your long-lost brother, you fall right into family stories, childhood tales, that sort of thing. But we talked away as if our mothers hadn't loathed each other, as if he didn't have forty years of memories of the father I'll never know. He made a couple comments here or there about Irving, about being in Greece, or sort of jokily referring to my having been better off without him. I told David that when I was fifteen I'd written a letter to *Saturday*

Night Magazine to that effect, after reading an article he'd written about growing up with Irving and Leonard Cohen. My response was a mean little epistle about how it seemed that the only thing I'd missed out on, not growing up with Irving, was knowing Leonard Cohen (man, I was angrier than I realized back then). David wryly said I probably wasn't far wrong. But it wasn't at all the focus of our conversation. The whole thing was much less of an ordeal than I thought it might be; he chided me for never calling him when Priscila had given me his number.

    I was getting around to it, I said. We agreed it was good circumstances had intervened.

    He has a novel coming out in a few months, so he said he'd invite me to the launch. It's very strange, of course, but not as strange as you might think. After all, I always knew he and our other siblings were around (though our sister lives in California), now it's just much more real; I actually can envision myself as the baby in a family of four. I never really thought about it that way before, but it's rather pleasing, this having a near relative in the city, someone with more experience in life who might get a kick out of sharing some brotherly wisdom.

In other interesting news, I sort of accidentally proposed to Mike last week. We were talking about embracing adventure and he said, Hell, having kids will be a kind of adventure, and I said, horrifying myself, Enh, I think we should just get engaged.

    I had said it as a joke – a way to laugh at our apparent need to leap forward into the great unknown. Still, it sounded remarkably serious hanging there in my quiet kitchen.

    Michael recovered with admirable agility, and laughingly agreed that marriage would indeed be an adventure. My suggestion having been flung out there, a conversation about the future could not but ensue. Part of Mike's fear, it seems, has to do with my wanting to write. When I met you, he said, You were so prolifically creative, writing all those songs, performing. I was kind of intimidated by you, actually, but I thought it was really cool. And then we got together, and you stopped writing so many songs…. It's like with dancing. You used to go out and dance – when we were broken up you'd go out with Joe, or with Eshe. I feel like you don't go that much anymore because I don't do it and you feel inhibited, maybe, like you think I think dancing is silly or something. But it's not like I think people shouldn't dance. I just don't feel comfortable doing it. I don't feel things the way you do, sometimes, and I don't want to make you check that part of yourself. Not that you consciously do, but we're together so much, and it's great, but I don't want you to bury that kind of unbridled… I don't know.

I was both refuting and agreeing with what he was saying. Being a writer doesn't require living some kind of "unbridled" life. I was thinking of Jane Austen, how she wrote all her novels sitting in her parlour, and hid what she was doing when people came in. This wild child speech seemed to me a justification of Michael's uncertainty about our future. I know he likes my wide open eyes, and often finds his own detachment frustrating, although his analytic distance can make my marveling – at budding trees, providential songs on the radio – feel childish. I don't mind that, though. The frightening thing is how dependent I have become on my vision of Michael and I married: he's the card which, if removed, topples the house.

Slowly, feeling bold as all love but glad to be finally admitting Michael's symbolic significance, I said, It's just hard to know if I'm on the right track. I imagine getting married because it would mean I've been wanting the right stuff, and that would go for the writing, too. When I start to think I've been misinterpreting things… that's what makes it hard to write.

Well, he said, If all it takes is an engagement to make that go away, then we should seriously think about that. I mean, let's do it.

No fucking way, man. We're not getting engaged just because I have some picture in my head about how life is supposed to go, and you're a great guy and want to make me happy.

No, he said, I mean it's probably what's going to happen anyway, right? If making it official is gonna make things easier for you, then….

We don't know what's going to happen yet. (I was not going to be proposed to accidentally, an agreement made at a kitchen table with the clock ticking loudly behind us, Mom's sleep apnea machine whirring from beyond her bedroom door. I don't need sky-writing, but this was just not how it was going to go down. Sitting by the dresser/dining-room cabinet, the Venetian glass clown with its head by its feet peering from between the Pernod and Vermouth like po-mo art. Why Mom keeps that thing is a mystery to me. Its expression was malicious even before its decapitation, yet we drag it from apartment to apartment, though we lost the broken-off hands along the way. Anyway, I was not prepared to talk marriage at two in the morning beside the headless clown.) You're gonna go somewhere, I said, We don't know where or for how long; we can't be getting engaged now. I gotta sort my shit out, you sort out yours; we have time to worry about it later.

Yeah, he exhaled, and looked downcast a moment, pet the cat that was smooshing his head into Mike's leg. But then he looked up at me with a sweet face, straightened himself in the chair and opened his arms for me to come to him, to his hard, separate, asking body.

The last piece of news: I finally wrote a poem – Mike came to the synagogue with Mom and me for our annual two hours of devotion. Or rather, tradition. Weird that fifty years ago my great-grandfather was the cantor there; my grandmother, the atheist, cutting up in the choir, pulling little pranks to make her fellow singers laugh at inappropriate moments. And then I suppose Zaida was only there for tradition, so we're carrying on that tradition. And maybe it was having Mike there, but suddenly, leaving the synagogue, I understood how familiarity can be stronger than love – how Mom, for instance, could have moved back to Forest Hill though she'd always hated it; but she couldn't fully hate it because it was what she knew.

Write soon, and Happy November.
xo Sam

        As I was walking from the Beth Tzedec

        Outside the synagogue, the Forest Hill
        Yom Kippur traffic havoc on Bathurst,
        Amid men with frayed prayer-books and kippahs,

Slim pampered wives, their daughters in Prada
Whose preciousness frightens me, I realized
This walk to our car, after the shofar,
Is September ending, marks a season's
Change. I wanted for you, love, my tall goy,
To see where I grew up, so you could know
Wherefore I loathed it, and it me, and how
Apart from it I felt, and was. Instead
A sudden joy, as though we were children
Sharing important secrets, and simply
Your knowing made the knowledge beautiful.

FALTERING ALONG THE FAULT LINES BUT KEEPING OUR BALANCE
01/02/2005

Hello Dearest Joe, and Happy New Year.

2005, isn't it crazy. Halfway through the "oughts," as Michael calls this first decade of the millennium. I don't know why, but I'm a bit sorry to see 2004 go. I liked writing the number 4, a contained, pleasing shape. 5 is a little wilder, messier, thrusting out onto the page like it does.

Or perhaps I'm just tentative about the coming year. Mike and I got our New Year's Eve started by having a rather rancorous disagreement about the news coverage of the tsunami. I said it was becoming a maudlin spectacle; he said it was getting its due attention. I said people are all bawling their eyes out over this particular horror but there are plenty of other horrors they can't be bothered to think about let alone cry over. He said people should at least be made to feel something. I said well isn't it convenient they can feel something that has no political consequences for anyone, being that it's a disaster caused by a big wave. The coverage is exploitative, really, because we're watching it like an action movie – oh yes, let's all get our brain chemicals stirred up by taking in some disturbing images, some brown people that don't really exist for us struggling for their lives. What entertainment!

We really got surprisingly uppity with one another – I think I was enraged by this feeling that he's starting to need such spectacle himself in order to be affected by the world, and I can't understand how that could be necessary, or how someone so savvy could be manipulated by CNN. I didn't bring that up, but we did argue all the way to the warehouse party we played. (He didn't love that either, of course – I mean he loved playing but then fled as soon as we were done, overwhelmed by the people and noise.)

I'd expected another pleasant New Year's loft-party, but there was a suspended feeling to the night that put me on edge. Sometime after three, when all the Special Occasion cocaine was snorted and the throbbing philosophical orgies exhausted, joints still being smoked but to no purpose, a hollowness crept into my stomach that made me shudder. Those four loft walls, the same ones I've been looking at for years; the red ladder to the alcove above the mustard-yellow fridge, the beige 1980s cupboards, Ty's weird wire-and-paper birds hanging from the metal beams overhead: I scanned it all like something menacing. What great insights had we had, tonight or any night, to justify all our sitting around? The loft I had always loved was stiflingly boring; I wanted to strip and run naked around the room and into the street, instigate an orgy or a verse-hurling mob, anything to break the pattern of our sitting and talking and smoking. But I was horrifying myself. This life – the dinners and downloaded TV shows and studiousness and eclectic music – isn't this exactly what I have always desired? Why this sudden rebellion against everything I hold dear?

I don't want to lose the pleasure of climbing the ladder to bed, Mike powering down his computer – programmed to shut off with James Joyce reciting "Well you know and haven't I told ya, every telling is a taling and that's the he and the she of it." I'm grateful each time I walk up the lane to the grey steel doors, shadows from the chain-link fence cobwebbing the uneven concrete at my feet. Ridiculously alive and happy in the condom-strewn back lot between the old factory and the GO Train tracks, looking out at the flat, contaminated land between us and the water, the unobstructed sky beyond the warehouse (which view I was admiring at eight this morning, while taking a leak behind poor desecrated Zippy, as someone was in the bathroom eternally). I love the weeds entwining themselves with the rusted, unusable stairs to the second storey, and the motorcycle restoration company with that inscription, backwards in black, old-fashioned letters above their door: Don't Let The Bastards Wear You Down.

Every time I take that path behind the factory out to the empty lot bordering Cherry St. I feel the world is mine, or rather I am its: a logical product/happy accident in platform boots and blue duffel coat, or catching a summer dress on the dusty stalks of Queen Anne's Lace, gravel in my sandals, aesthetic desires completely satisfied.

Suddenly on New Year's it seemed like a trap, this loft and the life that revolved around it: a red herring that had caused me to misread the clues of my life, and consequently to furnish a false ending. I thought our story thus far indicated what we would accomplish. But why should we believe that the lives we all imagine were germinating in our beloved hothouse of ideas and camaraderie? Because back in the golden past bohemians lived in abandoned warehouses? Because the urban industrial decay we have surrounded ourselves with symbolizes our foolish society for us?

I became almost frantic thinking of all the people, right then, who were engaged in good work, real work, affecting the real, physical world. People who volunteer at the Food Bank or homeless shelters, who do thankless advocacy work in cramped strip-mall offices. We had on some trance shit, I suppose to be party-like; I couldn't decide whether in other circumstances I would have hated it more or less. At the moment it inflamed my sense that we were just a cell, and not even a particularly healthy or useful cell, in the organism of our generation, our country or world.

Undressing in Mike's bedroom, I looked out into the loft at the familiar view. Cinderblock walls and cracked wooden window frames, my friends sprawled throughout the space. This will soon be a memory, I thought. They won't let it stand forever, it'll be torn down, or anyway our lives will change and we won't be here anymore. Perhaps I am becoming eager to know what happens next.

In the morning we went out for beans, then dragged back to the loft through the grey, wet day and listened to Martin Luther King's "Why I oppose the war in Vietnam" speech. Sitting on the floor of Mike's darkened room, I took in Dr. King's beautiful voice intoning, They must see America as strange liberators. At first I was only despairing. That he had been killed; that I'd missed the time he was alive; that there are no more Dr. Kings now – not in North America anyway. He had seen the direction history was taking; he had done his best to change it, but it hadn't changed. The revolution of values he predicted had not come. Yet I was lulled by the speech's incantatory beauty, the thought of the rapt congregants. I ain't gonna study war no more.

Later Mike and I listened to another speech, in which Dr. King explains that Life is a continual story of shattered dreams; he cites India and its tragic partition, the disappointment that has been the League of Nations. But he reminds us to be grateful that we do have hearts. That they're complicated and at war with themselves is certain – Lord make me pure but not yet. Being a good man, being a good woman, does not mean you've arrived in Los Angeles. It just means you're on highway 80. I'm a sinner, says Dr. King, Like all God's children, but I want to be a good man. What's in your heart this morning?

Finally, the pall of last night's musings was lifted; the dread of our futility and irrelevance was calmed as the congregation became increasingly fervent. All kinds of confused, difficult people have still done some good in the world; we aren't the first ones tripped up by our own natures, who don't know what to do or how to act. But, in our uncertainty, trying at least to flesh out ideals we can stick with, create lives that won't betray us too much.

So that was New Year's. As for Christmas, Mom came to the Bobbies' for Christmas day for the first time. I wasn't sure she would relish the change to our usual routine of opening presents, eating a bacon-and-eggs breakfast and lying around all day. Nor was I sure Michael would appreciate the linking of families implied by having Mom there. But it worked out great: Michael is always particularly sweet with me around his family, Mom got a huge kick out of Mike's grandmother's surprisingly ribald sense of humour. And Sheila, being Rosicrucian, had plenty to say about spirits, energies and reincarnation; Mom sat with her much of the night, Sheila sitting daintily in the rocking chair, Mom leaning in and laughing confidentially about the weirdness of premonitory dreams. Everybody got tipsy on eggnog or Scotch, the birchwood fire crackled away, and the night ended with Mom, Janice and I standing in the kitchen flushed with heat and drink harmonizing Joy to the World (as in, Jeremiah was a bullfrog, da na, he was a good friend of mine....)

Sending much love (also from Mom, Mike, Eshe and Flo). Everything good for 2005, sweet Joe. xx

MOTES IN THE ATTIC
01/20/2005

Dear Joe.

This is the first email I'm writing you from my own room, having at last gotten an internet cable that stretches far enough.

The rest of the birthday, after I spoke to you, was okay. Mom got me a book by Howard Zinn: *Voices of a People's History of the United States*. I thought this would be interesting to bring to our continuing discussion of how individuals have the power to affect society, Mom said, pleased with herself, though hot and harassed in a tiny table near the bathroom of the Starbucks in the Chapters on Bloor, into which she had just thrust herself in search of said book. The cover is a black-and-white shot of a huge, interracial crowd around a corner of the Washington Monument. In the front their faces are visible and as they stretch back they become dots, symbols of unity and progress. My first instinct was to be overwhelmed – you know, Oh, god, here are all these people involved in a fight for change. Then again, I thought, maybe it'll teach me something. That's really cool, Mama, I said. How did you know about Howard Zinn?

I saw him on Jon Stewart.

How's Mike, Baba asked. She likes asking about Mike, because she likes Mike and also because she likes to follow up her general inquiry with, When's he going to marry you?

Couldn't tell you, Baba.

Why doesn't he shit or get off the pot already! He's maybe waiting for a better deal to come along.

I don't think it's like that.

You don't think, you don't think but you don't know. I married Jack after –

Mother, do you want to let it alone? Kids these days sometimes live together for years before they get married. People are in school longer; it's a whole other world.

Live together. Phooey! I don't know what all this business is with living together. You move in, you move out. I say, you see the man you want, nab 'im. Like I always told you, Grab 'im, squeeze 'im and kiss 'im. Of course, you may have to put up with who knows what but you just do. So what if beautiful women were coming up to your grandfather all the time. I knew they were and why not? He was a king of a man, tall, handsome, generous, everything had to be the finest. Sure, women were throwing themselves at him wherever he went. But what did I care, at night he came home to *me* (and she drew herself up, pointed a finger at her own regal form).

Oh, sure, sneered Mom, What did you care. Phah! That's a good one. That's why you nearly killed him when that woman showed up at the door.

Yeah I was bad.

Bad! I thought you were going to murder him.

I'm sorry, what happened?

This woman rang the bell one day and your grandmother answered it and some woman was standing on the steps, saying she just wanted to see.

To see?

To see who it was Jack was married to. What kind of woman I was that she couldn't get him away from me. She was standing on our steps in a fur stole, a stunning woman, lovely figure, hair done, and that's what she said. I just wanted to see.

That's crazy, I said. So what did you do.

I said, Well now you've seen so get lost.

And then went berserk on Father when he came home, although he insisted he'd had nothing to do with her, Mom added.

Well, who knows whether he did or whether he didn't. But you see? Your grandfather was some prize. And I'm sure he dipped his wick on occasion –

She laughed at my astonished face, then drew her arched brows together and lowered her chin into a 1940s pose of roguish feminine testimony. Oh sure! You didn't know he was being wooed and maybe screwed by every varlet, harlot and starlet in Hollywood! But you don't leave a man for that. All these women who run divorce their husbands over something like that, I say forget it. He comes home to you, that's good enough. And of course your grandfather treated me like a queen.

He sure fucking did, said Mom. Not that it stopped you from making his life miserable. Your whole life was a fairy tale and all you ever were was miserable.

I know. I wish I could have been different. Listen, you think it's easy being me? I'm nuts.

For a birthday party, I did what I've been thinking to do for awhile – a kind of "salon," down at the loft. It was just a party for a good couple of hours; I was loathe to interrupt people and say, you know, Gather children, it's poetry time. I was too happy padding through the place in my hand-me-down beige wool skirt and bare feet, coming into a conversation here or there, looking at everyone arrayed around the room. They made a lovely tableau standing around the teak table spread with food, white candle stuck in a beer bottle in the centre; someone igniting a match on the stove's pilot light. Above them in the alcove people held wine glasses, sent smoke scuttling along the black ceiling, tipped their heads back and laughed. The whole scene could not have been more prettily haphazard, or a better paean to Youths on the Cusp of Adulthood. Aesthetically speaking the only thing missing, my dear Joseph, was you.

For one moment, though, coming into the crowded room, I felt strangely out of place. Not out of place exactly but divided; my brain flitted home to Mom and our apartment – she'd been at the party earlier but had gone by then – I wondered what I was doing here among these happy folk. I knew many in the room were my dear friends but in that moment felt quite invisible, as though the whole scene would exist just as completely without me.

This was no salon; just a university party for which we had decorated the walls with poetry. What was I trying to conjure with this ritual, and what right had I to try it? I felt people were expecting some kind of event, though, so Ty helped me set up the amp and a mic, and I gathered the company. They seated themselves with more anticipation than I expected; the performance seemed a logical interlude in the night, somehow. After me, Matechuk stepped up, and another classmate; then Jamie read a short bit of Hegel, something about "walking backwards into the future." Flo performed a Shakespeare sonnet – this one we loved when reading to each other recently that ends, "You had a father, let your sons say so." Mike gave a short rant on Hummers, to various Yeahs and Fuck Yeahs from the audience.

So in the end I was elated again. In the grim fluorescent stairwell light I saw people off, waving them down the driveway, wisps of snow blowing onto the concrete floor; I could hear their voices long after they disappeared around the corner. As I mounted the creaking wooden stairs, I thought how for every such gathering recorded in books, thousands of equally marvelous ones must have taken place, about which we know nothing. And that fact itself was marvelous, the ceaseless and ever-changing iterations of a particular ideal.

These days the talk is that I'm moving into the loft in the summer. Ty is of course delighted, and Mike seems… to find the plan acceptable. I can envision it and also not. Sometimes I think how much easier it would be to have no ambition but to live with Mom, look after her, maybe scrawl some poems in my free time. Like a Victorian girl who was too poor or too ugly to marry, or whose suitor was killed at sea. Alas, the past two hundred years' progress has made such choices seem unnatural. No one sacrifices themselves for their parents anymore. The only kids who live with their parents into adulthood are those mocked as basement-dwelling stoners.

Alright Sweet Joe, to bed with me. I'm glad your holidays were good, and your Dad feeling well; you are a good son to help look after him like you do. It's crazy they can replace hips and knees, eh? I'm sure I'll need new ones someday. Hooray for your Dad's good health – I can just see the two of you working on your car, all ruddy and happy. And I'm glad old Ray's got his new shocks.

So, onward into the year! Much love, Samantha.

FEAR AND FORMLESSNESS

02/09/2005

Dear Joe,

I've just returned from the launch of an anthology of young Canadian poets. Depressing how intimidating it was. In Fiction class last week Susan was talking to me about my novel outline, our most recent assignment. There's wonderful material here, she said, But there's no story arc yet. I haven't got a clear sense of what will drive the story forward, or where the denouement will be. One idea – I don't know how you'll feel about this, but can the Mom become seriously ill and die?

I must have looked at her with some horror because she said, with an understanding smile, No. Maybe not. Well that's okay, it doesn't have to be that, but there will have to be a point where everything comes together. And where's the Dad? That could be a pivotal thing, especially if you have him be political like Sam but she doesn't like him. I don't know; give it some thought. I think this could be really great, though, Sam, so keep at it.

At the time I felt encouraged. She thinks it could be great! I won't kill anyone off, no; I refute the notion that for "something to happen" someone has to kick the bucket. Something else will put the brackets around the story, give it a shape. Perhaps it will be Love, like in an Austen novel: Love and Society. And I'll have to think of what to do about Irving....

But now I'm back to thinking it's futile. Instead of the reading, I should have gone with Ty to the meeting the Kensington people had about how to proceed with the car-free Sundays.

x

OF WHAT IN ME IS SLEEPLESS

02/18/2005

Hello Joe,

I hope this finds you well. I miss you badly tonight. Remember when we lay in bed talking about the bar we would open called Jack's Porpoise – laughing at our imperfect sense of purpose, our poor poise on its precipice?

I returned last night from Montreal, where Mike and I went for four days of Reading Week. We took the overnight bus, which was actually not bad, and got our first slice of Montreal at about seven a.m. walking up the silent, sunny, frozen rue looking for breakfast. We were booked into the same B&B on Pins, and though we got there early the lady who runs it let us in; we got to chatting as she showed us our room, and Mike and I told her the significance of the place for us. Which, combined with the fact that February is not the most popular month to visit Montreal, led her to give us the gracious front room for the same price she was going to give us a cozy closet at the back of the house.

We went to see Irving again, back to his cell in the massive concrete hive of Maimonides, a geometric structure rising from a mound of wheelchair ramps. An institution designed to handle a high volume of activity, and horrible because the activity thrumming from it is death. When we arrived he was sleeping so we had to wait, during which I once again went through the whole Why did we come can't we just go routine. And once again Mike convinced me to stay. I had my shameful, unstoppable cry in the bathroom and then read *Childe Harolde's Pilgrimage*, waiting for the end of Dad's naptime. Eventually the appointed hour arrived, so we ascended to his darkened room, and looked around at the paraphernalia of his former life as he was toileted and made presentable. There are books and portraits, pictures stuck to a particle board; there's even one of me, when I visited him in his house eight years ago.

His caregiver Diana gave me a book that was Mom's but which Irving had on his shelf: *On Creativity and the Unconscious*, by Freud. It has Mom's slanting, perfectly regular signature in purple pen on the inside, and Diana thought I should have it. On flipping through it I saw many things underlined, which I assumed was Mom's work, but on closer scrutiny I found marginalia in Irving's almost-illegible hand. A strangely fitting gift. I wondered if I'd ever read it.

Diana wheeled him to a day-room on the first floor. A few feet from us by the window a family was eating cafeteria food, drinking juice boxes and hollering pleasantly at a woman in a pale yellow cardigan who seemed to wince into the blast of her family's well-meaning attention. By the door, a woman with dark wiry hair energetically held forth on tests and therapies to a woman with wiry white hair. Diana told us a bit about how Irving's been doing, people who'd been to visit and so on, and tried to engage him in the conversation some, but he never answered. Trying to speak, I didn't know which of the two strangers it was more appropriate to address – the one who might have loved me, or the one who understood what I was saying.

We left as it began to get dark. How badly I wanted to smash something, or shoot heroin, or do anything with the taste of annihilation to it. Or at least to have a car, to get into a sealed-off world of my own and drive away toward the city, instead of standing there trapped in the brown slush with my dying father behind me.

I couldn't have felt less like going to Mike's cousin's, which was where we were going, but it ended up being pretty fun. Though my brain was doing strange things, it was just as well to be in a warm kitchen, talking about our lives as young people are supposed to do. Joanne is Brian's first cousin, one of the passel he grew up with in Kitchener – which was apparently full of socialists and communists. They were all over Ontario, Joanne was telling us; her family used to attend communist dances and youth events, picnics – she left at twenty-one for the Ukraine, where she lived for several years. It was a perspective on 1950s Canada I'd never encountered, which is kind of fascinating: how much can disappear, even from memory, in a generation. Baba's father, my namesake Sam, was a socialist (though they lived in the States), but none of his children can tell me anything about his political activities except that he was always getting fired because of them. Baba once mentioned that he'd been a union leader, but when I pressed her for more information all she could say was, I don't know. Who knew from anything? I was all day in the closet practicing my violin.

Back in the Plateau, Mike and I meandered toward Pins through the sharp, twinkling night; we admired the bricks of old houses, buildings Irving and Zaida walked past as boys. Michael put his arm around me, and I watched our feet stamping their impressions into the virgin dusting of snow, wondering if someone looking at our prints later would see the even step between us. As we went back to walking independently, I thought of the many – the hundreds – of bodies that had produced these two bodies; ancestors and ancestors whose lives resulted in us, our unforeseeably matching strides. The imperious wind shushed my brain a moment; I was carried forward through the dark air, old as any animal. Michael put out his hand to catch the snow, and his peaceful face reminded me that there is nothing new under the sky – except us.

xo, Sam.

HOWL, OR ROBERT JOHNSON BLUES
03/10/2005

My dearest dearest Joe,

you know what fucks me up? "Howl" fucks me up. The first time I read it, I cried over its beauty, over the intensity of this era I missed. I just re-read it now, and cried because no work of literature will ever unify people like that again. Imagine what it was like in that room in San Francisco, this wild gay Jew making gorgeousness of a generation's gore. His hearers "digging" that this poem, this moment of the poem's arrival holds the possibility of changing art, and perhaps society, forever.

We have no certainty like that of our ancestors.

Today my half-brother was informing me about New Spain. As often happens, our conversation has left me feeling young and stupid – run down, as Ginsberg said, by the drunken taxicabs of Absolute Reality. David reads so much, provides example after example to prove that everything I think about the world is simply ridiculous. Predictable bourgeois lefty bullshit I'll grow out of in ten years; less.

We went to see *Capote*, which begat a good discussion about writing and ethics. From the theatre we went to some swish bar in Yorkville where David is clearly a regular. Walking over we were arguing about *Hotel Rwanda*, which we had debated seeing but the timing didn't work. He thinks it's grand they've made a movie of it; I think it's perfectly indicative of our twisted culture that we'd do sweet fuck-all about the genocide, and then appease our consciences by watching a movie about it. Oh the heroism, the good one man can do. Let us applaud him.

David said, Well would you rather it was just not an issue? You might appreciate this film as a kind of progress, because historically people haven't really given a fuck about the death of people in some far-off country. And maybe, Samantha, maybe if enough people go see *Hotel* fucking *Rwanda*, next time there's a genocide about to happen, people will step up and call for intervention if that's what you want. Not that it's necessarily a good idea – you might remember, for instance, what happened when the States tried to intervene in Somalia, which was a different situation but you see what I mean. Or the intervention in Bosnia which the Administration was given so much flack for. But at least you can't say they were idle.

Are the options really bomb the shit out of a country or let it destroy itself?

Well that's a whole other issue. We're talking about Rwanda and if what you want is for people to give a shit, Samantha, then here you are, people give a shit.

It's not a sign of people giving a shit. It's a sign that people feel bad about not giving a shit. And not just about things in far-off countries we can't really affect, but about stuff in our own society. People are stepping over homeless people to line up for *Hotel Rwanda* so they can bury that twinge of guilt they had stepping over a person.

I was happy walking through the narrow Yorkville streets having this rancorous conversation with my brother. He was waving his arms and smiling belligerently as he made his points, always seeming a little like he was taking the piss out of me but always eloquent, delightedly ignoring the stares of the neighborhood's patrons. Settled on the bar's heated patio he bought the drinks and told me about Cortes and those two brothers whose name starts with a P. Who conquered the whole of Central and South America by sheer will, brawn, fearlessness and ruthlessness. You see Samantha, he said, That's what human beings have always done, that's how this world we now enjoy was built. You have to respect what's been accomplished, even if you despise the means. Humans are violent animals. So you want a world with no more genocide well, sweetheart, I hope you get it but I wouldn't hold my breath if I were you.

My mind is a petrified havoc of images. I think I opened Ginsberg to read someone who cares desperately – thought he might remind me of the potential good in looking hard, even with reverence, at awfulness.

But what do I see?

Empathy – the word keeps surfacing in my brain like a water wing. This clumsily bobbing hope that there is a moral purpose to these visions of people suffering which crowd my brain during political conversations. That to feel sadness and anger for the fates of others – to refuse consolatory resolutions – is part of believing we can lessen our travesties. I hold these hopes even as I know my mind is reproducing images created to inform me about the world, and my place in it. As one who watches, who is informed; who is learning what my brother knows, that This Is How The World Works.

I feel there is something wrong with David's explanations, something defensive and predictable in his proclamations about humanity – but my feeling itself seems defensive and predictable.

Michael says if I can believe in anything, I must believe in love; the drawing toward. And I want to, unequivocally, but then love, too, can seem a lousy trick, a crossroads deal: You shall know beauty and make it live, tend it chained to a bone jutting from your plot on this mass grave.

We can trick the devil, though; win out on the bargain. Chained to ugliness, we sometimes carve the bone beautifully – make it a flute. Stare at our compulsions and hypocrisies until they can be wrought into instruments that conjure our better selves.

xo, Sweet Joe

PART III:

In which we remember visions are a first step to decisions.

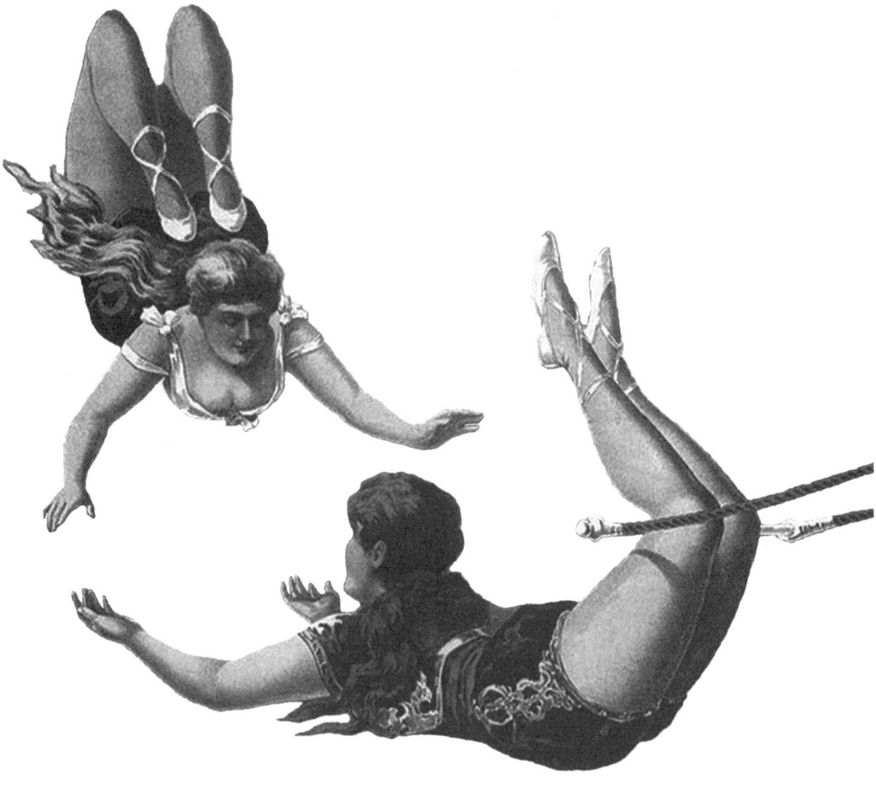

MIXING MEMORY AND DESIRE

04/02/2005

We're on top of the world right now. Too bad we can't appreciate it.

So said Flo, as we surveyed the ice breaking on Lake of Bays yesterday in the sunshine. It had been one of those diamond-clear days and we were messy-haired, wrapped in wool blankets, listening to the ice cracking all around us, a sound like embers dying in a fire. I had never heard that before, innumerable drips and snaps magnified across kilometres of frozen lake.

Flo's pronouncement made me laugh: her twinkling cheery pessimism. Or self-flagellating optimism.

I don't know, I said; I think we appreciate it sometimes.

And we returned to reading aloud our Gwendolyn MacEwen: "To follow you one does not need geography. / At least not totally, but more of that / Instrumental knowledge the bones have…"

With Flo's words I christened the new writing book you gave me; it was a delightful thing to have with me there – its rich colours, the embroidered paisley and flower a perfect complement to Mrs. Shaw's Victorian cottage. And to a lovely weekend generally, one of those brief moments where everything seemed important and good. Finding the Neil Young cd at just the right moment or bursting into song as we set the table, like characters in *The Big Chill* but without their thirty-something nostalgia. With our twenty-something nostalgia, I guess. Mike seemed reasonably happy given his impending freedom from school. He was wide-eyed quiet in the earth and pine-smelling woods, listening attentively to the birds' chirps and caws, face upturned to the streaming branches, a little smile on his lips. He ran around like a kid, dodging tree branches and leaping over rocks, and I watched him like a mom, proud of his supple body and his enjoyment of it. Outrunning "It" – the encroaching part of himself obsessed with the need to Do Something – for a little while longer.

Last night we sat in a circle, smoking on the porch, and I made a ghost story out of a grisly part of Hardy's *Jude the Obscure*. Jude's eleven-year old son, Father Time, hangs himself and his baby siblings after his step-mother informs him of the meaningless suffering that is life. (Father Time: Then if children make so much trouble, why do people have 'em? Sue: O – because it is a law of nature. F.T.: But we don't ask to be born? S: No indeed.) Lit by the one candle that glowed on the white wood floor I recounted the tale, getting a good collective shudder from Father Time's suicide note: *Done because we are too menny.*

Aaahhh, trilled Florence, giggling; That's horrible. And we pondered briefly the horribleness of it before shuffling back inside, wool blankets trailing, to the warm nucleus of the living room.

As Michael stoked the fire and Bri strummed the guitar I thought poor old Hardy never could have imagined this. Not much more than a century after he lived and here we are, three university-educated girls and a dreamy-headed but scholarly boy, sensibly terrified of how we'll make our ways in the world but at least not as likely to be crushed by life as poor Jude or his cousin-love Sue. Sure the poor are still piss poor but Hardy never conceived how big the middle class would get (in industrialized nations, at least), how very close to self-determined our lives would look. Well, "self-determined" is kind of a stretch, and who knows what will become of us when there's no more oil, or when Canada quadruples its population with refugees from ecological crises, but for now it sure is sweet. To be privileged enough to know those privileged enough to own property like this, and so indulge myself periodically in some youthful fun in the woods. I could feel my brain thawing with the lake's ice, a bleary melancholy that's been between me and the world for the past month melting away. Coaxed out into the world again, the natural progression of life asserting itself.

So I taught myself "Martha My Dear" on the upright piano, baked chocolate chip cookies with Flo, heard stories from Bri's trek around Lake Titicaca as we made chickpea stew and Mike spun around in his socks laughing at "Titicaca." Almost terrified to find myself happy again, knowing it will seem absurd later, but knowing it's more absurd to be willfully miserable – who wants to be that kind of monkey? It's all a merry-go-round with me anyway, so I might as well cheer when my pony is up. Hoorah! What a beautiful view.

This morning we walked to the mailboxes for the paper, and then Bri taught us the sun salutation on the government dock. The poses felt good, and it was warm enough to be in short sleeves though the wind made all our skin pink. Afterwards we carved our collective family name, BERSHABOB (a long-standing silliness) into the dock's old wood. Mike accompanying our etching with tuneless falsetto cheese, *Friends forever, carving their names in the dock, friends at the cottage, in their early-to-mid twenties, carving their names for posterity....* A Hallmark Productions song for our Hallmark moment. Mike humming and chuckling even as he put some finishing touches on the 2005 beneath our name.

And, thank god, I finished my final story for Fiction. I spent most of the last afternoon at the cottage following a patch of sun on the floor of the screened-in porch, wrapped in my Moroccan blanket and tapping away on my laptop. Happy in the brief certainty that I was doing what I ought to be. Michael came in as the light was fading and squatted down behind me, his arms around my chest; Is it going well? he murmured, kissing my head. I leaned into him, said, Couldn't be better.

As ever, your Samantha.

COME TOGETHER

04/24/2005

Dear Joe,

What a strange time it's been! First, Mike – super-cautious, ever-vigilant Mike – left his backpack on the subway. That wouldn't be any catastrophe but that every last note for his final essay was in the backpack, and the essay was due in three days. It's particularly ironic, because he's been trying so hard to be diligent. He'd done most of his research, just had to go home and write, and then the subway incident. Oh, was he pissed off. And when Mike's pissed off he's inconsolable, body a barbed wire STAY OUT fence. He got his bag back late the next day, but the damage was done. Of course the essay turned out good, though a day late – Human Rights and Marcuse – but I think he's still angry about the backpack, further evidence of his ambiguous relationship with aspiring to anything.

Moving on. Last weekend, after a party at a classmate's, I went down to the loft to spend the night. I was already in bed and Mike was opening the window before he came up, when I heard a thud and a Shit! When I got no reply to my Are you okay, I scrambled down the ladder and saw Mike standing with a huge gash on his foot. He'd been propping the window open with this glass thing, and it had slipped. He sat down on the couch and I went to get some gauze, but when I came back he said he thought he was going into shock and maybe I should wake Ty up. So I did, and he said Mike was indeed going into shock so got him lying down and bundled in blankets and whatever else you're supposed to do, and then bandaged his foot for the trip to the hospital. (Luckily, I had borrowed Baba's car that night.)

Meanwhile I wasn't feeling so hot. My stomach was roiling, and I was thinking what a sorry scaredy-cat I was. What'll I do when I have kids and they get hurt if this is what happens at the sight of blood? As Ty was helping Mike to the door I ran to the bathroom with a wicked upset stomach. But I thought it was just the horror of seeing Mike so pale and hurt, so I got myself together and drove him up to Sunnybrook. Whereupon I ran to the bathroom and was violently ill, almost relieved to discover I had food poisoning and was not just pathetically thin-skinned. (I had been late to the curry competition….) The next few hours passed in a haze of vomit, a North Toronto boy regaling us with the tale of his wound sustained in a clubland brawl, and more vomit. Eventually Mike was seen and his foot sewn up with five stitches. At about five a.m. we drove back to the loft; I woke up feeling like a family of gophers on meth had made their home in my stomach lining, and drove home.

Then yesterday I was at work, a lovely spring day all dripping and sunny. I had taken my bike in for some minor repairs, and on my lunch break went to pick it up. There I was coasting down Clinton in the gentle April breeze; there I was digging the budding trees and happy pedestrians; there I was on College heading for a sandwich from Riviera; and then there I was dodging a van pulling unlooking from its parking spot, getting my tire caught in the uneven road where the new streetcar track is going in, and flying over my handlebars.

I stood up, shaken, but thinking I was fine, scraped-up elbow but nothing serious, grateful I hadn't flown into traffic or hit my un-helmeted head on the curb. A couple of concerned passersby asked if I was alright and I said Yeah, took myself to the corner and leaned against the wall, where I realized I had a huge tear in my pants and also some kind of wound. I walked back to the store, thankful I was wearing an oversized hand-me-down shirt that covered my flapping pants, and went into the washroom, where I looked at my bloody thigh. I came out and found Mike waiting for me, so I took him back into the bathroom and showed him my gash. He took one look and said, Well, there's sub-coetaneous fat coming out; I think we're going to the hospital.

Where Michael held my hand as I got my five stitches; the doctor said I was lucky, had missed muscle by millimeters. I lay there thinking this is what it would be like if Mike and I were really responsible for each other. How it would be to navigate the world together. I know it's kind of revolting, but this week of injuries and illnesses has bonded us. Or felt like a successful dress-rehearsal, if that's any better.

Other than these incidents the month has been fine. I was reasonably pleased with my portfolios for Fiction and Poetry, though it's always a little disheartening to see how little I've really produced over the eight months of school. When will there be enough poetry for a collection, *vey iz mir*. I was extremely happy with my final poem, however, so I shall attach it for you.

It's funny, doing creative writing in school. I don't ever talk about it with Baba, for instance. She just knows I'm in university and getting good grades; she has no idea what I do there. I think she sort of knows I "want to write," but it doesn't get discussed. And yet I feel she is coming to understand me. She doesn't call me "tough" anymore, I realized recently; that used to be one of her big complaints about me. Like after Mom's anaphylaxis when I was seventeen, Baba would go on and on about how horrible it was and I would just assent, not saying much. You're so tough, she said more than once; You're hard. What's the matter with you, you don't care? (Because in that situation and others like it I refused to cry, or lament; because simply doing what needed to be done was all I was capable of, and it seemed like listening to other people freak out was part of my job.)

But now this practicality seems to please her. And gradually perhaps I'm starting to prove that I do help my mother – not enough, but at least I help. I went to Harbord Bakery for the Pesach macaroons and cakes, which I enjoyed, and which allowed Mom to say, in an attempt at jocularity at the Seder table, I think it's wonderful Samantha should go to Harbord, it's carrying on a family tradition. I know you've never given much of a shit about that, Mother, but I think it's worth something anyway.

No, Baba said, It's worth something, it's worth something. That's where your father would take the family's dinner. Where all the Jews would go with their dinner, for the Sabbath.

That's right! said Mom, willfully ignoring the slightly disapproving tone which Baba couldn't help – she was thinking about the absurdity of this Jewish observance, the trouble and public life implied in hauling cooked food through city streets. Well, whaddya know, Mother! That's right – people would bring food they'd prepared on Friday, and Harbord would leave the ovens on so that when Shabbat ended you'd have a lovely cooked meal. Father would be hauling Annie's brisket through the streets, right Mother?

That's when he was being a good boy. Not when he was throwing rocks into his uncle's basket of eggs…. And she made a cheeky face at Michael. For whose presence everyone was grateful, and who later enlivened the conversation by postulating that the plagues in the Pesach tale are an allegory for Jewish terrorism against the Egyptians.

Our final fiction class was held at Susan Swan's charming Annex cottage to make up for a class we'd had to miss earlier in the semester. It was a sweet way to conclude my time in the program –a fire in the hearth and all us kids crammed into the funky, comfortable living room to critique the last stories, the last we would do together, which seemed far more promising than a year or two earlier; there really was that supportive atmosphere Nashira talked about in our first fiction class, and it had produced some good work. Then at about nine o'clock we streamed through Susan's white picket gate, past the budding but still-bare tangle of stems in her garden and into the quiet street, our bodies and their shadows taking over the pavement beneath the clear and deepening sky. It was a lovely little image, meaningless in the grand scheme I suppose but positively pregnant with possibility at the instant; Matechuk was beside me so I linked my arm with his, and we strolled evenly together. This feels good, he said quietly, and I nodded.

How can we aim toward anything if none of these moments that seem so meaningful are what they seem? Those quiet moments where I ask a question of myself and the answer is Yes, a fast, unconditional Yes. The conditions come later, of course, but in those moments I do believe, don't I really? I think I do.

And, the last and best bit: my plane ticket to Heathrow for June 1st. Mom is very kindly giving me some of her points from all her business travel (as she said, I've racked up enough of them, and God knows when I'll get to use them so go have a good time. Even with your ticket I still have enough to get to Europe again, as if I'll ever have the money to do it).

Guilt, glee. I'll see you in a month, sweet Joe, and you can show me the life you've come to know.

xxo

Sam.

In Memoriam: A Letter

My bible tells me that Good Friday comes before Easter.
And I have not lost faith, I'm not in despair. I haven't lost faith
because I know that the arc of the universe is long,
but it bends toward justice.
— Dr. Martin Luther King

Dr. King, you were disappointed with America.
You saw the horrors of its wars, knew the
causes. You called them out. Like a good father
whose smart child does a stupid thing, you
expected more, asked for it by loving. Of course
a country is not a son, countries have other,
simpler ways to dispatch obstacles. More complete.
Guilt is so light dispersed amongst many.
You would say, I suppose, I shouldn't be bitter:
My bible tells me that Good Friday comes before Easter.

Dr. King, you saw freedom rise, people willing
to die for it. Sundays your church must have
overflowed with those who believed your proclamation:
*Out of the wounds of a frail new world, new systems
of justice and equality are being born.*
But they were stillborn, Dr. King. Your wraith
and theirs haunt the nation, illuminate
these dark hours of history, when Beauty has all been bought,
Love sold, and God has died, intestate.
And I have not lost faith, I'm not in despair. I haven't lost faith

yet daily I lose faith, lose heart. To mark the first
day of this year, my friends gathered, and aimless,
tired, sunk in a guilty ennui, we let your sermon rouse us.
Reverend Dr. King, religion is to me as some half-sibling gone wicked,
in whose bad deeds are manifested all my secret flaws,
and faith the siren's voice that lead his weak mind wrong.
Yet when you preach, half a century collapses, I am calling
amen with your congregation. From you I will learn how to struggle
gracefully, learn to whistle a nightingale's song
because I know that the arc of the universe is long

and my lifetime short. That is a comfort. Dr. King,
I am alright with unfinished business
and *walking the streets with a burdened heart*
some days. You were right. To try is enough,
to love, in spite of reasons not to love.
If I must believe something then I will believe this:
humanity is a great tree that reaches out into a dark sky,
memories of millennia stored in its trunk; it grows
heedlessly, without purpose,
but it bends toward justice.

BEEN UP SO LONG IT LOOKS LIKE DOWN TO ME
05/01/2005

Dear Joe,

thanks for the email; reading about real people, who need real things, which you can really help to provide them with, was comforting. I spent seven hours on the phone with David yesterday. Talking to him feels like jousting with a noodle. Somehow everything I know and feel to be true ends up sounding like undergraduate claptrap ideology, like one of those horrible conversations you hear at university pubs – a mash-up of Chomsky, Marx and *Adbusters* magazine. It's so embarrassing to be the source of it, but I can't help myself; I don't want to end the argument and I won't agree with him.

David on the Vietnam war: Necessary. Absolutely necessary and if you don't understand that you really don't understand global politics.

I had said something about Irving being on crack regarding Vietnam, that for all his love of justice and hatred of oppression he backed that war and that seems insane to me.

Without breaking a sweat my good older brother set me straight, or rather, threw a half-hour summary of countless history books at me. His coup de grace: And now America has fully normalized relations with South Vietnam, with the same regime they were trying to overthrow and *couldn't*. So what kind of a monster is America? If they're so awful, if they're so self-serving and this terrible destructive imperial power, then why the fuck are they trading with Vietnam?

I of course have absolutely no answer for that. Free-market capitalism something. But I should have known better than to start in on that subject without Mike around.

Capitalism is apparently the deliverance of mankind. Look at Russia, he said to me, And you goddamn lefties (he's laughing), you *goddamn* lefties were making the same excuses you're making for Cuba today for Russia in the fifties. In the *fifties*, for godsake, when if you had the remotest desire to know what was going on in the Soviet Union it was obvious –

I'm not defending fucking Stalin, I splurted, Or that demented Chairman Mao but that's not necessarily communism any more than what we have today is a free market. (Again that undergraduate pub-speak, the elephant of my passion sitting on the April ice of my understanding). That was just state-run capitalism (thank you Mikey for that reasonable-sounding phrase). Inevitably when there's a revolution, the factions that really want to let the people run the country, that are really trying to change something are killed off. Like in the Spanish Civil War and Stalin-sponsored Communists were crushing local Anarchist and Syndicalist movements so the same bigwig bastards could keep running the country, and that's what always happens. If anyone had listened to Emma Goldman when she came back from Russia in the twenties, it might have been different.

Okay, but no one did. No one listened to Emma fucking Goldman and no one wanted to believe it when they started hearing about the camps and the purges. And it's the exact same thing with Cuba. The exact. Same. Thing. You're here with your Well but they have really great health care and who gives a shit, Samantha? They're an authoritarian society, they have no freedom of speech, their economy is shit but everyone only wants to talk about the doctors.

I made some last lame attempts at questioning the appropriateness of the sanctions, the cruelty and power-lust of the "bad example" theory, trying to dig out the fragments of a Bay of Pigs documentary that made the States look responsible.

Look, honey, there's always a superpower, and there's always bloodshed and that's just how it goes, that's history. Yes it's ugly and it's horrible and you think it should all be different and I get that, I do. Listen, I used to be just like you, I used to – I grew up in the seventies for chrissakes, and I used to sound just like you. People were freaking out then just like you are now, there were no jobs, the economy was, you can't even understand; you think it's bad now, in the seventies it was just like no one was working. I mean you're at Starbucks and it's terrible and all that but when I was your age there was no Starbucks, there was no *nothing*. Nada, okay? So everyone myself included was freaking out and we were thinking the world was going to end just like you, protesting nuclear proliferation and environmental abuses and all the rest of it. And the world hasn't ended. And it isn't going to end. People just like to talk about it ending, they like to complain, especially when you're young and that's okay. You're supposed to be questioning everything and feeling horrified at everything, that's what you do when you're young. But when you get to be my age you'll start to see all this hysteria –

Your age? Stop talking like you're an old man –

No, I know, but really, you'll see, just give it a few years. All this shit about America, like they're the evil empire. What you really have to understand, what you'll come to appreciate is that America is the best superpower we can possibly hope for, they're certainly the best the world has ever seen. (I wondered if those were the same things, but he went on....) And all this modern imperial bullshit, Samantha lemme tell you they've done more for developing nations than has ever been done in history. Colonialism, I mean come on, you have to have a really willful misunderstanding of colonial history to think that way. And all anyone wants to do is whine about South America and lousy health care in the States. It's madness.

Every fact I had ever known was dissolved in the acid vat of David's argument, which ended with: Samantha, all you have to do is look at the Dominican Republic. Shares a border with the nightmare that is Haiti but they opened their borders, and now have full trade with the United States, a booming tourist industry and they're basically a first-world country. No one wants to talk about that Samantha, no one wants to talk about how, if you cooperate with the States you're gonna grow, your economy's gonna improve, your people are gonna have jobs. Everyone just wants to shit on the States and really, Samantha, what's going on is, you don't want countries to develop, you don't want all the picturesque peasants to move into shiny new apartment buildings and that's the problem. The problem with capitalism isn't that it doesn't work but that it works *too well*. It's like this woman I met in Barbados, she'd been to the Dominican Republic and she hated it. Too modernized, too touristy. She wanted the *primitive* experience, sweetheart, she didn't want to see big new buildings and good roads and golf courses, she could get that at home. Samantha lemme tell you I spent a lot of time in Greece. Growing up, right, with Dad and all that, and I remember when the Greeks were living in hovels, okay, I mean you can't even imagine how poor they were. They were impoverished, truly, people living with no electricity, no plumbing, no proper health care, it was appalling. They were really, really poor and they'd been totally destroyed by World War Two. But it was beautiful. I mean, Athens was a stinking shithole but the countryside was stunning, these little fishing villages and olive groves, it really was like the Greece of antiquity in a lot of places. And it was so cheap, Samantha in 1970, Dad and Leonard could rent these little houses on Lesbos for twenty-five dollars a month, it was unreal. You go back now and it's, there's nothing left of that. In thirty years it's completely changed, it's a modern country. That way of life is done, it's gone. And I mean it's kind of a shame, Samantha, it is, because you'll never see that Greece, you go there now and they all have new homes and it's cleaned up and the villages are full of tourists and it's not as *interesting*. It's certainly not that cheap. But that's the tradeoff. Spain is the same thing. Right across the Mediterranean – thirty years ago these were impoverished nations, you can't even imagine. I think you have to be honest with yourself and admit that you don't care about development, you're not really mad about brutality and this and that, I mean you are, because you're a nice person and that sort of thing is very ugly, you know, but I mean I think you have to be honest and realize that what you're really lamenting is that development, changes that really improve people's lives, makes a country bland. You don't want to admit that it's *in your best interests* for these places to stay poor, because then you can go there and it's a whole other way of life, it's exotic, and it costs nothing. But that's what capitalism does, that's the genius of it and that's the terrible thing about it and I agree with you (with me?), it's very beguiling to have these places, not where you'd want to live or I'd want to live, but for other people to struggle along under whatever horrible system, because it's different, there's something different going on in those places. But I think it's hypocritical, Samantha, to say you want people to have a better standard of living and then deride, constantly deride the country and the system that makes it possible. The problem with capitalism is it gives you too much goddamn choice and people don't know what to do with it, *that's* the fucking problem. You literally have the rope to hang yourself with, capitalism makes everything possible (except, I thought, a living wage for my mother) and the *tragedy*, Samantha, is that you have *too much* goddamn freedom and you need something to be angry at. I know what it's like. Oh yeah, the punk scene, all angry at the Man; I had a mohawk for chrissakes. But you'll see, you're a bright person and eventually you'll realize that all this *sturm* and *drang* is just a youthful pastime. You'll wake up one day and you'll see, Mexico is getting rich, other nations are following in the footsteps of Malaysia, South Korea, the Dominican Republic, and you'll see all this anger is just unnecessary.

After I hung up I lay on the couch in a stupor, mind full of the clever comebacks I couldn't find earlier. Because sure, David is right, it is all a question of what we happen to call beauty. It is not true, however, that in ten years I will find it beautiful to look back at my young self, and mock her political ideals as a conventional absurdity. Perhaps some of the aesthetics, but not what they meant.

Write soon. x

CEREMONIAL PRACTICES OF THE MODERN YOUTH

    05/18/2005

Dearest Joe,

Congratulations on getting all your work in! You are now trained to Do Something Out In The World. Do you feel it?

It was Flo's birthday on the 4th (a Taurus like Mom, another similarity between them), and I was house-sitting for Priscila and her partner Chris. I closed the store, then called Flo as I was heading back to Priscila's; Flo had just met Paul (the guy she went to SARSstock with) in a park (in keeping with the apparent compulsion in everyone we know to return to the scenes of our childhoods), so they headed over to meet me. We smoked a doobie on the porch and he told us about growing up in the St. Clair West neighborhood we were then in; I asked him about high school and he said Oakwood but also Central Tech, briefly Northern – I think there was another one, too.

Oh I hated school, he said, grinning. I mean, I liked the social part, but the classes? No way, man, put me out on the lawn, the fuckin', south doors at Northern, right? Some of the teachers were cool, but oh, fuck. I just, I hated it. I was good at some stuff, but. That's why I'm going into the trades. Big money, no university, oh yeah!

He made me think of the fellow you've been working with – like if he'd just had access to another kind of school, he would have had a lot more options.

A few days later Flo and I met up with Paul at the Cannabis March. We missed the march, but sat in the May sunshine beneath damp trees in Queen's Park, surrounded by a predictable yet wonderful rabble of kids in tattered black T-shirts and combat boots, kids with dreads playing hacky-sack, hip young things in low-rider jeans toting their baby-faced boyfriends through the crowds; girls in pot-leaf bikini tops and pot-embossed toques; a girl with wire-and-cloth pot leafs sprouting from her back like wings. A band set up in one corner of the park, cops walked benignly through now and again. The paths were a curving bazaar thick with food, hemp clothes, locally made clothes, pot advocacy literature, pipes and paraphernalia, fruit smoothies. Two guys were camped out in deck chairs smoking a hookah and getting their picture taken. Later Ty and a few people from Samba came by with instruments and we played as the day was ending. The cops were nice about it despite our having no permit, so we got to play a few songs, our most ardent admirers being a circle of tripped-out kids, barefoot and flailing. They whirled around in front of the drums, while straighter folk –

students and passersby, young parents, suburban pot enthusiasts, and my suddenly appeared Mom – bopped their heads. And I have to say that banging my drum in the spring twilight, joints being passed all around me, the stately stone Parliament building visible through the batik-hung trees, something stirred in my breast dangerously akin to patriotism.

I'm glad I came, Mom said later; It was interesting to see how this generation is doing it. I was surprised, actually, that it was all you young things, that there weren't more people of my generation – I mean, what, no one smokes anymore? And then with your peers... I don't know, it was a nice vibe, nothing bad, but it's the same thing I used to notice at Northern, all the colours are dark, it's no more the pretty dresses and flowers on people's cheeks. There's not that... gentleness – there's less laughter, that's one thing I noticed. People are more guarded; there's less reaching out, less interconnectivity. Everyone is just there in the same place, but not to be with each other.

So there's the T.O. scene I will be leaving. And now, to bed. Soon that shall be next to you.... Thanks for being my audience now writing class has ended.
xo

THE RESTLESS TWENTIES

06/02/2005

Dear Eshe;

Sunday evening, between stacks of schoolwork and cds at Joe's desk in the corner of his apartment, beneath bookshelves and the Pollock print I gave him. We had breakfast at three o'clock, then put our feet on the table listening to one of the BBC's million stations, smoked a joint at 4:20 as The Talking Heads came on. Now behind me Joe's asleep on his couch, head by the open window, which is filled with the leaves of an enormous tree. Joe loves this tree, though he partially blames it for his respiratory problems. We are by the sea, he said, Which ought to blow us clear of all this. Then he sneezed, and laughed, Ah, it wouldn't be the same if I weren't having some sort of breathing difficulty.

The apartment is full of plants. The first thing we did upon my arrival was put on the Modest Mouse cd I brought for him (*The Lonesome Crowded West*, which he loved immediately), and godknowswhy dusted the plants. Smiling at each other in the grey British afternoon light, leaves and little wet sponges in our hands.

But now I can't quite still my brain. Sitting staring into Joe's caramel-brown eyes, saying nothing, I was troubled by the feeling there's something I ought to be doing. I couldn't help but wonder if it was like this in the early days – those three months we had – but I decided no. Then it was truly moment-to-moment, unquestioned. So, what now? Boredom? No. Restlessness, but not because there's anything I want. I came for the quiet, and the frame Joe's presence creates. Only I can't shake this feeling that with every moment I must be molding my future, fashioning A Life; *What should I be doing* the unchanging ticker-tape scrolling through my consciousness. Maybe it's just guilt about leaving the Mom; she always has so much to do it feels wrong for me not to. But at this particular moment, there is nothing I'm supposed to be doing. School is done; I'm on vacation. Candles flicker against the crooked walls, squash soup made by Joe earlier in the day simmers in the tiny kitchen; our tableaus etch themselves into my brain, explain my nature to me. How extraordinarily lucky I am.

He's just stretching himself now, and looking fondly at me tapping away at the keyboard.

More soon. Big love, Sam.

IT'S ICONOGRAPHY OR THE POPPY
06/07/2005

Eshe, that's funny what you said about heroin – to think of you having apocalyptic fears on account of a heat-wave! No need to run out for that bag of junk yet, though; keep eating your cherry popsicles like there's no tomorrow, because I'm inclined to think there will be one. Though yes, the disappearing atmosphere is terrifying. Your email was also funny because the first day I got here Joe, too, was talking about his curiosity vis-a-vis the good poppy; and then today, on the way home from driving around rural

Wales we put on a mix tape and the first prophetic beats of "Heroin" began. The highway hum melted into their mounting, uncanny drone as my familiar hand with the big smoky quartz on the third finger suspended a poorly rolled cigarette out a window filled with the blurred, many-splendored greens of Welsh vegetation bathed in white gold sun. Puckish Joe's beautiful face happysad and quiet next to me, a sight that stops me laughing when the clichés of my iconography are about to make me cynical. He is too real: pulsing life and terrifyingly fragile. And all around us, nestled in between the lush valleys, huddled the bleak hardened villages and their crooked rows of lives that Joe had just been explaining to me. I don't know, I've always liked the song but today every discordant mangled-machinery note made perfect sense – both in itself and in the scene, different as it was from the world that produced the Velvet Underground. Pulled by the notes' violent cascade into an all-encompassing calm we rushed over the chicaning motorway in Joe's miniscule car which seemed an impossibly flimsy barrier between us and a thousand things that could kill us, none of which, at that moment, frightened me. The song's screaming distortion was like something ground out of the ancient, rusty machinery of existence, which I see as I write it sounds absurd but is honest at least, because that's how it seemed, as it also seemed that the voice coming through the stereo pining for a uniform was like so many men we know, wishing for a purpose, a nameless place on a clipper ship back when there were physical unknowns left to find.

    Which made me think of you and I recently on Euclid, saying But we're *not* like them, are we? Abashed at our "men are like this, women are like that" – loose talk not befitting young women of our generation. In the car enveloped by the Underground with Joe poised as he always is between loving this life too much and wanting to leave it, I felt again what we were saying that afternoon as we watched the kids showing off for their Annex Moms and Dads, that men really are taking the brunt of this modernity business. We may all be staggering blindly forward, and we may all be ambivalent about it, but in the end the girls we know don't want to annihilate society, where some of the men kind of do – sometimes even those who don't think they do. And if they can't get at society, there's always themselves.

So then there's that question of irrational faith — and I know you'll agree when I say that listening to "Heroin" turn into "Gimme Shelter" on the mix tape I thought *but crazily, some of them lived* — they made art of the destructiveness. Saved by irrational faith, by visions that might be hallucinations. Belief in those visions the most dangerous, the only cure.

Joe says that all the men he meets are angry. Rich, poor, comfortable, fucked-up, they're all angry. (Mike says anger is the same as fear, but that fear is for something that can be lost, whereas anger is for something that can't be gotten.) Half Joe's job is bureaucracy, it seems — helping people fill out forms, deal with the bullshit minutiae of existence — and the other half is convincing people that they want to live, and be sober enough to continue filling out these forms so their lives can be slightly better.

I sit quietly and memorize his features for when life will not include this sitting and listening to the world so carefully, to a whole album or the same song again and again without speaking; when he won't be there to softly strum his guitar, reminding me, in the simplicity of what he plays, to take pleasure in the smallest, almost imperceptible changes between chords. Thinking how it's possible for songs which are no great works of genius to powerfully affect us, how even rather prosaic lyrics can tell us about our lives. He'll hand me a smoke, smiling at me as I take it, drawing his hand away slowly, and I wonder that such a simple act can contain so much of what I want my youth to be. That I can know in those moments it will all be written down, that I am built to build this iconography, have been granted the gift of irrational faith.

Though I wonder if, of the two of us, I get the better deal. Walking downtown yesterday he looked at some new buildings and said, How horrible! so earnestly and Britishly it made me laugh; but his face was sad and it made me laugh more, that he could be so miserable and yet make me happy, because his misery is so aesthetically pleasing. It feels like my enjoyment should be cruel and yet I know it is not cruel. It seems unfair, though. He does everything I need him to, whereas I suppose I do everything he needs me to but it isn't enough: my love for his misery can't make it easier for him. So I got sad that I cannot save him from sadness; in my hubris, I almost imagine sometimes that I can, because I shall put him in a book – as though my translation of his pain into images could make him any happier. Though in a way, too, I know it does; that I am here to see, to take my portraits, think about what they signify.

I look forward to seeing your dear face… hope all's well….

Love, Sam.

FACTIONS, FASHIONS, AND TRYING TO READ THE BLOOD ON THE WALL
06/11/2005

Hello, Dear Mike, and thanks for the email.

Yesterday we went to a fundraiser put on by this anarchist group Joe is sort of affiliated with – the same ones who put on that protest where Joe was the only person who stopped to speak to the sixteen year old who'd come out to join them and was timidly tagging along. Anyway Joe's friend R., from school, has been involved with them for some time (she has a big crush on one of the guys), and so we met her and took the train to this grungy pub in Newport, a gritty little city about thirty kilometers from Cardiff. Up the stairs, into a dark room with wide wood plank floors, punk music on the stereo. I got a vodka and lemon (a new drink I've found I like – you have to drink something here, people think you're weird if you don't) and surveyed the scene: what you'd imagine, pretty much. The requisite type of young people (plus the one obligatory over-thirty-five with the slightly queasy smile): sort of dirty, more guys than girls, and a hierarchy within what appeared to be the "core group" of anarchists (apparently all male), which I thought was funny – based on looks, level of involvement, and height, seemingly in that order. R.'s crush is the tallest, most be-studded member, rather stand-offish. It's so sad; in my head, I hear "anarchist" and envision a bunch of earnest, impassioned people talking politics and strategizing – maybe even greeting strangers who come to their meetings with a, Hullo, never seen you before, what brings you by? Or a, Say, friend, did you hear about [insert injustice here]. But I just wandered around the room, looked at some pamphlets, bought some coffee from a collective in Peru, and eventually they started a film.

It was a documentary about the G8 Summit in Genoa, and more moving than I expected. The footage was shocking – blood streaked on the floor and walls where protesters had stayed, in the Indymedia centre a carnage of equipment and more blood. I hadn't realized the scale of either the protests or their repression. When that movie finished I was fired up, determined to do my part; for a moment the packed room seemed full of promise, a little cell in the body of people that would change how things are done. A band set up and eventually the lights dimmed again and the kids started playing; incomprehensible words were screamed, spit and sweat flew, drunk kids bopped around. I tried to feel part of what was going on, tried to hold on to that feeling of inclusiveness I had momentarily felt watching the movie, standing in the dark with all these other rapt people as angry and hopeful as I. But all I could think of was the scenes of revelry in Genoa before the shit came down, and my feeling, watching those scenes, that I had missed out, was forever missing out on whatever youth movement was going on. All those cool protesting kids with their necessities in well-used backpacks, eating together on the pavement, dancing the sundown radiant with the brief, intense camaraderie between them. I always wonder, seeing kids like that, where their parents are at, if they're close. Of course, there were so many people at the protest it's silly to generalize – whole families came, and married couples, and students; but the centre of these scenes, and certainly the most militant scenes, always seem to be comprised of people free to take responsibility for the world in general because responsible to no one in particular. But perhaps that's just my fantasy. My excuse for not being among them, simpler than the other thing, which is this sense of not knowing who to join, what to do, what outcomes to demand. I mean, what were the protesters' goals? There are so many: open borders, fair trade, environmental responsibility, labour ethicality. People Before Profits, that utterly logical utopia of which we all dream.

I am glad I can dream it with you.

See you soon,

S.

OBLA DI OBLA DA

06/14/2005

Oh, Joseph, I always miss you worst right after I leave.

The day I arrived to was dishwater grey, thick as clam chowder. Mike and Mom came to pick me up, which was kind of them (though they were late, Mom delighted that she'd shown me the inconvenience of waiting, and the error of my belief that it is not necessary to arrive at the airport when the plane is meant to arrive). Mom was harassed from having to leave the office early, and from the heat. Mike sat in the back seat, happy to see me. Highway traffic was bad, of course, but "Obla Di Obla Da" came on so Mom and I sang along, which gave us a smile. Then she bitched about her week, which was shitty as usual. We went back to the apartment, and shortly thereafter Flo and Paul came by, pissing Mom off even more. She doesn't seem to think much of poor Paulie – when I went into the kitchen to say they'd only stopped by for a quick visit Mom hissed at me, I don't understand exactly who this Paul person is, or why he's here, but, if that's what you want having just gotten back.

I realized she probably felt slighted that the first thing I wanted to do was smoke a cannon on the balcony with these two "very big-energy people," as Mom put it. And it wasn't necessarily the thing I wanted beyond all else, but it was what was happening. So smoke I did, and as we lit it the rain came; Florence's migraine and my headache began to abate, and the changing light made the nasturtiums, the salvia and basil plants glow. As Florence smiled mischievously and told me about her week-long trip out to Halifax with Paul, I was glad she had come: Flo who will enjoy my entreaty to notice the familiar smell of rain on Toronto streets, the fat raindrops bouncing off the asphalt as drenched, smiling cyclists coast by – will understand just what I mean then return to her madcap tales…. And then off she and Paul went, very unified-seeming, a little storm of talk, slapdash clothes, and careless hair swirling out my door and down to the ancient Jeep they now co-own.

Mom, Mike and I had dinner together as the evening cleared, and Mom's mood cleared, and the familiarity of it all was good. I tried to tell them about the Nicaraguan poets – they looked at me indulgently as I got too excited about it, spilled haphazardly the bundle full of images I carried away from your kitchen table – Somoza's expensive stones upturned in the street as barricades... the writing on the wall: The Triumph of the Revolution is the Triumph of Poetry. Mom liked that, as I knew she would.

Soon, to work. We'll see how the familiarity of that strikes me.

Good luck with the job hunt.

All love,

Samantha.

THE RAT SINGS LIKE A CANARY IN THE COALMINE
06/27/2005

Dearest Joe,

There was a dead rat rotting in the loft. A horrible smell emanating from the bathroom for days before one morning Ty, with his excellent sense of smell, rooted it out and removed it. It was beneath the floorboards under the sink – he had to pull up part of the floor to get at it, and he said the smell was so vile it became a sound, like a high whine in his head. It seemed like a portent of bad things to come – on top of the messiness that prevails now that neither Michelle nor Jake lives there, this dead rat: the Valley reclaiming its territory.

The bad omen yielded an eviction notice. Ty of course intends to fight it; but it is almost certainly the beginning of the end. The city is cleaning up the Don Valley, and part of the reconstruction project is an artificial hill to protect the homes they plan to build from the river, which floods about once a century. Why they can't make this hill start fifty metres further east, and preserve our building – which the good taxpayers of Toronto recently provided with a new roof – I don't know. I'd like to think that Ty will team up with the other tenants and they'll forestall this lunacy, but how long can a handful of people hold out against Progress?

I have scrapped the idea of moving to the loft, both because it may not be there for long, and because of my aversion to further debt. Then there's the larger uncertainty of the time period. The question of what Mike is going to be doing and where, and will I go with him. And the fact that I don't think Mike wants me to move in. He said he was okay with it, had even seemed excited about it sometimes; I'd been casing his room to determine how my furniture would fit. But then the other day we were at the kitchen table discussing it for the fiftieth time and he said, I don't think it's going to happen, man.

I was strangely relieved, but pissed off at what seemed his reluctance. I'm reluctant too, though. Mom thinks it would be silly (the debt, she says), and I dread leaving her. The past few years have been tumultuous with us; I'll move out soon enough and then I won't live with her again, at least not for a long time (I rather like the idea of living with her when she's old), so I want to enjoy our time together before I go.

Write and tell me about Gleneagles.... x

FLUNG FROM A FLYING TRAPEZE
07/17/2005

Dearest Joe,

So you have run from helicopters, thrown your body into capitalism's path and halted its motorcade for almost two hours. I love thinking of it – your weightless moment. Early dawn, Snickers bar in your pocket, dodgy anarchists dodging the chopper's spotlight in the wet Scottish field – I imagine your hands spread wide at your sides as your arms pumped, you wheezing all the way to the road. Good for you my dear Joe. At least you were there.

But I can see how you would feel it was pointless. On one hand the dissent is encouraging. On the other, the protests always seem like pageants set up in the mud outside the castle in which a far more lavish pageant has been going on for centuries. If only the people in there could see how absurd they look.

Mike and I were discussing this a couple of nights ago, after watching this documentary called *Girlhood*, about two girls in the youth justice system in the States. We noticed that the film was partially funded by George Soros, so got to talking about him and some of the progressive stuff he says and does, and I was seized by one of those spasms of optimism. Do you think it's possible, I asked, That people could get to a point where being a multi-billionaire starts to look stupid? A radical revolution in values, like Dr. King said. If all rich people did like George Soros, that would radically change the world. And if everyone does it, there's no incentive not to do it.

I wanted to know how Soros made his money so Mike looked him up on the Wikipedia. Stocks, something, Black Wednesday, and I wanted to know what was that so Mike read it aloud to me, stopping to put it in layman's terms. Which I did understand, and am intensely grateful to have someone who'll explain things so clearly and well; and I'll be following along for a good while as Mike's deep voice good-naturedly intones these complicated ideas, and then I'll realize the words he's articulating have begun to sound meaningless. Inflation. I think no matter how many times inflation is explained to me, I'll never understand it. But I keep trying because this is how the world runs and I'll have a moment of glory remembering Trade Deficits and GDP Deficits, a flash of knowing these things for Labour and Globalization class, parts one and two. Mike valiantly decoding, yet again, this business of buying and selling money, interest rates. And I listen and think I understand but then I'm thinking how I'll describe this moment to you: the length of Michael flung on his burgundy chair, me curled on the couch in the room's 1930s hue.

This is how the conditions of the world are determined, these numbers, this disembodied money flying through the air, and I can't understand it. I'm annihilated by it. As far as I can tell, the world is strapped to trapeze artists who can never see the rope they're hurtling toward. All laws of reason dictate that sometime they will miss.

All I was trying to figure out was whether Soros' wealth was acquired through immoral means. Oh all these guys, said Mike, None of 'em are angels. Someone else is always getting poor for them to get that rich. But it matters whether they do better or worse stuff with the money – as you suggested before, more or less rational –

At which point Ty came in saying, Rational? What's fucking rational, nothing is rational. (And he hurled himself onto the couch, groaning. The MCAT is in a month and he's freaking out; as if the MCAT isn't enough, he and Michelle aren't speaking, and, because he has to pay the bills, he's spending more time than a prospective medical student should on getting the Kozlik's Mustard man – whom he befriended at the St. Lawrence Market – an expanded factory that's up to code for him to start supplying supermarkets.) Except maybe you guys, he said. The way you guys love each other, that's rational. Oh why can't Michelle love me, Sammy, the way you love Mike? Am I really so awful? I need her. I have to write this test and I need her. I don't even want to sleep in my bed. I'm glad you guys are home. It's been lonely.

So passed our first night back from Timmins. Where Michael and I listened to a lot of CBC North, hollering Bread and Circuses every time they talked about the Olympics. Cursed the Vancouver bid. We heard about the London bombings and cursed the Iraq War.

Our second-last day we were sitting on the screened-in porch with Mike's dad and cousin Gary, and somehow got onto the mess the world is in. I was shocked as always by the optimism of the Boomers. (You were depressed by Live8 too, eh? My mom thought it was wonderful.) Brian thinks everything is going to be just fine. But look at Greenpeace, I said; Great organization, respectable, even. Beginning to win the hearts and minds of a large segment of the population. That's great, it is, but it's fingers in the dam. The real problems, the general trends, haven't changed at all.

But, Brian said mildly, More efficient energy sources are going to make a big difference in your guys' lifetimes. You'll see. Solar power and wind power are going to take off – and I also really think mass communication is going to change the playing field for all of this.

The internet is a huge tool, said Mike; And there you go – the military started researching that technology so in the event of a nuclear blast there'd be some decentralized means of communication. But they couldn't predict the effect that would have; he took a swig of beer then added, Look at the Zapatistas.

I was imagining the well-informed and the well-meaning sorting their NGO pamphlets over breakfast on a Saturday morning: the writing of cheques, the reading of neatly folded papers containing updates on reforestation efforts or Haitian hospitals. It seemed so sweet, ritualistic and hopeless. We couldn't even stop the GTA from amalgamating, I said, Even though we voted against it. Harris, our fucking elected representative, just did it anyway. So who's going to stop suburbs from devouring arable land, or garbage being dumped in the ocean, or manufacturing jobs leaving the country?

Oh lord, Gary said, No kidding. The schools have been really affected the way things are going in manufacturing. When I was teaching back in the '70s there were apprenticeships, you could learn a trade so that by the time you graduated you could work. He told us more about what Timmins, and the school system, had been like back then, and it sounded wonderful. Certain I was romanticizing, but enjoying the vision of it as Gary described it, his giant brown hands steady, held out. He concluded his brief, practical discourse on how his world has changed by saying, But you guys're doin' great.

And looking at his calm, mischievous eyes before he turned to Brian, who was asking about wood for Gary's expanded deck, for no particular reason I believed him.

So that was the cottage. I wrote one serviceable poem and two that need work. Now I'm back at the 'bucks, not working many hours. Our new manager gave me a talking-to about Ty's hanging around while I was working (talking, I'll admit, loudly and agitatedly, and not necessarily stopping as I served); but all her rule-abiding doesn't mean she can get through more than a five-person line-up without looking like she needs a valium. Plus, we have a crop of new hires who haven't learned the fine art of not giving a shit yet being proficient at their jobs. All the full-timers are ready to slit their wrists. The Golden Days of the College Starbucks have clearly passed. Not only that, but Ariel is closing Flavour Hall: her mom is renovating the space, renting part of it out and turning Ariel's apartment into an art gallery. So no more *hekdish* haven to visit on breaks, no more Jamie or Ariel sweeping into the store to enliven my shifts. It's the end of an era.

This was further affirmed by the death of Michael's beloved cat Monty, friend of his childhood, walrus-shaped alter-ego. He was old and sick, and Mike and his Mom put him down a few days after we came home. Mike said he burst into tears when Monty went limp in his arms, and said he was surprised how hard it was. I was like, Are you kidding? Of course it was hard, I said, amazed someone could be so emotionally detached that he wouldn't have expected it to be. Yeah, he said; I loved that cat. But also it feels like (as though I didn't know what he was going to say), it just feels like another sign that my childhood is really over. Like I had to say goodbye to another part of what I used to be.

In other news Mustafa's back in jail. Mike had a feeling about that while we were away, so was sad but not surprised to return to the message from Mustafa's roommate about his arrest. He'd been in the coffee shop across the street from his apartment and felt that a guy was looking at him funny, so had started to argue with him, and the guy had called the cops. When they came Mustafa was sitting quietly drinking his coffee, but the cops searched his bag and found an X-Acto-knife.

Mike spent two days last week at Finch and Whereverthefuck waiting for Mustafa to come up on bail court. If you ever want an interesting field trip, he said to me, Go sit in bail court for a couple of days. Then you'll see how the other half lives. People in for pathetic little crimes that middle-class people find it easy to avoid – assault, drug offences, petty theft, forgery. All of the accused were men, without exception. The judge looked like he enjoyed gritting his teeth in his spare time. They bring the jailbirds in three at a time and deal with them, bing bang boom and on to the next bunch.

Mike was asked to testify and so spent about half an hour telling the court Mustafa's whole story, how deleterious the effect of jail would be on his psychological well-being, the difficulty this educated man had experienced finding work, his financial struggle, how he respected his friendship with Michael and had demonstrated obedience to his authority as surety on the previous bail. He was even asked by the court to fill in details of Mustafa's record which were absent, contradictory, or invalid in the police reports. As the judge deliberated, the defence attorney gave Mike a note, which said something he interpreted as a dig on the prosecutor. The note said "cheque arrest record," which, while amusing, disturbed Mike with the fact of the defence attorney's not being able to spell.

Later Mike flipped the note over and found that the attorney had written another note, presumably to his colleague, that said "What an intelligent individual, and likeable! Most people would have abandoned Mr. Murza." It made Mike smile briefly, and he kept the note.

Mustafa just stared blankly at his feet, hands behind his back and didn't move an inch for the whole thing. The judge ruled against bail and they marched him out exactly as he came.

Mike is working full-time at the currency exchange these days, but has decided to conduct an interview with Mike the Tailor, one of the area's homeless men who uses Mike as a bank and has an interesting story about how he ended up on the street – he used to be married and own a business. For years Mike's been getting bits and pieces of the story and now he wants to formalize it, maybe turn it into an article for a paper or something like that. I'm glad Mike has a project. He's also been attending a weekly class run by the Anarchist Free University – he saw a poster for it in Kensington, so we went to the information meeting, which was about twelve guys in the back of a restaurant in the Market. The class – Anthropology – is taught by a guy who used to be a professor in Texas who moved here out of disgust with American foreign policy. It's good to know that such an organization exists – at the cottage we'd been talking about starting a Subterranean University, to keep our brains limber as we age.

So that's Midsummer in this city, sweet Joe.

In case you can't tell, I miss you.

ON TODAY'S INSTALLMENT...
08/20/2005

Florence is having a baby.

Or at least, Florence is pregnant, which means it's very likely that she's having a baby. She's going to Cuba in a few days with a friend from school to celebrate their graduation, and when she comes back, she'll make a decision.

Three days ago she called me; I was down at the loft, and Mike and I were planning to go up to Flo's parents' house to visit her and Paul. She got me on my cell as we were getting into Baba's car, and asked me if I could please pick up a pregnancy test kit. At first I thought it was just Flo's usual paranoia, for she is neurotic about her health (while abusing it most tenaciously); but she said she'd already done one test and it was positive, so she wanted to do another. There was something in her voice that got my attention and I wondered if it was just that giddy way she has about her sometimes.

When we got to the Shaw house, Florence and Paul were in a state of high excitement. We proceeded to the basement bathroom and stood outside it as Florence aimed her pee into the little plastic thing. Paul's guarded brown eyes were flickering under thick brows that went up and down as he spoke – Oh, you're gonna be an auntie, he said. I can feel it.

But it might just be a false alarm, I said, not believing it really.

No, I know. We conceived that night on 'shrooms.

Oh, yeah, Flo said sheepishly from the bathroom, We think we might know when it happened.

But have you been using anything?

Uh. Not really. Not, reliably.

We now stood around Flo, and watched one blue band appear. Two was no, one was yes. We waited for the second one, and had a brief debate on whether a second one could be seen, but decided against it. There was the one strip, the colour of antifreeze, signifying that another human being was in all probability at that moment taking shape in Flo's body.

On the way home Michael and I discussed: he was, as I suspected he would be, rather surly about the whole thing.

But you know she's always wanted a baby. She even always said she thought she'd have one at twenty-seven, and that she'd probably get pregnant before she was married.

Sure, but just because she said it doesn't mean she has to do it under whatever circumstances. They can't take care of a kid, look at them.

Yeah they don't know if it's raining or half past four, as Zaida would say. But then again, who does? Who's ever ready for kids?

Well, I'm not saying they have to have a nursery all set up and a life insurance policy, but like, fuck, man, they conceived on 'shrooms? That's not cool. And they've been together what, two months? Are they even together?

They co-own a Jeep.

Michael looked at me skeptically: I don't know, man, I mean, I'm a cautious guy, right, maybe I'm just not good with these kind of sudden major life decisions, but I don't think it's such a good idea.

I think if they decide to do it they'll be alright.

But it is worrisome. Paul wants a Lamborghini. He wants to retire at fifty. He wants to scam the taxman, live in a mansion in the 'burbs where you can get mad acreage and build what you want, have a pool, a ten-car garage, a basement with a club-quality sound system and no neighbors to fuck with you. He thinks girls should be like his ex-girlfriend, now an escort, and just not give a fuck, though whether or not he believes that prostitution is a viable career choice depends on the day (this has lately engendered several interesting debates between Michael, Florence and I). And I marvel at Flo's ability to accept anyone, if they're interesting enough; how she can accept others' values without acceding to them; how she'll mold herself to them ever so slightly, an inflection here, a hand motion there, and none of it is outside herself – and all the while Paul's ex exerts some kind of sorcery over his mind, and Flo takes it all, all of it. Only when Paul revealed that, since being tied up and robbed at gunpoint by some black guys in Alberta, he's not too hot on black guys, did Flo balk at Paul's beliefs. This came up recently in the context of Flo's ex: Flo mentioned that he'd called and, I don't want to think about it, is what Paul said. You with a black guy. And off he went on why not.

So I said to him I don't know if I want to raise a child in a household with a man who holds such views! It was what I wanted to say, and I so rarely actually say the thing I wanted to say.

Oh, it's so hard – how do we even know what we want to say anyway?

She took a gulp of cranberry juice from the blue glass I'm always afraid she'll break (Mom's had it since I was a kid) and said, Well, I would've maybe wanted to say other things too, but it seemed like one of the things I should have wanted to say.

Well, maybe after he's been with you awhile he'll start to see things differently.

I hope so, man. We're really different people, I'm starting to see that, you know? He was out on his own by sixteen, living with Lindsay by seventeen – his views on the world were sorta forged in a crazy, uh, kiln? – she giggled – No, but you know, he's been through some shit. (An inflection I don't entirely recognize; his, it must be). But he always wanted kids, always. That's sort of why we weren't using anything – well, that and he didn't think he could get a girl pregnant. Because he thought he'd done too many drugs! And then I thought, because of what that doctor said to me, that I might have trouble. So we kind of thought it couldn't happen, but I think we also kind of wanted it to happen. I don't know. That night we did 'shrooms we talked for hours and at one point his face, it was like, almost grotesque to me, like it was almost too real or something. I don't know how to explain it but I remember being sort of, *repulsed* I know that sounds awful. But then it became beautiful, like, everything about it made sense. Linda Goodman, in that Love Signs book I was reading, she says sex between two Tauri can be likened to a psychedelic experiment, isn't that funny? I can kinda see that….

Mom and Mike are in agreement that for Florence to have a baby now is lunacy. They point to her moodiness, her dependency, her complete lack of domesticity. She still smokes. They say she should take her time, figure out if she's doing more school or what, see where this thing goes with Paul, then *decide* to have a baby. But now?

I say, people have been having children for which they're not prepared since time began. She wants kids, isn't getting any younger, and this might be her only chance. Also, it's not like the Shaws, after they get over the inevitable shock and horror, are going to disown a grandchild of theirs. They're going to adore it. So what are we worried about?

And I'm surprised at myself – to find myself arguing for irrationality, for such a major action based on nothing, no logic, except the logic of Flo's-family-has-resources-and-loves-her. But I think it is this business about deciding. Mom and Mike seem so hung up on it, and I would have thought I'd be too. Instead, Flo and Paul seem emblematic to me – funneling through one tornado of a couple the randomness we're all enacting. I know that there are consequences to everything they're doing, and they might not all be so good, and that people are people and not symbols. But maybe I don't know it as well as I ought. Because it seems like what they're doing is what most of us haven't the guts for – to live as though we have no idea what the fuck we're doing, without even the pretense of a grand plan. Stripping the word "decision" of all its magical power.

This cavalier attitude is distasteful to Michael. Discussing this again yesterday morning as we were getting dressed, I willfully risked provoking him further by saying, Maybe I'm more my father's kid than I thought. I mean maybe there's a kind of irresponsibility in how I'm seeing this situation because I just want to know what happens. I do. I find their life interesting, the recklessness of it interesting. Except I don't have the stomach to live like Irving did, to take all the drama into my own life, so I encourage it in other people's lives. Kind of cowardly, really. Like making reality TV of my friends. Of course, if I write the book I want to write that's exactly what I'll be doing.

But to my surprise Mike defended me: No, he said, the creased T-shirt he was about to put on hanging in his hands, You'll be telling a story that your friends help you depict. It's not just a question of, like, we live lives like these, aren't we special – that's reality TV. These stupid little dramas set up for the cameras – it's not even reckless, it's just fake – I mean, the consequences are it fucks with your life, every time you have a drug-fueled mental breakdown it's news, you're just a train wreck waiting to happen, but. Sure you're fascinated with other people, but you're not one of those people who, like, live off drama, like the alien presence in *Star Trek* that thrives off discord – sorry, I'm a big nerd. You're not making reality TV out of Flo – you're not goading her on, you're just supporting her as she tries to make the decision and not judging her on necessarily the same criteria as I am or your mom is. I mean god knows, I can be sanctimonious enough – it's that puritanical streak in me – always something I've known I had to watch in myself. Nothing of the Dionysian in me; so Flo's like, hedonism is troubling for me and then, when you bring in the possibility of a kid….

Why is Mom freaking out about it so much though?

Your mom? Because I think she doesn't like to see the decision to have a kid get taken lightly. I mean she's always kind of identified with Flo in some way, but your mom, when she decided to have you, that was serious business for her. She constructed her life around being a mom. That's what she thought it should mean, that's how she wanted to do it. So Florence over here, just flinging herself into it, gets Harriet's hackles up, it's offensive to her values. It's not that I don't see why you think Flo could have this kid. It's just, ugh, I dunno (he gave his shoulders a series of little shakes, as though the frisson of their craziness was tickling his back); It makes me uncomfortable. But I don't think that it's, like, bad of you not to be uncomfortable with it, and I don't think it's just prurient interests, or some displaced desire for craziness. Everybody is attracted to some amount of craziness, even I am – I mean, I knew Flo before I knew you. And when you and I got together I knew it was gonna be complicated and I did it anyway. Why? Because I was intrigued, and because maybe I was looking to get knocked around a little bit. It helps you know you're alive; you're *involved* with shit. So of course you're kinda fascinated with the whole Flo-Paul thing. But you've always known what kind of life you want to have, so you're not inclined to go looking for the same kind of trouble that your father did. But I don't think that makes you a coward.

Generally when Mike talks about the clarity of my life vision, if we can say that, he gets a sort of equivocal smile on his face, a kind of queasy, unbidden acknowledgment that he is implicated in this picket-fence life I desire. And this time was no different. As generous and ready to defend me from my self-criticism as he was, he couldn't prevent the little smile from creasing his cheeks when he mentioned the life I want.

Of everybody, only Eshe seems to be in agreement with me. It's crazy, she said, But Flo will be an awesome mother, I can totally see that. Although, she's also really self-centred. But maybe having a kid will help. Anyway, when *isn't* having kids irrational?

Indeed. But they scramble up anyway and that's how the world gets made.

Ah, planning versus spontaneity – it's a fine balance. Ty and I were discussing this with regard to Pedestrian Sundays in Kensington, as we loaded drums and headed toward the Market last Sunday.

Why do you think it's even on Sunday, Ty asked me.

'Cuz it's a day that a lot of people have off and some of the stores are closed so we're not messing with their business?

Yeah, that. And also because that's when we practice. That was part of how it got started, when Shamez first said he wanted to close off the street, Rick said, Do it Sunday and I'll bring the samba band I'm playing in; and we had a barbeque outside La Palette and played. And then in 2002, this really kind of monumental thing happened. You weren't there, you hadn't joined yet; it was right in the middle of the summer, there was a party in the street but the cars kept coming through and disrupting us as we were playing and so finally, this one car came in and I walked in front of it, and the whole band sort of swarmed around the car. I mean we circled it in samba, and so then the car backed up, and it became this kind of great symbol for Car-Free Kensington. We pushed out the car. But then we had a meeting, in 2003, with business owners and a city councilor and discussed what to do, how to proceed. Because originally the idea was to make Kensington a pedestrian mall. But we were concerned about hurting the businesses and irrevocably changing the neighborhood. So this year PSK is every other Sunday and it's gotten really big, lots of people want to play, there are more activities. Which is incredible. The giant chess, I like the giant chess. But time slots. Okay, we'll take the last two and just play until we're tired. (His cheeky Sephardic haggler's voice, its certainty we are entitled to play when we please.) That's the trade-off, right? I don't know, as this thing grows, if people will realize how incredibly serendipitous it was. It wasn't a big organized thing, it wasn't… it fell together, you see? That's the beauty of the thing, that's what allowed it to become what it is.

I sat there marveling that a boy who was literally crying on the steps of Starbucks two days earlier could be heading with perfect calm to the very restaurant where his beloved's current lover works. He bolted through the city in the conditional sunshine as though his life were all in one piece, talking to me about Kensington as if there were no MCAT to write (which he did over the following two days), no Kozlik's mustard factory to renovate, no distended line of credit to pay off, no surveyors outside his home. Just him, his gearshift and a trailer full of instruments, and me listening to him claim the world with his talk. And I loved the familiarity of being his passenger, my trust and slight terror of Ty in his aviators knowing the timing of the lights on Richmond and getting us across town in ten minutes flat.

Sitting on the curb across from La Palette after we played I said to Mike, There's no way around it, it's going to gentrify. But if it's going to happen, it might as well happen like this. With people who at least care about the community aspect – like, I think there'd be a big fight against a gigantic condo or some shit. People care, too, about the actual neighborhood and not only about some utopian vision like having a pedestrian mall, which would inevitably just become an expensive little museum.

Sure, Mike said; If enough people care about keeping it cool it helps the vibe stay the same at least. Sort of, although it's already changing. And like, people were pissed about the Loblaws thing, but they came anyway. And stole the name, what, Zimmerman's is it? Yeah, stole the name and pretended like they'd been in the Market for forty years when it's fucking Loblaws. Insidious motherfuckers. And people spraypainted and whatever, but it didn't do any good and now people shop in there and don't even realize.

The neighborhood kept the Nike store out.

It's true. That was at a time, though, when Nike was taking a lot of flak generally for its labour practices. Not like everyone else wasn't doing the exact same thing, but it got out about Nike somehow and it served as a lightning rod for people's wrath. And even if there's no Starbucks or Nike store or whatever, you can't stop the rent from rising. And you're right, this is downtown real estate, man, there's no reversing the clock on that shit, the value is going up. It probably costs well over half a million dollars to own a house here. So you won't be able to stop the boutique shops moving in, and whatever trendy thing. We're the kind of people that're making it happen. People like us want to go out and have beers from microbreweries, or eat a nice meal sometimes –

I don't know about that; like, I can't pay sixty-five dollars for a shirt, I come here for the used stuff.

And the character. These kinds of street parties and stuff are really fun for us, but it makes the place an attraction; it increases interest in it and that's not all bad, like you said it helps preserve the area as something kind of special –

A sense of its history is preserved at least –

Sure but its interesting heritage also raises the rents.

Ah, the love of my life, the buzzkill.

Sorry, man, he said regretfully; I don't mean to be a curmudgeon, it's not like I don't enjoy these things. I just don't want to see the place become another Queen St. West. Or Yorkville, more aptly.

Oy vey iz mir bite your tongue.

So that's the story, morning glory – so much change to greet your return to the parental computer – a charm against feelings of stagnation. How is life back with the folks? I'm sure you're being, as ever, the helpful son and patient brother. I'm glad to hear the move went smoothly but did you have to leave absolutely all your furniture to be happy? It was such a comfortable couch. I suppose that's the appeal, isn't it – just driving away with what fits in your car. I'm glad you took the shelves, at least. Good luck on the apartment hunt, and the job hunt and – don't tease me – are you really thinking of coming to T.O.?

Let me know,

I'll have the welcome wagon ready.

xo

INTO THE WOODS

09/07/2005

Dearest and best of all possible Josephs,

once again you have sent me a book at just the right time. I filled up the red and purple one just before I left for B.C., where I used a little spiral thing, very functional and uninviting. Its front pages are crisscrossed with Mike's hand jotting numbers of car rentals and friends, addresses, directions. A nice memento, but I'm pleased with everything about this new book, so thank you for the present. I'm glad there was no paper in your brother's old room so that the book's first pages are inscribed with your inventory of his old belongings, your few transplanted ones. And of past and present – did you realize your back-and-forth? From the new home you will soon make to the sound of your father's breathing coming through the wall when your pen stops; from the just-started magazine you have searched out for me (incidentally, a magazine originally started by Shelley, dormant for two centuries) to the books you will read because you've already read them, or failed to when you were supposed to previously (the thought of you throwing your hands in the air with Stendhal in your twenty-year-old lap made me smile). Mind full of your prospective job as you drive your Mom to the mall – and the bookshop where you worked as a teen now a DVD store....

So yes, B.C. One of those periods of life that make me say, Maybe when I'm older my self-wrangling skills will be better. Get to know the nature of the beast.

I was nervous about going in the first place, probably in part because I felt bad about leaving Mom for the third time this summer, but I didn't figure that out till later. Beforehand all I knew was apprehension about the whole endeavor – didn't have what to wear, frightened of all the strangers. You'd think I'd have been pleased as punch to go, Michael and I on a real traveling vacation together, and to the wedding of his oldest friend. But the day before I left, it was all dread.

He was as he usually is traveling anywhere, considerate and a little curmudgeonly. This was our first time on a plane together, and it was weird to see his body I know so well squeezed into the garish velour seat with the plastic wall by his head, to hear his voice through the unworldly airplane drone. We got into Victoria at about eight o'clock and headed to the restaurant where Jesse and Kate's bachelor/ette parties were beginning. We had missed supper but were meant to report there for the treasure hunt that was the night's activity. As we traipsed around the harbour with our packs looking for the correct seafood place, Mike on my cell phone taking directions from Jesse who was clearly yelling over a roomful of people, I was full of criticism and condemnation. We wouldn't be able to clean up or have dinner; we didn't know where we were sleeping.... But I thought of Baba spoiling all Zaida's and everybody's occasions, thought goddamn it I guess I got her disease but I'm not going to be symptomatic if I can help it. Who cares where we'll be sleeping; when have I ever?

We got to the place, white stucco and low light, and I was briefly mortified to be standing plane-smelly and with a huge pack in the foyer of this classy joint in the midst of its Friday dinner rush. Then Jesse came lumbering out with a smile to light the world, pulled Mike into a brotherly hug, and we made our way to the large table where a group of healthful-looking youths were eating, drinking and talking. Michael was given a place next to Jesse, and I tried to be brave and make conversation with the unknown fellows sitting near me. By the time we left the restaurant my brain had realized it was time to travel, to be a part of whatever environment it found itself in. I guess Michael had come to the same conclusion: the night's finale took place at some big club, where he, to my wonderment, got up on a stage where the others were dancing, and joined in. Dancing in a club with loud music and flashing lights, on a stage for the world to see. Now that's love, I thought, spying him doing his graceful, cagey, quasi-martial-arts dance moves as though that's what he'd be doing any Saturday night.

Michael and I slept on couches in the bride's home. Kate's mother knew who my father was and asked me questions about him. Answering in the affirmative the inevitably embarrassing question as to whether I also write, I felt even more separate – the strange Yid come with pretensions from Toronto – from the bright, active kids busying themselves in comfortable camaraderie with tasks around the house.

Two days later Mike and I drove out to the camp where Jesse works – a branch of the same one he and Mike attended together as kids. We'd brought a tent, but it was Mike's four-person and very heavy, so Jesse gave us a smaller one as well as a stove, water purifier and some other things. We loaded it all into the rental car and headed north, stopping for a night at Jesse's godsister's place. Grum, broad-shouldered, fascinatingly taut, with whom Michael tree-planted (at which time she dubbed him Bobbo, a nickname that has stuck among that crowd), recently bought a place outside Courtenay. The bungalow now called The Homeshtead looks to have been built by hippies in the seventies; it recently had its plumbing fixed by Grum, who also grows most of her food in the enormous backyard. This, Mike said, Is where we want to be if shit ever really hits the fan.

I agreed, feeling the helpless, wasteful city girl I am.

We smoked some pot, a whole bunch of us on the floor and in various chairs around the kitchen. The talk was slow, about parties, work, neighbours; our hosts were animated but without urgency. Every time Mike or I opened our mouths, I had the feeling we were in a different dimension from the rest of the room; we were speeding through every sentence like language was about to be erased. I tried not to talk.

We set off in the late morning to Cape Scott national park, at the northernmost tip of the island. In the late afternoon we arrived, parked our car and marched off into the forest toward San Joseph Bay, an inlet about a half-hour's walk from the parking lot. We set up our tent on a patch of white sand and I didn't understand why I was anything other than delightfully happy. Heading off to collect water I found myself becoming frightened. It was getting dark. We had to find an appropriate place to collect water that could be purified, and I was afraid we wouldn't. We are not this kind of people, I muttered, close to tears, as Michael and I walked along the beach looking for a tide pool. Mike knew something about where we should look for water, but I had no idea and was terrified we wouldn't have any. We are in the middle of nowhere and completely unprepared and this was a terrible mistake. Mike smiled and put his hand on my shoulder and told me it would be fine.

Cooking dinner in the peaceful darkness I apologized.

No worries, Sammy; you always freak out a little in these situations. You weren't raised doing this kind of stuff. It's always hard doing things that are unfamiliar. Plus we're off the grid, your mom can't get in touch with you and that always makes you anxious. Like that time in New Mexico....

It's the wind! I said, to make us both laugh. (At the beginning of our road trip with Bri and Flo, we stayed a night in a stunning national park, on a high cliff with a constant wind, and whistling, incessant wind often makes me uneasy. It was early in the season and the park was mostly deserted. Also, it was Mom's birthday and my cell phone didn't work. In the morning I had what I later learned to identify as an anxiety attack, and Mike did chi gong on me until I fell asleep in the back of the van. Only years later did I figure out that the problem was not so much the wind, but the fact that I had been unable to call or be reached by Mom on her birthday.)

The morning was misty, with clouds so thick and close I wanted to dissolve them in our coffee, to lick them off Mike's thigh or chest as we lay in the sand-filled tent. There was a fine rain but it was warm, so I put my raincoat on over my underwear and followed the shoreline to where the forest meets the beach. Rocks jutted from the creamy sand, some crowned with a crooked little thing like a bonsai tree. Rain and mist warm on my face I let my fingers explore the grey-black rocks and autumnal coloured lichen, the trees whose trunks seemed to be swallowed at their base by the wet sand. A young, outdoorsy couple emerging from the woods startled me out of my reverie, the ponytailed girl looking with a moment's confusion at my half-smiling face. The joyous insignificance I'd been feeling turned to self-consciousness – the remembrance of my thighs exposed below the yellow slicker, the peculiar, rapt expression I must have been wearing; but then I thought who cares? And laughed.

I saw Michael walking toward me, faded cargo pants rolled up, wearing the serious expression I've seen in pictures of him as a kid. He would be getting antsy to head off soon. But he came toward me and smiled, tucked a wisp of hair behind my ear, looked around silently at the rocks and trees.

I admired his smooth, ruddy cheeks, the fine curve of his jaw covered in light stubble.

I felt younger than him, and also older – young because deeply and frighteningly in love, at his mercy was what I thought; old because I am without the type of terror I feel in him and many boys his age. Though he stood close I could feel Michael isolated from me, sheathed in the young, hard masculinity he pulls around himself without realizing; but I wasn't afraid, didn't feel that if he leaves me my life will come to nothing. I, too, was solid, separate from him, thrumming with everything alive, ancient and impervious around us.

We packed and proceeded into the forest for the five kilometre hike to Eric Lake, an isolated point along the thirty-or-so kilometre trail to the tip of the park. It was raining but we didn't care, just planted our walking sticks and mud-soaked boots firmly on the slippery wood bridges and groaned merrily when we stepped in a big puddle; we kept up a good clip, stopping briefly to drink water from the bottles we had strapped to our packs. We are this kind of people, I thought, as we took photographs of each other beneath the dripping canopy.

The rain had grown harder and colder by the time we reached the point. There were a few campsites under the trees, and one sandy spot of beach before gravel led into the narrow lake. We quickly pitched the tent in the sand, and Mike tried to get the Coleman stove going for dinner. We'd been having some trouble with it and now it didn't want to light. He got it going and we put water on to boil, but lost the flame. I relit it, having learned the day before how to operate the stove. This went on for awhile until Mike was ready to eat gorp for dinner, but I was determined, and so for three hours lit and relit the Coleman stove, smoking wet cigarettes and listening to the rain on the trees and water. Mike wandered around seeming a little out of sorts.

To get him talking about it I said, So, your oldest friend is getting married.

Yup, said Mike.

Looks like they've got a good corner of the world carved out for themselves.

Yeah. I think the west coast is where Jesse belongs. It's probably a good place to be, considering what we're probably looking at for the next ten, fifteen years.

He went on about the economic meltdown, and environmental crises, and unsustainable suburbs.

It's true they're not viable how they are, I said, trying to be constructive. But if we were to, say, actually develop our public transportation then we'd be like most of the rest of the industrialized world, where people could live in outlying areas and take trains into the city centre for work.

That'd be great, said Mike, But they'd have to start that, like, now. And the city just doesn't have the resources. I don't know, maybe I'm wrong. Maybe the economy will bounce back, maybe capitalism is more resilient than I think. But it just seems to me that every so often in history there's a major upheaval that redistributes resources. And old Mother Nature is going to give us a reminder that she's still in charge.

I could feel myself getting heavy, limbs weighted down with the dark ages to come. Mike saw this, said, But who knows? Maybe these predictions are just something in my psychology.

I sat awhile, thinking that if he's right about everything to come, it's bad; if he's wrong, it's bad. He always says it's the other way around – if he's right he gets to be right, if he's wrong then that's good for everyone and he'll be happy.

Finally I said, I think I'm not as good at these conversations as I used to be. That frightens me. I used to be able to think about this stuff with more of a sense of adventure, like we're going into the great chaotic world and whatever it is I can take it. I mean I guess that's still true, but now....

I know what you mean, he said, surprising me. It's like I can barely keep my head above water.

To my raised eyebrows he said, I feel like a passive observer, a scientist. Detached, free to make any predictions I want. (And that's the thing that kills me: that he can talk on and on about the terrible changes for which we're so ill-prepared, and it's as though he's making predictions about the weather.) His face was grave. That's what's become of the feeling of fluidity

I used to have as a kid, he said. You know, when you met me I still had that sense of possibility based on this passive acceptance of the world. That feeling that I didn't need to strive or take control of anything, I could just drift through the world and some transcendental quality would allow me to make my mark on it. (He rolled his pronouncements off his fingers, let them rest on the tips; held his hand open so I could take his proffered thoughts. I pictured him as a kid, propounding, his grandfather calling him Professor. Here he was still, offering words, thoughts. Not realizing now, any more than he did then, that these words and thoughts are him.) And I felt like that ability, he said, – To not want anything in particular – was my strength. But these past few years… I dunno. It's gotten harder and harder. I don't know what happened, how I got off-kilter. It's like when I was sitting on Jonathan Rooke's porch when I was four years old, I'm still sitting on his fucking porch, not knowing if I want to go with him and his Mom or not. Wanting neither thing, wanting the option to not exist, to have never been given to me.

Okay, but the thing is there are ideas in your head about how life is supposed to be, about what it is and isn't good to do. You've been thinking about this shit since you were a kid. So that's your guide. If you can't know what exactly you want, well, who does, really, but you have principles that inform your decisions about how to act.

I could see I'd struck a nerve; his face became hard, forming a rebuttal. A shell around the larva at the core of himself which at all costs must be shielded from development. A suspended amorphous goo of possibility, beyond everything.

But that doesn't help this flatness, he said, This feeling like there's a note in the chord of life that I'm not hearing, a richness that's lacking from what I remember the world being like as a kid. But, that could just be what happens to the brain as you age.

Then why don't I feel like that? (I hate this explanation he occasionally offers, some myelin bullshit for why life will never have the golden glow it has when we're four.)

I don't know, you have this way of looking at the world, of making meaning out of it. Sure, you falter sometimes, but in general you have a story you tell yourself. Although even you, I mean you worry about why you want to write, or why you want the life you do, you worry that it doesn't come from inside yourself. And that's the thing, we don't know. But you, you have a way of making peace with the uncertainty. Don't you ever feel like this? (I could see him turn the conversation away from his vulnerable core, from what he might have to do to be in the world.) Like a passive agent, in terms of how you interact with the world as a consumer, or seeking a job, or your cultural identity – that these things are formed by things beyond your control?

Obviously, because they are. But that's not the – look, ohholyfuck look, there's a bubble! I poured the macaroni into the pot, and the stove went out. I relit it. Ha, I said. Boil, motherfucker.

You're a trooper, Sammy, he said, referring to my persistence regarding himself, I think, as much as the stove. He began walking to the tent, saying, Bah, just typical twenty-something nostalgia. Like you say, the end of university, all this shit needing to be decided. It'll be fine, he said, waving a hand behind him.

I felt very tired. Hemmed in by trees and the low, pregnant sky. We've had some permutation of this conversation so many times; I thought we might be trapped for eternity on this stony outcropping in the woods, mourning all the dead unreal Michaels, worlds of them slain by this dastardly foe Reality.

Surely not. I could feel myself drawing toward my image of our future selves as toward a warm body in bed, instinctive, seeking comfort.

Just as it began to get truly dark I drained the pasta and proudly handed the pot to Michael in the tent. When I tasted it, it was the best thing I'd ever eaten in my life, until the moment I realized that Mike had dumped about an ounce of crushed chilies into it. He felt terrible and I didn't have the heart to scold him. Meh, it's edible, I said, mouth burning. He's one of those people who are frustratingly hard on themselves, so hard that to state one's grievance is only salting a wound. Yet I was struck by the thought that this particular fuck-up was a kind of declaration, an assertion of incompetence. Better to give him the benefit of the doubt, though.

We lit a joint and he picked up a strand in our never-ending conversation, voices muffled by the tent and the rain beating against it. Exhaling into the starless night he said, Maybe I was always setting myself up for this. I mean, I thought I should have written a novel by twelve – I was always the kind of kid who set these expectations for myself but never met them. They were unmeetable; but I had to have them. So maybe I got what I deserved for my, uh, lack of realism. I just, I thought there was this *quality* I had, that allowed me to just adapt to my environment and which would result in my doing something, whatever it was I was supposed to do. But I'd do it through not trying, he laughed dryly. And I thought failure was noble.

Yeah well failure is a lot less terrifying in the abstract. But you still have that quality, I think. It's just that adapting to your environment, or expressing yourself through it, is an act of will. And that's problematic, especially for you.

Yeah, what is it? It's like a pain, like something grinding in my teeth.

The knowledge we're going to die, I said grandly, wanting to see what he'd say.

No, he said. Death – it's almost a relief, a comfort that eventually we're all rendered down to our original components. The story has its conclusion and therefore its meaning.

I felt a little ill: the shocking ingratitude of it; how he could sweep away our whole existence as lightly as he'd brush a dried-up cobweb from a corner. But I attempted to sound impassive, said, It's fascinating about men and death. Almost all the boys I know are so compelled by it. The war movies and computer games, the eagerness to contemplate catastrophic situations that will demand action and/or death. But it seems to me a fear of life that breeds it.

Sam, there are so many dead people right now, so many generations of people who lived and are now dead. Dead people are what's going on here. My brain, everything I can think or do, everything I am is because of dead people. Ancestors, philosophers, politicians. I'm just a brief glimmering manifestation of the dead. And when I'm dead I'll be part of all that too;

whatever my life is, I can't have no effect at all. So after death the meaning of whatever it is that I was will be clear.

I fail to see what your dying has to do with what the meaning of yourself is. I mean yes, when you die your life takes shape as a story in the people who knew you and survive you, and in those stories, maybe even in how people perceive your era, some "meaning" is ascribed to you and how you lived. But you're here now. Your responsibility is to be alive, and put to the best use possible this troublesome thing called consciousness with which we all are burdened to a greater or lesser degree.

But it's so painful – he was laughing at himself, telling the truth.

I thought of his aesthetic preference for struggle, how I'd always thought it would help him navigate and draw meaning from the stormy passages in his life. I'm surprised to hear you resisting pain, I said. You who used to tell me how you respected the hero on his long journey, becoming what he is through trials and suffering.

I guess I need to remember my love of pain, he said, stubbing the joint firmly into the sand outside our tent and sticking the roach in his pocket. He sat staring out into the wet darkness, and I could feel him steeling himself for the decades-long battle of adulthood. And strengthening the fortress walls around the abstraction at the core of himself, his nonexistence.

Sometimes, he said, It just seems there's not enough beauty to justify all the ugliness. But I don't believe that's true. I guess, I guess life is just death harnessed to thwart itself. And how could that not be ugly sometimes? But that's what we're doing here, so we might as well do it.

I knew he wouldn't like it but I told him I wanted to smoke; he changed places with me, took off his pants and got into the sleeping bag. I dragged on my cigarette, hating it a bit but wanting the smoke in my lungs, wanting like a fool to laugh in the face of death. I thought of Mom, how she'd loved to smoke. Knowing that, like her, I would be forced to give it up, if not for love of myself then for someone else (in her case it was the dying wish of her beloved cousin Ken). But what happens to the recklessness? I'll give up the cigarettes but not the recklessness. Not the will to rebel a little against this life I love too much.

Do I love it enough for Mike and me both? Maybe, I thought; but no. I might be able to create the world for him, but I can't force him to love it.

I closed the tent flap and undressed. Mike said, In my choice of lover and mate, that's one place I have choice, more control than over other choices.

And though I wasn't sure I agreed, I knew he was asking me to believe in love the way he believes in it, as a force against entropy, a brave thing, unquestionably good. A joining together in a universe that wants to pull itself apart. And with that I do agree. I got into the sleeping bag and kissed him. The fecund rot of centuries was the warmth behind his young, soft lips and I devoured it, covered with my kisses this brief face on the immortal body of death.

Yes my love, here we are among the living.

As he turned on his back to sleep I suddenly wanted to write something, had a very clear phrase in my head to describe an understanding I'd just had about the future. In the dark I began to scribble, but didn't begin with what I had intended, making a sort of journal entry instead, and by the time I had gotten to where we were I had forgotten.

Learn from this, I warned myself; Pounce on the moments of certainty.

The next day we somewhat unwillingly returned to the car and headed south, stopping for lunch in Port Hardy, a town at the northeastern-most tip of the island and the most hardscrabble place I've ever been in Canada. We checked into a cheap motel outside Courtenay, because all the 'shtead residents had already headed down to the wedding. While Mike showered I looked out the window at the exotic emptiness, loving the unknown cars speeding past and the quiet, half-country smell of the outskirts of everywhere. The "writing delusions," as my mind wants to call them, had me in their grip; they were gaining strength from the life Mike and I were sliding into. Images I've always had that grow clearer each year like photographs taking form in their chemicals. It's more mundane than I thought, this life – the smell of rental cars, the feel of chunky, unfamiliar keys and the slight irritation as Mike examines a map, misses a turnoff, angry with himself. Young people traveling to their friends' weddings; taking photographs muddy and triumphant on a forest trail; composing speeches for the wedding celebration; fighting fear of ourselves, each other, the future. More mundane than I thought and breathtakingly beautiful. And I keep telling myself my own story as it is happening, transcribing what I know I have to remember, what I will want later when the time comes. The sureness that it will come, the sureness that it won't, familiar as my own voice.

Heading to the wedding we realized that gas was even more expensive than it had been the day before – was up nearly a full cent. Sweet Jesus we picked a great time to go on a road trip, I said, and Mike said, Don't worry, it's not going to get any better. Everyone's saying Oh it's only temporary, oh they'll increase production and the price will go down, but it's bullshit. Oil's only gonna get more expensive, you'll see.

We had lunch at a White Spot and got to talking about families and neighbourhoods. Mike was reminiscing about his and Jesse's childhood, the incredible Jackman Public School playground Mike has been lamenting since the city replaced it with something safe and boring. The conversation turned to Grant and his childhood friends, one of whom is now addicted to smack. He recently resurfaced, supposedly clean, but then stole Brian's guitar. It's the strangest, saddest thing about John Milton, Mike said; I used to babysit him, and he was the loveliest kid you ever wanted to know.

Must have been fucked up by something.

I don't know, man. I mean, his parents were divorced and I don't think it was too pretty, but he had a stepdad, and they seemed like just another family living in Riverdale. Maybe home life doesn't account for everything. I mean, how is it that Grant and I grow up in the same household, and my oldest friend is getting married this weekend, and Grant's oldest friend is getting high on junk he bought with my Dad's guitar?

As we debated the role of parents, the waitress placed our food in front of us and Mike said, Maybe the best thing for him would be a stint in the military.

Are you fucking kidding me?

Well better the military than jail. I mean, at least in the military you can feel useful. And if you've already got one foot in the grave because you're addicted to drugs then, hell, at least you can turn that disregard for your own life to some kind of account.

Account! I'm surprised at you! And the military brainwashes you. Drugs brainwash you. Jail makes you a better criminal.

On it went like that, until I looked around and saw a couple of women at the next table glancing our way. I laughed and said to Mike, Anyone would think we were having a lover's spat.

And Michael smiled, looked up from the little packet of jam into which he was digging his knife, saying, Well they don't know this is just our form of entertainment.

Speaking of which, I think I shall have to tell about the actual wedding tomorrow, for Itay has just arrived at my door with an eye for *The Daily Show*. To be continued…

xx

INTO THE WOODS PART 2
09/08/2005

Alright, the wedding. We returned to the camp; all the campers had left a couple days before, and it was now filling up with wedding guests. Everyone else was staying in cabins or camping in a couple of large areas, but one of Jesse's friends took us up a steep hill behind a supply cabin where there was a clearing perfect for a small tent. I was feeling shy and out-of-place, and was grateful to have a spot away from the other guests.

That night there was a party by the lake. Michael and I ambled over as it was getting going, he in a gregarious mood greeting people he'd met before, me tagging along trying to be bold in my hellos. In other circumstances, I thought, talking to people is such a pleasure. Where's that Sam now? When it came time to line up for food, I was horrified to find that I'd become the chubby girl I'd been at my one year of sleepover camp, hungry and ashamed to be seen eating. Everyone knowing each other but me. As I watched Mike dive into his second hamburger I knew my shame was lunacy but couldn't do anything about it; I ate lightly and went to sit on a log where an older man with a beard was sitting. He was Grum's father, lovingly called Yeti by the young folk. He's a professor of religious studies at Guelph, so I asked him questions about the trip he'd led, an educational trip to India which Jesse and Kate had gone on, and about how he knew Jesse's parents; he asked me questions about my schooling and my plans, like older people do. He had an odd, kindly face and I liked listening to him and thinking of the decades of friendship between his family and the Rocks.

When it got dark and everyone had eaten, people started dancing; Kate's brother is in a couple of bands, one of which played cover tunes on a makeshift stage near the water. I tried to dance a little but was too self-conscious – not so much for fear that I'd look bad but that the dancing would look like the effort it was. So I stood by a fence and watched the performance, the audience in groups or pairs talking, dancing a little, cheering the band with faces lit by the fairy lights strung above us. I went back to my seat on the log. A couple of people I recognized from the bachelor/ette party smiled and motioned for me to come dance; I smiled back and called, In a while. Eventually Mike came over and sat by me, looking with a wistful smile at the dancing people. He put his arm around me and I asked what he was thinking, a thing I rarely do.

That I'm really happy, he said. Looking at me, his pupils very large in those wide, mysterious eyes he kissed me, said, I'm happy I have you.

And it was alright, all the people in their uncomplicated revelry and all the things I don't know and am afraid of and want to be; all of it was good because there we were, two strange city kids with our heads full of thoughts, holding each other on a perch between a forest and a party.

The next day was one of preparations for the bride and groom and their families, but they had planned activities throughout the day to keep the guests occupied. Michael was with Jesse and the other groomsmen. When he came back to the tent briefly for something he seemed excited and distracted, answered tersely that he'd jotted down some things for his speech but had decided he was mostly going to wing it. He seemed very manly, or rather, very much a young man, executing a rite our society has no good language for. The boys were at Jesse's cabin drinking whisky and telling stories.

Had I been feeling bolder I would have gone on a nature hike or a canoe ride, but as it was I clung to the tent, reading and smoking, grateful for the time alone. I had a minor panic when it was time to shower – the showers were communal, down the hill from where we were camped. I dreaded nudity in front of any of the taut, healthy girls I'd seen around, couldn't stomach the idea of exposing myself to them. Appalled to be performing this compulsive comparison – competitiveness and vanity, blights upon womanhood and me perpetuating them. Weakness. Weakness and habit. And probably some shit about Mom. Great. A fat girl with Mom problems, making myself laugh at my own viciousness, impelling myself toward the shower. Where this whole problem was null because I was the only one there.

It was a rocky beginning to a rocky night. For no apparent reason but that I was unable to reverse the time warp back to nine-year-old Sam I had inadvertently caused when I entered the camp, I hated what I had brought to wear. It was a long turquoise skirt like people are wearing this year and a white sleeveless blouse I had heretofore liked, and a cream coloured Celine cardigan with gold buttons I had borrowed from Mom. This cardigan was the main source of my mortification. Looking at myself in Mom's big blond wood mirror I had thought it was sort of thrift-store old-school, and intended to hide the ostentatious buttons and the fact it was a little too large by wrapping it tightly around myself. The corded wool on the arms looked cozy for the cool September nights. Here in the woods, though, I just felt like I was dressed in my mother's clothes. Or my grandmother's clothes. Rich old lady clothes. Rich old lady clothes and a cheap little skirt: a walking museum of my family's rise and fall. Nothing to be done about it, though; it was too cold to go without a sweater, and everything else I had was covered in mud. The only thing about my outfit that made me happy was the shoes, little brown flats I had gotten just before I left. Easy to clean, easy to walk in, sweatshop-free. I looked at my feet, hiked my skirt and marched down the hill.

I followed the line of guests making their way to the ceremony. It was late afternoon and the sun was shining brightly, an uncommonly clear day for B.C. (When I asked Jesse earlier in the weekend what would happen if it rained, he looked at me, said, Ah, it won't. A bold statement for this part of the world, I know, but I have faith. If it does we'll figure something out.)

Beneath tall pines overlooking the lake was a little wooden stage which had been decorated with yellow daisies and blue hydrangeas grown for the occasion by a friend of Kate's family. I took a seat on one of the last risers, and smiled to two friends we'd met at the 'shtead, one of them – Sam – wearing a shiny silver jumpsuit and holding one of those big foam hands people have at sports events with Number One Wedding written on it.

Soon Kate was seen being rowed across the lake in her white bridal gown; she stepped smiling from the canoe and up the little dirt path onto the stage. Yeti performed the ceremony – he spoke about the couple's responsibilities to one another and their community, told stories from their time in India illustrating the correctness of their union. In a suit and sandals Yeti stood fondly, gravely between the young couple; the four men, four women – they seem too young to call men and women, but boys and girls isn't appropriate either – well, the bridesmaids and groomsmen arrayed in a semi-circle around them, all of us encircled by trees older than generations of our ancestors.

Jesse and Kate kissed, and then rowed off together in the canoe to the sounds of their loved ones cheering and clapping. These are happy people, I thought. They have enough money but not too much; they know how to love and how to have a good time. The parents have their own world and the children have theirs, and where they meet there is respect, interest and affection. I knew I was making generalizations, and that my assessments were designed to imbue this world with some magical quality I felt was lacking in my own. What did I know, after all? Everyone has their secrets and sorrows. I knew this and yet couldn't help feeling that these people were blessed with a lack of complexity impossible in the city I know, or the families.

Thusly was I tormenting myself as I waited for Mike, the other guests murmuring happily off into the forest toward the reception. He came, eyes shining and distant, and told me they were going to have photographs taken, he would meet me at the dinner hall. I took myself in the opposite direction from everyone and found a little wooden bridge, where I sat and smoked, hoping to focus my brain on the joy I knew was in me somewhere. Instead the chest constricted, and the eyebrows; and the chin that was trying to be stern wavered and gave in to shameful tears. I was sure then that Michael would never marry me; the world seemed so large and I would only bind him to a difficult city, a difficult family, my own difficult brain. I didn't want to be responsible for that and so cried over the beautiful life that was not for me, contemplating how to make it easy for him to get away.

When I met Mike at the hall I did my utmost to look happy. He told me how on their way to take the pictures the whole wedding party had stopped as a family of deer crossed their path. How they seemed almost like spirits, they were so silent and unafraid. Then he looked in my eyes and asked, What's the matter?

I think I'm gonna sit this out, I said. I'll just go back to the tent, and turned to go.

No no no, he said gently, placing his hands on my shoulders. Why?

I don't know. I wish I could have hit this from a different angle, I said, starting to cry.

Oh, Sammy, it's okay, and he folded me into a hug that stifled my sob. Again I thought of Baba, how Zaida had to harangue and cajole her to events, even parties in her honour. Of all the traditions to carry on, I thought. But she was a genius, so she had an excuse.

Mike convinced me to come in and eat at least, so I pulled myself together and found my table. Mike was at the head table of course, and I was seated with Kate's friends from university. After perfunctory introductions I sat quietly and watched, trying my hardest not to radiate discomfort and sadness. I examined the pretty piece of handmade soap with a sprig of cedar in it that adorned the place settings. Each table was named for a tree or flower, and the MC informed us that each one should come up with a cheer to be performed sometime throughout the night. Resisting the urge to run I waited my turn for food, Mike ruffling my hair as he passed by on his way to the roast.

Finally, the speeches. A chance to sit quietly and enjoy hearing people say nice things about each other. When it was Mike's turn I was so nervous for him I couldn't concentrate on what he was saying – the only thing I remember is him talking about the Best Man pact they'd had since they were kids. I kept being afraid he'd forget his train of thought (silly, because one of his great skills is to return a long diatribe to its original source), or would go on too long (a less unreasonable fear), or would forget the things he'd told me he wanted to say. Whatever he did say must have been lovely though, because for the rest of the night and next day people kept coming up to him going, Bobbo! Great speech! And apparently someone told Jesse: I'd like to have a friend like that Bobbo.

As it grew dark my discomfort began to abate. People were getting intoxicated and standing in groups beneath the trees surrounding the dining hall; Michael stayed close to me, his face full of sweetness and pleasure for his friend, and because I had stayed and was beginning to enjoy myself. Grum in a black leather jacket (a 1980s-looking thing you would have loved) and the colourful dress she'd made came over to me and we chatted awhile; I was more comfortable with her than I had dared to hope, given how different our lives are. We got Mikey and a few other people and smoked a joint. Later I saw Jesse's younger brother walking around by himself and I asked where his girlfriend was – I'd met her at Kate's Mom's house earlier in the week and she seemed a sweet girl – Jackson to my surprise answered that she'd been feeling anxious and had drunk too much, so had gone to bed. Mercy, I thought, I'm not the only one. To Jackson I said, Well, these situations can be stressful.

Oh, our parents are all depressives so our generation all has anxiety, pronounced the handsome, gregarious youngest Rock child, before weaving off into the darkness.

Mike and I went down to the dock and were soon joined by Jesse. I'm dumbstruck, he said, and sat quietly. The cluster of our bodies was like a pupil in the giant eye created by the parabola of trees in front and behind us and Mike, looking upward, said, It is incredible, isn't it. There's no one out there watching us, it's an endless desert as far as we know, and here we are, the only non-desert forever and anywhere.

Behind us, music and laughter, then shrieks to our right as someone dove into the lake.

Up by Grum's big dirty van with her and a few others, Mike said, This is some wedding. It's a high bar to set, you know? When we returned to the hall Kate's brother's band was playing, and as they started into "Harvest Moon" Mike put down his beer, took me in his arms and we danced. I thought of how in the car before I left I'd heard "Angie" on the radio, and imagined dancing to that song with Mike at the wedding. *Angie, Angie, ain't it good to be alive?* The grand romance of it, strings sweeping through decades. Then of course I'd realized it isn't the best wedding song. But "Harvest Moon" is, and as our bodies swayed together at the foot of the stage I thought for a moment Mike would propose right there; then I thought fuckit, felt his arms around me.

The next day we took down the tent, packed our gear. Mike was quiet and sombre. I wanted to make love in the grassy clearing between the pines and we did, but I felt Mike was only giving in to me; his mind was elsewhere. Afterwards he dressed quickly, walked around the hill: a pensive boy on a grey day, kicking at stones. He'll leave me, I thought; he has to leave me, is right now pondering his escape. But then, too, this disquiet is something we share; the disquiet and also the desire to not let it compromise our ideals. So perhaps he will stay.

We returned to poor miserable Ty, who despite being half-mad with grief still has the wherewithal to say things like, Mikey, you should be a journalist.

This had never occurred to me but as soon as he said it, it made sense. We were sitting on the patio at African Village waiting for our foul, Mike toying desultorily with abstract notions of making a living, and that's what Ty said, as if it were the most obvious thing in the world. I saw Mike's eyebrows go up and his head lift. A journalist, eh, he said.

Sure, said Ty. You know what's going on in the world. You can write. Be a journalist.

Then the food came and Ty started in again on Michelle's jealousy, Michelle's callousness, Michelle's loveliness, how Michelle is hanging out with all Ty's Kensington friends, people she would have been too shy to talk to if it weren't for him. She likes what my life provides for her, he said, But she doesn't like me.

Speaking of jobs, I quit mine. I called when I came back, asked when I was next working, and the dipshit new manager said, Right now; I said, My new schedule, which was supposed to begin in September, says I can't work Wednesdays. Today is a Wednesday. She said, Well you're supposed to be here now and I said, Okay, I'm done. The only really bad thing about it is the old-school people – Deanna, Katrina – who I'll miss.

Finally there's Florence and her baby. She has told her parents, who were mortified of course. I had received several miserable-sounding messages from her on my cell while we were away, but by the time I called her she sounded much better. She said Cuba was kind of rough because the friend she went with is going through a religious conversion, so had a lot to say on the topic of Flo's pregnancy. But now she's stopped smoking and is looking after herself; Paulie graduated from his course and is working with an old-school taper named Fat Joe. Flo feels sick all the time but is taking it well; mostly she misses coffee. Both she and Paul hope the baby's a girl.

So that's that, my friend. xo

Your Samantha

JOSEPH OF THE SHEFFIELD DRUGWORKERS
09/10/2005

No, sir, Joseph of Arimathea has nothing on you as far as I'm concerned, though he is an apt patron saint – I looked him up. Hurrah and congratulations, my sweet Joseph Clark.

It's been a momentous week. I received your email when I came home from going to Flo's first ultrasound, early in the morning before she went to work. At first it was kind of peculiar to be with Flo among the other expectant mothers beginning their days at the clinic: one with a man, some with small children and none of them, like Flo, speaking with hushed urgency about the twisted state of affairs between her boyfriend and his mother. Strange seeing her undress in the little cubby and put on the institutional cotton robe. The Flo of messy bedsheets and pretty glasses in the garden, the crying hypochondriac Flo on the phone, Flo of the reckless laughing eyes dealing officiously (as she learned from her mother) with the nurses and technicians and climbing onto the raised medical table in the darkened room. And yet the strangeness was that it wasn't strange. There was a seamlessness to it, to the girls we've been together and the girls we were in that room and the women we would be in other rooms like it; there was no rift between the times we lay around trying out the names of our future children and the moment when on the black screen before us appeared the tiny pulsing light that is Flo's baby's heart. The kind Eastern European lady rolled the plastic wand around Flo's not-yet telltale stomach slathered with ultrasound jelly, and I had a weird sense of relief: that glowing technological moment, the light signifying the unseen life in the room, did not make that life any more real than it had been before. Ever since the one blue band came up outside Flo's bathroom, ever since I saw the wild, tender look in Paul's eye when he saw it, I've understood that next spring Florence will be a mother.

Oh the times they are a' changing.

And not changing.

I'll see you at the airport. x

WORDS

10/04/2005

Dear Joe,

I loved your paragraph, your tiny epic. Rather a perfect summation for our strange four days. "i went missing" bold in my inbox, and clicking on it I could already see you on your first day back – a panicked, aimless drive through the countryside. The description of your flight home made me sad, the Eliot Smith junk dreams and your pain seeing your Dad smiling at the airport at four a.m.

And then, too, it seemed you'd stopped yourself short – the sudden "happy rosh hashanna" like a hurried seal on something that had to be sent though you knew it was futile.

I keep thinking of the night down at the loft when the talk got too much for you, how we walked the neighborhood for hours, out of cigarette filters, smoking the shag at the bottom of the tobacco pouch. Me thinking you wanted to keep going, or rather, not knowing what I could do for you, and hoping you might tell me. Thinking how before you came you were writing every week: visions of domesticity in Toronto, Toronto a blurry horizon at the edge of your vision as you watched the plums drop in your Mom's garden, as you filled out forms for your new job, as the university friend who used to cry over songs with you discoursed on the perils of black tea and white china. Trapped on your cloudy island, everything you wanted to hear or say murmuring in your head until nightfall or a weekend afternoon, when hotmail would deliver droplets of it to me. And then you're here drifting silent through the east end; or on my balcony, telling me that to my friends you are like my lap-dog! That you are not smart enough for them. It couldn't be less true and some part of you knows it, but the part of you that wanted to debase yourself was bigger. Or rather, debasement was what emerged from the tumult, having grown strong from it.

I'm not saying don't be unhappy, Joe; you know I think that's crazy. Some degree of anxiety and pain just seems reasonable and necessary. Oh I know it's habit that keeps you, when there's finally the chance to say all the thoughts in your head, from doing it; an adaptation to the circumstances of your childhood and in some ways a very sensible one. But it seems – like my mom once said to me – that you think it's wrong to be happy.

Sweet Joe, I shall counter the accidental curse your mom put on you with her fear of your lifelong loneliness and unhappiness, which was only a fear of your living a life she couldn't understand at the time. Maybe it's an equally terrible curse but I'll say that for you I envision a life full of possibilities. Only instrumental suffering need apply. x

OF SHOES AND SHIPS AND SEALING WAX

10/24/2005

Dearest Joe, you have nothing to apologize for, for I will have you quiet or talkative, happy or sad. Thanks for the email; of course I'm glad you came, and relieved to know you were too. Also that you've got yourself a place to live. Sheffield sounds cool. Send me pictures?

Yes I have been hard at work. It's marvelous to be done with the 'bucks – to be a full-time proper student. Of course being broke kind of sucks, but hey. I'm tutoring the Korean exchange student that lives in Eshe's Mom's house, so that's a little money; I was worried I wouldn't know how to teach (and I don't) but she's very laid-back, we mostly just shoot the shit and look over her work from school.

I love all my classes, but best of all is the Independent Study with Susan, which we've decided to call Memoir and Social Criticism. When I show up at her lovely Annex cottage, I feel like I have finally come to that sweet spot in university life where I know what I want to know. Last week I stood in Susan's chaotic but comfortable office as she shuffled through stacks of books, papers, looking for something she wanted to lend me. For a moment I had to will myself not to imagine having her life, to be happy I had mine, was a student standing there beneath her professor's bookshelves. A lovely place to be (and maybe one that leads somewhere…). Susan looks at me with those keen eyes and I feel she sees something in me, something worth her time. The largest portion of my mark is for "production of an autobiographical novel which addresses today's social and political realities through examining their effects on the book's narrator" – I'm quoting from the course description we made up. The book may not be finished, of course, but at least it will have been begun.

I started off reading Augustine – not compelling but necessary. You'd find the book I'm reading now interesting – *Heroine*, a memoir about a bunch of activists in Montreal in the 1970s, all of whom are terribly self-conscious and yet can't seem to tell the difference between aesthetics and politics; although, it's hard to tell when she's being deliberately ironic and when it's an accident.

Michael didn't come to synagogue for Yom Kippur, but he came to dinner. I did the shopping. I've found I rather like driving up to United Bakers and standing in line for my buckets of gefilte fish with the well-groomed Yids, these faces I grew up seeing. Dark, straightened hair; Dior's Poison, Oscar de la Yenta. Women with diamond tennis bracelets on their tanned, veined wrists. Frumpy women with frizzy hair and flowered blouses, fancy shoes from discount stores; pushy women in tight, expensive shirts, impatient with the cadre of Filipino women behind the counter; well-tended women gossiping with small children on their shoulders; *haymishe* women with loud, warm voices and faces that light up when they see their friends come in the door; older women with their immobilized ash-blond hair stepping gingerly into their husbands' waiting sedans in the bumper-car parking lot. It's a big chore and Mom finds the *hekdish* a hassle, though she understands what I mean about liking the familiarity of it. I like to go in a little stoned, nothing like anyone else there and yet belonging there as much as anyone, see the familiar manager in her haircap, holler Bernstein across the counter and bask in the sense of continuity it gives me.

We had Thanksgiving dinner with Michael, Baba, Eshe and her mom Erica, Ty and his younger sister. I wondered how the company would get along but it worked out great, except that Baba couldn't hear anything Erica said. Baba told stories from her singing days – always a subject to get her lively. She recounted the time Stravinsky told her to take care of her voice and Baba said, I'll try and Stravinsky said, Don't try. Just do. Mom told the story about when Baba and Zaida went to meet Prince Philip for a Variety Club function: Baba wore a white satin gown with embroidered black flowers, a tiny pearl hand-sewn at the centre of each one. As she and Zaida walked the long hall guarded by a row of RCMP officers, Baba turned her face toward Zaida – but she was too close to him; smooshed her face into his shoulder, smearing her makeup all over his tuxedo. As the Mounties worked to keep their faces rigid, Zaida just looked down at Baba, said, Why did you do that?

It's sweet yet mildly disturbing how enthusiastically Mom tells her Baba stories. She is so beaten down by her, so burdened, it's always surprising how as she tells the stories Mom seems proud to be Baba's daughter. Like a weird Stockholm Syndrome: Mom as a child a prisoner of her parents' narcissism and elegance, and after all these years still strangely devoted to those qualities.

Perhaps even stranger, Baba has conceived an intense fascination with Florence's pregnancy. She who does not like children, and who never cared a fart for most of my friends, asks me every time I speak to her, How's your pregnant friend? She must really be getting old. Sometimes she asks me more than once in a conversation. Last summer she had surgery to remove a little lump in her neck; it was nothing, but she was consumed by fear about it and we hoped removing it would make her feel better. Instead, it seems the operation has made her more dazed. Like when you were here, she was less engaging than she used to be. I expected her to ask a million questions about your life (rather than only her favorite one, and the funniest one she could have asked you, Are you happy?), but she seemed not to know what to say. She's quieter and more confused. I'm terrified that she, too, will slowly die from Alzheimer's. The other day on the phone she began a sentence, said, I – I, I, I. I nothin', darlin', I nothin'.

Ty is making a last-ditch attempt to save his home from the Don Valley Reconstruction Project. After going through city archives, acres of microfiche at the library, and learning everything there is to know about the history of this loft, he's petitioning the Heritage Society to save it. The brick building next door is staying; it was the Dominion Wheel and Foundry. They made wheels, obviously, and railway ties, railway casings, munitions shells during the war. The loft was where the metal went to set; that's why there's a crane between the two buildings – you know in the stairwell there's that window and you can see a piece of equipment outside? It's to move the casts from the front building to the back.

We sat in the wan light at the kitchen table and Ty told me the history he'd learned, full of information, dredging it carefully up from his memory for me. He told me this history, and bits of what he's been doing to try and save the place, like he's told me anything, but for the first time he seems tired and without much hope. He went to New York last month for an interview for a medical school in Australia. Apparently a lot of Canadians end up doing medical school in Australia; they actively recruit us, knowing that Canadian students have an absurdly difficult time finding a place in their own country. It's disgusting; I can barely think about it.

Also it appears that as of sometime early this month he and Michelle have reconciled. She rode up to him on her bike in the rain in the alley outside the loft, a box of strawberries in her basket, and he said, No. That was at the end of August. I repeat this now because he repeated it to me so many times, the bike, the rain, the strawberries. How he said No, oh, he couldn't stand how he'd said No. And now something about sitting in the car and saying that when they got together he was at a turning point in his life, it was a new phase, and this too could be a totally new phase or it could be the continuation of what they'd begun. A new story or a new chapter, it was up to her.

And now it's no longer over, even though Ty might move to Australia. Perhaps because he might move to Australia – they reconciled just after he had the interview. Which is fucking infuriating, because if they could have just reconciled in the summer then Ty could have concentrated better on his MCATs, and maybe he wouldn't even need to think about Australia. His test score wasn't terrible but it wasn't fantastic, and that's why he's despairing of getting into a Canadian university. And he knows all this, yet what he wants is her. I love her, he says. Mike, Jed, Jamie, they all think it's crazy. They think Ty and Michelle fight too much, even when things are "good." And it's true, they do. There is literally tearing of hair and gnashing of teeth. Yet in a way I'm glad they're back together (is it just because it's familiar? I can't tell). I'm beginning to understand how two smart, well-meaning people can torture each other beyond all reason.

Jake is back in the cubby above the kitchen, having left the nonprofit he was working for in New York. Now he's fundraising for a documentary on the role of education in the Israeli-Palestinian conflict, so of course there's been much talk about that whole question. And one day finally Ty was passing by the couch as Mike said something about Gaza, and Ty said, You know what? You guys are always talking like you know what you're talking about, but I'm Israeli, and do you hear me spouting solutions to the problem? No. And do you know why? Because you could sit here until the moon turns into blue cheese and still not have any idea what you're talking about. You make it sound so simple – oh, the Israelis should do this, the Palestinians are getting fucked over like that. As though there were some system on which all of this is operating. There is no system; there's no clear evil. But you know what's definitely not going to help? A lot of armchair academics pontificating like they have all the answers. Everybody just slags off Israel because it's so easy. But if the problem were so simple, it would have been fixed by now.

Mike and Jake listened, chastised. Not because they agreed, but because Ty is indeed Israeli, and they both felt the insensitivity of incessantly ragging on his homeland, a place his Dad fought for in two wars. A place where a mango tree, planted at Ty's birth, still grows in the garden of his grandparents' house.

That night after Mike was asleep I wrote an application for some federal scholarship. Richard, my former poetry teacher whose class Love and the Novel is quickly becoming one of my favourite classes ever, said I should do a Master's in Interdisciplinary Studies. He knows I want to write a book and said this way I could do it and get a degree, do a scholarly portion and a creative one. Sounds pretty good really – I can research what happened to the 1960s youth movement, and memoir, and…. I still can't believe I'm now the kind of person who likes school. One of those privileged brainiacs indulging in a glut of knowledge, getting my pats on the head for ideas well-produced. Ah well. Like Mike said, If you need to dig a hole and someone offers you a shovel, you're a richer person for the shovel, but you're not a sissy-puss. What can you do? You have to be the best rich white girl that you can be. Just try not to be ballast in the vessel of the commonwealth.

Mustafa is finally out of jail, and is planning on going back to Syria. He's been away seventeen years and misses his family. He spent a lot of time in solitary, began thinking of suicide. He told Mike he'd felt like a soldier in a war against the world, but decided that was the wrong track. He wants to make peace instead. We went up to his place last week, the large apartment with parquet floors and not quite enough furniture, two pictures of fruit in peach plastic frames by the kitchen table; on the big balcony Mike played the oud and Mustafa the guitar, and he did seem like a man in the process of making peace with the world. Laughing at himself a little, but not despairingly. We talked about Virginia Woolf, and later watched *The Corporation* on Mike's computer. Mustafa loved it; it got him fired up about politics, and Mike likes it when Mustafa's anger is focused on something real. And there is the example of the Interface Carpet man, the CEO whose awakened consciousness is a reminder of what humans are capable of.

Mike thinks Mustafa's returning to Syria is a good idea, and it looks like to ease the transition, Mike's going with him.

Last week, David took me to his reading at the International Festival of Authors at Harbourfront. He picked me up in his wife's black Saab looking very dashing in a tweed blazer and green shirt, gave me a warm, distracted kiss and bolted south. We were late. His driving style is aggressive and watchful, kind of like Ty; he's like a twenty-five year old with the life trappings of a forty-year old. And the life trappings have brought that aura that older people have of being settled in themselves, the skin a little thicker, a kind of sureness that emanates from the body, says *I know what I'll be doing when I wake up tomorrow.* I feel like a kid with him but not shy, simultaneously naive and worldly. A familiar half-reckless, half-responsible Sam that pleases me. He too seems half-reckless, half-responsible, but I think it's from the opposite direction – like, he was born to irresponsibility, had no one to look after but himself and so didn't, but eventually learned enough to survive. Whereas I was born to responsibility, and claim a certain amount of fuck-it-ness for aesthetic and philosophical reasons. David read well, was engaging and clear; most people can't read worth a shit but I knew he'd be good. Afterward a bunch of people (including my half-brother Max, who I had not seen since Irving's tribute) went for drinks and a late supper at a glass and burnished wood restaurant on the other side of the parking lot and through a building full of shut-up shops. The restaurant was expensive – half-full of tourists and Lakeshore condo owners – but David is generous, and ordered lots of food. We were squeezed into a round booth with black leather seats and wine bottles behind us on a high shelf under pot-lights. The talk at our table was fast, loud, and literary, and I liked it. Priscila was telling stories in that serious schoolgirl way of hers, her dark curls down for the evening (she always wears her hair up when she teaches), and David would embellish or ask questions. There were so many of us we changed the air of the restaurant, brought something heedless and mildly disheveled into it. Max and I went out to have a smoke and a question occurred to me. I ought to take advantage of the situation to learn something about this family of mine, I thought.

You know that poem to you and David, I said, Irving's poem that's about all the different kinds of Jews, the wandering Jew, the cultured Jew? You know the ending where it says "Be none of these my sons, my sons be none of these, be gunners in the Israeli air force"? Did Irving actually mean that?

Oh yeah, said Max.

He wasn't being ironic?

Ironic! No, why would he be ironic? Dad was horrified by the Holocaust, you know, it affected his work very deeply.

Well what's not to be horrified about, but that doesn't mean you have to be in the Israeli military. I mean, I thought maybe he was making a statement on the atrocity of further war, of taking up arms in a conflict that's not winnable through arms.

Not winnable – Samantha. Listen, Dad believed in Israel, maybe not as the holy land where the Messiah will return and all that, but after the Holocaust the need for a Jewish state was clear....

And off he went on why. He has the same eager, confrontational style as David, but with Max there's no comforting hint of self-mockery. I wished Mike was there to challenge these seemingly irrefutable points, but I'd left him inside talking to Max's wife about the state of education in Ontario.

A couple of days later Max called to say he hoped I hadn't been offended by the discussion. I can get a little wound up, but I hope you didn't take it personally, he said. I assured him I did not; I love a feisty conversation as much as the next Layton came into my head but at the same moment seemed ridiculous. I just said, No, talks like that are one of my favorite pastimes, and he seemed genuinely relieved. You're from a different generation, I said, It's interesting to hear that point of view.

Scary though, for I feel so ill-equipped to make a new life from the old.

Ah well: Equip, equip, although you're not equipped, as Mike's subconscious exhorted.

xo, Sweet Joe

THE TREACHERY OF ARCHITECTURE
11/01/2005

Dear Joe.

Cinderblock is worth nothing in the eyes of history.

So said Ty, as he explained that the loft would be coming down. I tried, he said, You know I tried. We were lucky, babe. We had the last of this place, the best of it. The last of these places in the city. But it's over. So we're going to have one hell of a New Year's party and then for all I know they'll cut the power on January 1st.

And in some devilish synchronicity, Ty was accepted to medical school in Australia. They've offered him a big scholarship. Fuck, said Ty, when he called me last night to tell me; I can't even get in here and fucking Australia wants to pay for my first year. I don't know what I'm gonna do, Sammy. I mean, do I stay here? What for? My home is being blown away, Michelle, well. Who knows what's happening with that. I can't stand the cold. So stay here and what? Finish my Master's and then try again? What if I don't get in? It could take years, years of more debt, more bullshit, and for what? I need to start doing this now. If I'm going to be a doctor I can't afford to fuck around anymore.

But Australia?

At least it'll be warm.

I got off the phone and cried and cried. Cried so much Mom said, Holy fuck, Samanth, it's not like he died.

But the whole time is dying, I sobbed, astonished that she didn't understand. I was crying for Ty, for the loft, for Flo's girlhood vanishing into her expanding belly. For the end of school with people I have come to know and now will never see. For Mike who leaves for Syria in three months. For all Ty's hard work not amounting to the vision I'd had for him, because despite doing everything in his power, and despite seeing very clearly what he wants, the life he's been running headlong toward isn't here but as far away from here as one can get.

He's going to medical school, that's his dream, and he's being offered a chance at it. Aren't you happy for him? (Mom was very tired.)

No. I'm not. Maybe I should be but I'm not. It isn't right. He's doing it out of exhaustion and fear and frustration. He's doing it because he's the most contradictory person in the entire world and so he would go on and on for years about community and family, and build a community and a family, and then fucking leave. He fucked up his MCATs because of the fucking breakup, because since he's the most independent person you'll ever fucking meet he's also the most dependent and he couldn't keep his shit together and now he's going to blow up his entire life just out of a perverse need to cause himself pain.

But Samanth, said Mom, trying to be patient, Firstly he hasn't even decided to go yet.

He's going to go.

Okay, well even if he goes isn't there any aspect of this that's good? He got a major scholarship. It's only a few years. He can come back.

Maybe, maybe not. Please don't say think of this as a great adventure.

I should have known. The first things I learned about him were that he wasn't from here, and there was nothing that could keep him here. Yet this is not the story I have seen for him. I thought his need to move around would be satisfied by travel, work – but we have talked so many times about our kids growing up together.

It's like we were building this big Lego structure, and somewhere in the process we started constructing different things. What frightens me is that this whole time, Ty has been working from blueprints neither of us understood, and I didn't realize until his section toppled mine.

So tonight I'm a frustrated child, unable to click together the baffling things in my unpracticed hands.

Sam

x

ON THE PROW OF A CLIPPER SHIP

11/20/2005

Dear Joe,

do you ever have moments where you see yourself and think, "aha, so that's me"? Completely real to yourself, you see what others must know and you cannot, except for those surprise instants – just now I was walking around talking to Eshe on the phone, and there was I in a cherrywood frame: neck extended, head in a red shmatah and eyebrows raised, a thought exciting my tongue I caught myself and knew.

Oh, how it gets distorted, though. That instant I fix the thing to deride myself for – the blemish, stupid sentence, unkind thought and it's all over, a mad dream; I want more than I can have, to be a better version of what I am.

Earlier this week I got a rejection from Event, another established Canadian journal. At first I just thought you stupid fuckers, like Mom taught me. But then I got to thinking how arrogant, and looking at my poems they seemed young and radical and silly. Telling Mom that my poems were rejected was of course the prelude to my "why should I write" refrain. Sometimes it seems wrong to be so fascinated by this tiny corner of the world, I said, But...

What?

In the hallway the cat started to hork. I looked to see he was on parquet not carpet, and my eyes grazed the carved wood bench that used to be in Baba's and Zaida's house; it was concealed by pictures we have no place to hang, the boxes our cell phones came in, a purse needing repair. I loved our beautiful bench with its placeless objects, the beautiful table with its stacks of bills and unread *Times Literary Supplements*, and I looked at Mom's brown eyes, laughing, spat, *I want to write this goddamned book that's what.* I just can't always see the point.

Art justifies humanity, she said, eyebrow arched, coming into her element. Jewish Mama Muse challenging her moody charge into action.

Really Mama, does it?

Washing dishes in the white kitchen light she stood tall, all aching five foot two of her haughty with the passion of her argument. We have always produced art, she said, The cavemen in their caves were making drawings on the wall. People have always suffered for art, people have sacrificed their lives for art. It's an integral part of our being and it helps justify, or not justify, but at least mediate the terrible things we do to each other that's also human.

But art also profits from those awful things we do –

Well of course, she said; Like I always told you Irving was doomed to foul his own nest. It was his tragic flaw and he knew it: that was the sad part. But he couldn't change, he was compelled to get himself into these situations just to see what would happen, and he would hurt people terribly. And he suffered terribly. But it was also a source of his creativity, and an expression of his curiosity about life, his insatiable interest. Like when he set himself on fire as a child because he was curious what would happen if he tipped the candle toward him.

That seemed like a normal stupid kid thing to do, I thought. Perhaps the particular thing was how clearly he remembered wanting to know. I'm always slightly uncomfortable at the Irving dissections, the Mom Dad revelation speeches, especially those that come back to the tired old Artistic Bad Behavior argument. You know, Joe, I've been having this argument for years, since I was a child. The "I don't believe art requires being an asshole" argument – I remember being shushed by my Mom in United Bakers as I was shouting about it, four-foot-nine Bubies turning their ancient Polish noses toward me perplexed.

To Mom I said, I think there are other sources of creativity than literally or metaphorically setting yourself on fire. You can have the curiosity without the destructiveness…

Mom eyed me, pleased, as behind her Ty peered into the kitchen, saying, Hey Bernstein ladies.

How ya doin' Tyela? He gave her a doleful look; she gave him a hug – which always turns him into a little boy, half resisting half delighted – and went to get ready for bed. When she was tucked in he went into her room, asked about her wheezing (her asthma's been bad lately); I thought how no one else except maybe Eshe would come in and sit on Mom's bed as she's ready for sleep beneath her pink sheets. It's like having a brother. I loved the contrast between his dark skin, the hard, dark boy energy of him in his secondhand wool sweater, and Mom's pillowy confection of a bed; loved his ease perched on it and looking into her eager, loving face. I could see where the worry lines are going to come in on his forehead. They chatted awhile about Mom's health and then he stood, said, Well, in a few years I'll be certified to give you health advice, Harriet.

You've decided? Mom said, looking up at him with curiosity and concern.

Yeah. My Dad's going to help – it's been a crazy few days figuring it all out. He said he'd give me the money, then he changed his mind; I was trying to figure out how much more I could get on my line of credit. Now I'm in debt to my Dad, my life is in his hands. If I don't pay him back he can't retire, so like, I've gotta make money fast.

Samantha said they offered you a scholarship.

They did, but they only cover the first year fully. After that it's international fees, and I hear living in Sydney isn't the cheapest. This whole becoming a doctor idea is not really designed for people without money.

What is, Mom asked with wry bitterness.

Yeah, well, said Ty, smiling his slightly world-weary smile. There is something touchingly old-world about him, the cumin-smell of his skin, the thick eyebrows arched for comedy and tragedy both. I looked at his narrow teeth, the plasticity of his well-shaped mouth. How well I know that mouth. Even though I know this is how it's always been, people leaving, men leaving to Do Things In The World, I don't understand how I am expected to just carry on without him.

We said goodnight to Mom, then went into the living room. As we assumed our customary positions on the couch I fought the urge to cry. He put a big warm hand on my knee and said, So Sammy.

So Ty.

It's into the great wide world with us.

With you, anyway. And Mikey.

Mikero. (Ty's pet name for Mike since Ty returned from Japan – Tokyo for two weeks in the summer with this kittenmouthed rich girl.) Yeah,

Syria's gonna be good for him. But he's lucky. He gets to come back to you. Four months isn't a long time.

Not as long as four years. But after that you're coming back, right?

I hope so, babe. Toronto's my home. You guys are my home. But we're gonna do great stuff. You, me, Mikey, Jake. I've got plans.

You always do.

What are you gonna do, Sammy? Like next year, have you thought about it?

More school, I think. I applied for the sshrc. Yeah, I knew you'd be happy about that. I don't know, though….

What? They're handing out money. If they're handing out money, you put out your hands. Better you than somebody else. You better get used to it, if you want to be a writer.

Guhhuh, I shuddered.

What, you have guilt? Look, we live in a civilized society, civilized societies have universities, they fund creativity. They allocate money so that art and ideas can be produced, and to instigate discussion that benefits us all. I mean, what better use should the money be put to? This is a society that makes bombs smarter than kids. There's already lots of money going to other things – it goes to technical innovations, and scientific exploration – look at Michelle, she got money to study beetle penises. And even that, I mean, great, fine. Someone wants to expand our knowledge of beetle penises, that's what society does with its money. If it wants to burn its excesses on thought, ideas, discussion – even if it goes nowhere, it's a better thing to do than spend it on what we spend ninety percent of our resources on. Saying it's frivolity and triviality – saying other things are less frivolous and trivial – I don't see the point.

He saw me scribbling down what he was saying and said, Why are you writing this down? It's not like we haven't had this conversation before, a million times. You've said the same things to me.

I know, but I won't remember properly. Anyway it's the context – when I put this stuff into the book, it'll have to be in the right place. We have every conversation a million times, but in the book it's the context that's important. Anyway I think you made your case very eloquently this time.

Which seemed to satisfy him. It's like I always say, baby, I stand on the shoulders of giants. Everyone does; every accomplishment, every great deed that happens is a communal effort. So you gotta take all the help you can get.

In what must have been an unconscious attempt to cement his leaving, Ty has crashed his Volvo. Plowed right into someone on the Gardiner, the car unsalvageable. Mercifully he was fine, as were the people in front of him – it was a truck, so he barely damaged it at all. His Dad is deeply unimpressed, and Ty could have used the money from selling the car, but oh well. He sold the Samba trailer. Now he's renting a Pontiac from his local rent-a-wreck, and seeing him driving this unfamiliar American car is the weirdest thing and makes me believe, more concretely than anything, that he's outta here.

All my love, Sam.

GOLDEN IN OUR IMPOSSIBLE CONFIDENCE
12/06/2005

Hello Dearest Joe,

I returned two days ago from Philadelphia – well, New Jersey, really; my great-uncle Mickey died. My grandmother's older sister's husband; Bonnie's father. She called him Daddy, and he was a very sweet man, called Rose his beautiful bride his entire life. He had pancreatic cancer so we've known for awhile the time was coming – I was worried, thinking there'd be no way I could go because of exams and papers, and Mom was freaking out at me that I'd even think of not going. But it worked out.

The first thing we did upon arrival was drive to Broad Street in search of a diner. The city felt familiar. Mom was pleased to be there and so was I; sitting in the plush burgundy passenger seat of the rented Ford reminded me of going to Florida with Mom when I was a kid, that excitement of leaving the airport and seeing the lights of an unknown city whizzing by in the night. I wanted to see South Philly, where Baba grew up, but it was late and we still had to drive to Jersey; Mom promised we'd come back for a proper trip, drive "down the shore" as she says, and see the Boardwalk of her childhood.

We found the perfect diner, called, I believe, the Broad Street Diner, sat at a booth with vinyl seats and ordered Philly Cheese Steak sandwiches. I'd never had one before so it had to be done (and I'd do it again, too). For dessert we ate rice pudding and reminisced about Mickey. His love and even temper when Rose was difficult (all the Cohen girls were difficult). How every summer when Mom's family would come to Jersey to visit the Weiners, Mickey would come in to wake Bonnie and Mom, who would have been up all night talking, and he'd raise the blinds saying, Up up up, chipper chipper chipper! Say good morning to the birds and good morning to the bees, and good morning to the grass and good morning to the trees….

I felt it was our mourning ritual, this eating of rice pudding and telling of stories. Invoking heritage, the known fragments of lives that preceded and produced ours, as a way to acknowledge death and its manifold progeny, life.

I was a pallbearer, surprised at how appropriate it felt to be helping to convey Mickey's body out into the bright morning, surprised too at how light the casket was. I was prepared for it to be very heavy, and to find it very sad. Instead came a kind of joy at my own strong limbs, and at taking part in a ritual that unites the living in respect for the dead. I felt the same as I took my turn to cast earth into his grave; the thing I found almost unbearable was watching Rose do it.

The night after we got back Mom made lemon broiled chicken, one of my favorites since childhood. I'll have to start writing out some recipes, Mom said, For when you're in your own home. And I wondered how it was possible to be delighted and heart-sore at the same time. Mike joined us for dinner, although I told him that I'd have to spend the night on schoolwork. As usual, having him at the table reminded me why I want to spend the rest of my life with him. He can listen attentively to all Mom's work stories, become incensed in the right places, join with me in excoriating the modern corporate world. After dinner I spun a joint and Mom said, Why do you smoke so much pot, you kids? It's not a criticism, I'm just curious. I mean in my day, when we smoked dope it was about transcending one's own limits, about increasing communication and awareness. You kids seem to smoke it like breathing. And your weed is so much stronger, like, wooo! – she opened her eyes wide, getting a whiff.

It's true, but maybe we smoke less, I said; Like wasn't it normal for people to buy like an ounce at a time? And I think it's still about communication and awareness. At least, that's what I get out of it.

But you're right, said Mike, We don't have the same kind of, like, ritual around it that you guys did. We are more casual with it – it's partly because it's just much less subversive now, because it's much less illegal. But drugs have lost that connotation you're talking about – we don't approach "altering our consciousness" the way I think your generation did. It's like, you can barely find acid any more, it's all ecstasy and other synthetic-happiness drugs. But it still comes from the romantic impulse to be a little bit bad, that defiant embrace of one's subjectivity, you know, looking for the sublime…

The impulse to be bad, it's true, and the destructive element – there certainly was that, even in the peace-and-love sixties. It wasn't big, in Yorkville, but like, I remember these guys you'd see around in their big red convertibles. They were hard, man, you could see they had money, maybe guns. I went, stupidly, for a drive with one of them one day. I took a female friend with me so there'd be two of us, if anything… idiot that I was.

Why did you go, I asked, astonished. (I thought of Eshe and me in New Orleans getting into the car with musicians we'd just met. Eighteen and feeling ourselves brash, breaking this cardinal rule of cars and strangers. But we'd done it because all our instincts told us these were reasonable people to trust.)

Why? I guess I was curious. I liked the danger of it, she said, widening her eyes and waggling her head to show how ridiculous it was. I was tantalized with it a bit, not terribly much, but. He drove out somewhere in the country and I guess started to hit on me and I wasn't having any of it. So he got mad and there was some disagreement – I mean nothing really bad happened. No, the one time anything really bad happened was with someone who was supposed to be my friend. So not all the peace-and-love hippies were really what they presented as. But anyway this guy got mad and, I don't know what happened I just know I was out of the car and refused to get back in. I guess we hitched back to the city. But there was another guy in that group, Isaac, I'd known him before, not well but I knew he sort of liked me.... Anyway, Isaac had his head blown off. I remember it was sort of a big deal in the Village, people talked about Isaac getting shot. Then there was The Vagabonds, of course – the biker gang in Yorkville at the time. I used to get in their hair. They'd come roaring down on bikes making a big noise, these beefy guys and those wiry tough kinds, and people would like Woooooh – she shook her hands – because on the street if someone would say something we were supposed to disappear or acquiesce and I wouldn't. But they were the fringe element. Much more it was kids from Etobicoke come down on the weekend to dig the scene. And then the core people who lived there – Tripper, Big Mike – everybody had names like that, Draino, Digger, like that. So there you go, that's my crazy hippie days, she laughed.

But that abandon, Mike said, That romantic quest for the unknown – you need that. That's why so often young people do shake shit up, because they have this – maybe foolish, or expressed foolishly – but they have this will to transcend their society. You need a kind of recklessness.

That's right, said Mom. It's like that time, Samantha remember I told you, when I saw that young couple on the ferry to Victoria. The beauty of this couple standing at the guardrails, the youth of them, backpacked, sandaled. I wrote a poem about it, I remember, something about them being golden in their impossible confidence....

And Mike said, Yes it's a gift, that confidence, because that's the only way things change.

In bed later, after I'd spent several hours revisiting *The Sorrows of Young Werther* for my final essay, I said to Mike, The thing about romanticism that drives me nuts is it's all about the immediate; this live-fast-die-young lunacy. It's so short-sighted, or like, world-denying in a way.

No, well, there has to be some vision that keeps you committed to the world as it actually is. But if you don't believe a little bit in the world as it could be, you end up building a fortress around your desires, because you think they won't survive contact with reality. The fortress becomes a prison, though. Life, at best, is a series of emancipations.

It's hard to tell the difference between running from and running toward.

It's true, Mike said, putting a hand on my face. Love is one thing, a way to know the difference. The only way around Sod's Law. With love comes the freedom of saying Yes, world, fuck me up, I'm one with you, you can smear me like a fly, I'm happy to be whatever happens. That's the real will to power.

Oooh, Mikey….

I started a poem. About the going of the loft. Ty and Mike had laughed their ways out the door, off to pick up burritos. Their laughing together as though everything were carrying on as usual sent a shiver through me like a fever-chill. I sat down at Mike's big black desk; looking out the window, I realized how rarely I'd ever sat there. Then I started scribbling something – it's barely anything yet. How strange it was, writing at the desk in the grey light, to know that I was for the first and probably last time living an image I had carried with me through all our years at the loft.

> The slow, sad days
> of your leaving, the knowledge
> that soon it will all be complete,
> winter's pigeon-coloured sky
> released from the concrete walls.
> No eyes then
> will praise this greying light,
> this bleak, muddy
> beautiful view. This scene
> will be committed to the private dream
> of history: mine, yours,
> some few others whose days were framed
> by this eaten, fissured wood,
> these rattling panes, a lifetime older than us.

VISIONS OF A DREAM I HAD AT TWENTY-ONE
12/18/2005

It's all done, my dearest Joe, and what a mad dash it's been. I've sort of loved it, in fact. My last exam was on the 14th. I felt well-prepared, talked to Ty on the bus from the station – Hey baby, he said, I just, was thinkin' of ya, wanted to wish you a happy St. Lucius day.

I finished at five and went downtown to meet Mike, who was taking me out to celebrate the semester's completion. We'd been out with his brother recently, and one of Grant's friends was telling us about this place on Queen East that sounded delicious, so Mike had said when I was all done he'd take me.

Michael Bobbie was sitting at the bar when I came in, but hadn't been there long, still had the grey scarf Bri knitted for him dangling from his neck. We took our seats and perused the menu; Michael surprised me by saying, Let's go crazy, and ordered appetizers and drinks and everything. We're celebrating here, he said, and toasted my completed semester. The restaurant, a modern-looking but pleasant place called Kubo Radio, was playing good tunes – all sorts of things, Blondie and Nirvana and the Supremes, a bizarre and perfect mix that we kept interrupting our conversation to enthuse over.

Mike has decided to apply to Ryerson's journalism school, a two-year degree for people who already have a B.A., so we talked about what he could send for his writing sample. Good thing he did that interview with Mike the Tailor, and the review of *Rebel Sell* (the book he gave me for my birthday) he published in Noesis, U of T's philosophy journal. Also he wrote this great thing, just for shits and giggles, called "Those Damned Toys," about how his political philosophy took shape watching *Star Wars* and *Transformers* as a kid, and then realizing that the ideals they were presenting were not borne out in society.

We discussed Mustafa a little, how happy he is that Mike is coming with him to Syria. Firstly, Mike said, He's glad because the hospitality he'll be able to show me is a way to repay me for standing by him with all the legal shit. But I think it makes him feel like he didn't just waste his time here. Returning with a Canadian, it's like, the seventeen years away from home weren't a total failure, some kind of bad dream. And I think it'll help him bridge the culture shock. But I wish you were coming with me, Sammy.

I wish I was too. But it'll be good for you to have time to just…focus on your Arabic and be out in the world.

I know you think it'll be good for me to be apart from you for a while. But I don't think I need that really. I think it'd be really cool to go together.

Someday, then, I said. (I distrust these late declarations of desire for togetherness. I know he loves me, and I know he'll miss me, but I really do think he should have some time alone.)

As we left the restaurant it was starting to snow, big heavy flakes landing on our coats and gathering on the pavement. Shall we walk? Michael asked.

We began heading west, the streets mostly empty; I held Michael's hand and put out my tongue to catch the snow. That's probably terrible for you now, he said. Full of atmospheric crap.

I know, I said. Even as a kid I remember eating snow and then wondering if I was going to die. We'd just learned about acid rain.

Oh man, I remember learning about acid rain and then getting caught in a storm and thinking I was going to melt, like it was acid that was going to burn my skin….

Joking about superheroes forged in acid rain we turned up Booth Street, where Mike's grandmother was raised. A lovely little east-end street lined with semidetached houses with wood porches and sloping roofs; Mike tried to remember but wasn't sure which one had been Grandma's. We padded through the new snow into the park and swung on the swings, unwieldy in our heavy coats, carelessly awkward.

Mike got off the swing and walked around the playground. I dismounted and walked over to him. I don't know quite how to do this, he said. Um, I have something for you.

You do?

He pulled a shiny black paper box from his coat pocket. A present? I opened the box and there was a ring on a bed of paper towel; is this it? A surge of joy, followed by a millisecond of wishing that there was a diamond, spasmodically obeisant to traditions I daily mock. I recovered and looked at the ring, a thick white-gold band with a beveled edge. You're proposing to me, I thought, but said, stupid with surprise and expectancy, It looks like a ring.

You see, Sammy, I want to marry you sometime before we're old.

Really?

Really.

Sometime before we're old?

Well, whenever we can afford to get married.

Baba will be thrilled to pay for the wedding. We can get married whenever we want.

So is that a Yes?

Is that a yes. Are you crazy? Yes, of course yes. Thank you.

Thank me? Thank you, Sammy. I wouldn't even know what I was if it weren't for you. The one person who really understands me, the only person I've ever wanted to hold me when I sleep. He took me in his arms. So you like the ring? Sorry it's on paper towel – it was rattling around in the box and I was afraid you'd hear it, so I went to the bathroom and stuffed it in there.

I love the ring.

Look inside.

I held the ring up to the streetlight and peered inside: it says DOUBT ALL BUT DOUBT NOT LOVE.

As I clasped him to me, my arms inside his coat, the snow falling on our faces, I felt that we were the only people on earth and also that all the Booth Street inhabitants were going to come out of their houses, stand in the warm glow of their porch lanterns and applaud.

I looked up into his face, that benevolent, boyish face and said, You are the most fascinating person I've ever met.

Really? You know a lot of interesting people.

It's true. But you're the most. (I wasn't sure, for a moment – it had felt true coming through my lips, but once I heard it said, thought but there's Ty, and Eshe, and my dear Joe... I wasn't comparing, though; I think I meant to say, You are the greatest wonder to me, the centre of my story.)

As we walked back along Queen Street, past the quaint and increasingly trendy shops' darkened windows I asked him when he'd decided to propose.

In BC, he said, surprising me. Yeah, that's why it was kind of annoying when I decided to go to Syria and all these people were like, you better get engaged before you go.

People said that?

Yeah, well your Mom for one thing, kept dropping these hints, like, you're not gonna fly off to the Middle East without... you know. And people at work. Ty. But I told them I'd already decided. Except your Mom. I didn't want her dropping accidental hints, and also it was out of a kind of stubbornness. I didn't want to be like, Yeah, yeah, I'm gonna marry her, really. I just wanted to do it.

Man, I had no idea.

Not at all?

No, not until you pulled that box out of your coat. And even then, I was like, trying not to get too excited.

I knew at Jesse's wedding. After that it was just figuring out when, and how.

Really? I thought you were deciding to leave me.

Leave you! No. I just, well, you know how I am. I had to talk everything over with myself.

We walked hand in hand in silence awhile and I thought of Mike on that hill the day after the wedding. In his grey hoodie kicking at stones under the big grey sky. How the distance I'd felt between us was the distance he had to travel away from me in order to make sense of his desire to bind himself to me forever.

You know how I know I'm really happy? I asked. I don't want to buy anything.

He looked at me quizzically and I said, Madame Bovary – the more miserable she was in her marriage, the more stuff she wanted to buy to make her life look like what she wanted it to be. But my life already looks like what I want it to be.

When we got back to the loft Ty was waiting for us, face full of excitement. I held up my left hand. Happy St. Lucius Day, said Ty, and we laughed. I knew, he said, What Mikey was going to do and I was so excited I had to call you, but I couldn't spoil it obviously so I looked up what was going on today and called about that.

Only you, Ty, I said. We sat at the kitchen table and recounted our evening; I kept admiring my ring, a stereotype of the newly engaged girl. Smoky quartz moved to the right hand, left ring finger newly encircled by this demure, solid band, changing everything. Then Ty launched into a lament about this girl in Samba he's crazy about, even though he and Michelle have just reconciled. I just want to bend her over a banister and give it to her, said Ty. Sorry, that's crude, but.

You? Crude?

Al a zain, he said, smiling, both hands gesticulating toward his crotch; a Hebrew phrase roughly meaning On my dick.

It wasn't until Mike and I had gotten into bed that I understood the magnitude of what had happened. I had been surprised, in the park, that no part of me wanted to cry; I had always thought I would burst into tears like a proper girl when he said the word marry, but it wasn't until I was next to him in our little nook beneath the sloping ceiling, stroking his hair, that I welled up. It had never occurred to me how different it would feel to be engaged. I had thought it would just be a formalization, a reason for a party, a relief. But it was different. We belonged more to one another, had agreed to move through the world together, and I felt young and humble, as though I'd just been granted admission to an ancient guild. City light coming through the window imprinted itself on the wall next to the bed, and I suddenly remembered very clearly a dream I'd had when I was twenty-one, a dream I've always remembered even though I remember dreams so rarely. In it I was lying in a bed in a room bathed in deep blue light, and next to the bed was a window or door with moonlight coming through. The remarkable thing about this dream, though, was the peace I'd felt in it. That was all I remembered: the blue room, the light beside the bed, and a sense of absolute peace. And lying there next to Mike I realized that this was the room in that dream; the light beside the bed was not a door but the reflection from the big windows, and the peace was not the peace of years of stability behind me, as I had interpreted it, but the awe of newness, the peace of knowing that this thing I have wanted for so long has really come.

In the morning Mike went to work and I to Eshe's. I called Mom as I walked from the station and said I have good news. Did Michael propose to you? She asked with more impatience than excitement, so telling her, Yes, he did, didn't have quite the kick I'd been looking for. That's good, she said, as if Michael had just avoided being branded an imbecile by her forever. Jeez, Mom, I said, It's not like this is exciting or anything. Sorry, she said. It's just, you know I think it would have been absolute absurdity for him to fly off to Syria – justamoment *sorry*? No, that one goes to Cineplex – sorry darling, it's madness here today. No no, I always have time for you, you know that. It's just I've already been on the phone with Baba not once but twice, and we didn't get our trailer placements – this is my life. But. You had a nice time? Yes? Well you'll have to tell me all about it. And we'll have to do a dinner with the Bobbies. Say hi to Eshe....

From whom I got my squeals and tears. Bless her, even-tempered as she is she'll bawl buckets over *West Side Story* and well up at other people's joys. Our lives are like a novel to her, I think, so even when people speak of relatives or friends she's never met, she gets invested.

I recounted Mike's proposal and then we sat in silence a while, thinking about it all. And I began thinking of "the book" and felt shockingly overwhelmed. Too much excitement maybe, but my voice caught as I asked her, Do you really think I can write it?

She just nodded, smiling her serene, knowing smile.

I think Mike and I will be married in the summer.

Happy Solstice and Christmas, Sweet Joe.
  As ever, Samantha.

HOW TO LIVE

12/30/2005

Dearest Joe, thank you for the Christmas email. I like that you got to carve the roast, and that your Dad heard "Angie" on the radio and turned it up for you. I'm glad your Mom is feeling better, and that you liked the card: yes, I thought "Live to the point of tears" appropriate for you.

In return I send you an enormous missive. But how could it be otherwise? It's not every holiday season, after all, that one is newly engaged – it is a wonderful time of year to make such an announcement! If one is fortunate as we are, surrounded by people who love us. I have been continually thinking of the assertion Richard made in class, that love is a community act.

First it was dinner with Michael's family, which Mom threw together for the Saturday after he proposed. She made a delicious roast, and got to use her Waterford crystal – wine, Scotch, and champagne glasses (although, she uses the champagne glass for ginger ale a lot – Save things for what! as she says). The first thing Baba said when she walked in the room? She looked at Mike's grandmother and said, What a pretty little old lady! (And later, quietly, to me: What a stupid thing to say. A pretty little old lady. I'm older than she is!) Sheila didn't mind; I think she thought it was funny. Baba was on her best behavior, although the Bobbies are probably just the type of "ordinary people" my grandmother would have spurned earlier in her life. The older Baba gets, the more I feel she loves me; she's even started to say "I love you" when Mom and I leave after visiting. (Mom asked her recently, What has prompted you to say this, having never said it in your whole life? I guess people can always change, said Baba.) Clearing the dinner plates, making tea, again I had that feeling of having just been admitted to a guild, a woman among centuries of women. A young woman in love. Mike put his arms around me and we posed for a picture. Betrothed, surrounded by family; taking our place in the ancestral line.

Then there is the extended family: a few nights ago we had dinner at Erica's – she wanted to make a celebratory dinner for the engagement before Mike leaves. She made us jerk chicken and regaled us with activism stories from the 1970s, a perspective on this city I could get nowhere else. And very informative on the whole process of how people try to be socially active.

A lot of stuff didn't get done because everyone was too busy being proud of themselves, she said. You know, it was a very exciting time, and people were caught up in Black Power this and Marxist that. Oh sure, the Marxists, or Trotskyites or whatever, they would have their meetings and talk their radical talk. I made sure I never learned even one quote of Marx, so I wouldn't accidentally say it and then they'd (patting Eshe on the back), you know. . .

Eshe: Think they had a convert.

Yeah, because, you know, they looked down on us, they thought we were wasting our time. They didn't believe in service. They were too busy with their meetings, arguing how the revolution would come about. They didn't have time for tutoring or workshops or whatever. One of them told me once (her light eyes glowing wide and mischievous), The revolution is going to leave you behind.

We all laughed. You're like, I don't wanna come! I said, which made her laugh more.

And Eshe was like, Yeah, it's the *Left Behind* series for Marxist revolutionaries, where only the true believers get into the new society.

Yeah, they were really stupid, proclaimed Erica in her slow, laughing way.

On the polar opposite of the political spectrum, I went over to David's house to see him before he leaves for Barbados. He is about to start another book, and I have a feeling this will be a major work. We've been out a few times – to movies, or bars on College Street with his friends, once to a literary party where he got hilariously drunk – but I hadn't yet been to his home, a lovely old house on Robert St.; the kind of place Eshe and I don't even bother to drool over on our walks. His wife was out of town on business, and Mike was seeing his brother, so it was just David and me. Much less strange than going to Irving's house – I realized as I went to the washroom and remembered being in Irving's basement washroom the first time I visited him, stunned by the unfamiliarity of it. In David's bathroom it was just like going to any friend's place for the first time – oh, so you live like this. Neat. He made some gorgeous garlic chicken and we sat at an antique table beneath absurdist paintings by an artist friend of theirs (one I particularly liked of a girl in a ballerina outfit and a man in a suit swinging yo-yos), and he told me a little of his life – here's a weird synchronicity: he and Max used to be currency speculators at Guardian, where Mike works, back in the eighties, before Dino (the hippest currency exchange cat anywhere and ever) bought it. How crazy is that? And he told me of writing his first book, holed up in the Dominican Republic in his early twenties. I like how he tells stories – how he produces the most poignantly metonymical details. And we talked politics, of course. Or rather, he talked, I listened. My favorite portion was his diatribe on the Jews.

Two thousand years later they came back with the same book. The same rituals. They came back with the same fucking language. They survived the Romans, THE ROMANS!! By the time they invade they've been ruling for five hundred years, they're not young and green and aggressive. And they say look – you gotta show respect for the emperor. You don't have to kneel and pray to his image, just put our bust up on your thing. Nope! Jews refuse. They refuse! And they end up stupidly, you could say idiotically – they were the first terrorists – the zealots, right – they fight the Romans, and they lose. They fight them like no one's fought them, except maybe Carthage. What is it these people felt so attached to? You could say okay that's one group of crazy motherfuckers and they're annihilated. But the Jews go away, and stick with it for two thousand years! So now they're sitting in this grubby little state, and they create an army of unsurpassed power. Literally founded by broken fucked-up refugees who came on rusty boats, who had to go immediately into war. Think of it – three years after the Holocaust, attacked by regular armies, and they won. It's kind of extraordinary. Desk-bound neurotics become warriors. So far, for everything that's happened, it's not, you know, not absolutely horrendous. Jews are still trying to keep a rule of law. Sometimes they're not doing a very good job but the numbers of times people have gone hysterical, that Jews have massacred… considering the strain they're under, where they came from. You can say you hope they'd be better, as a nation, and yes there's something about Israel that makes people clamour for some kind of moral superiority but Samantha look. There's only twelve million of us, I don't know what we are, it's astounding. The fucking Jews, they won't go away. What's the purpose? We're unlike any group anywhere ever in history. People have been doing Passover, that ritual, for thousands of years. They did it after they were kicked out by the Romans, and they did it in Israel. The Babylonians gave them pardon! And there they remained until the Romans kicked them out five hundred years later. You've survived Babylonian exile, you're not going to bow down to any fucking idol. You've created monotheism! They gave birth to it! One God, indivisible. Judaism is about a stern motherfucker up in the universe. It ain't about the afterlife, ain't about hell. It's about this life, and what you do in this life, and how you conduct yourself.

Then there was Christmas Eve with Shelagh and the kids. After they left we watched *It's a Wonderful Life*, and Michael actually stayed for it – and managed not to make fun of it, even when I got all choked up at the end when George comes home and the top of the banister comes off like it always does and he kisses it, he's so happy to be alive. That always gets me. Mike did say It'sh Chrishmash! a few times like Jimmy Stewart, but that was cute.

And of course Christmas Day at the Bobbies'. A big tree with presents beneath it, Christmas crackers on the dinner table, roaring birch fire in the fireplace. The only thing that made me a little sad was coming into the kitchen and hearing a conversation between Mom and Janice: Janice was talking about putting out good vibes – touting this intentional living business that's all the rage now – saying how if you put out what you want then you'll get it. And I thought Mom would agree but instead she said, I don't know. I've been doing that for years and I'm really not too sure anymore.

Which surprised me, and sort of made me want to cry, which also surprised me. I thought I'd be happy when Mom stopped believing in her New Age mystical crap. Be in the world as it is! and all that. But her new-found realism frightened me, made me think she's losing some essential component of herself, that her faith is being beaten out of her by the exigencies of living. I hated it as a child, but Mom has always had her crystals and meditation, her psychic flashes and her belief that war really can, like John and Yoko said, be over if we want it. And as much as I love to argue this with her at the dinner table, I guess I don't want her to stop believing it.

Now, this woman who never gave two hoots about politics wakes up on Sundays and puts on *Meet the Press* (she loves Tim Russert); and her powerlessness against the relentless demands of her mother and The Man has seemingly awakened her to the powerlessness of us all. So while she still believes an individual's actions can make a difference in the grand scheme of things, she seems to be losing her sense that people have control over the conditions of their lives. I always wanted her to see that will only goes so far, but I didn't want her to give up envisioning a better life for herself. Well, maybe at one time I did, because I thought it would be easier for her if she could be content with what she has (and maybe because I thought she wanted the wrong things. I still think that; think, if she were intentionally living toward a more reasonable life, the intent would have results. Though perhaps that is a residue of adolescence, a need to find fault). But I also think she's had brutal luck.

On the way home she was a little quiet. I asked her if she was all right and she said, Yeah, I'm fine. Just, I don't know, it's a little strange, in some way. These people are going to be family. And they're good people, they're nice people, don't get me wrong. And I know you like them and I'm very glad. But it's just…weird. You go along in life and you fall in love with someone and then you decide to make a life together, and it's not just the two of you, it's a whole family. Two families who might have nothing in common get joined by two people who have a tremendous amount in common – I mean, how does that happen?

That's the crazy thing about modern love, Mama. The unpredictable child born from the stormy union between courtly love and social custom.

But the love. The love is what matters. And Michael really loves you, that's plain to see.

Then last night people came over to the apartment; I gave out the truffles and cookies I'd made as gifts. When I told Ariel the story of Mike and my engagement, her big blue eyes filled with tears. Oh Sammy that's beautiful, she said, throwing her tiny arms around me and pressing me to her famously ample and unbound bosom. It always amazes me that, practical and scientific as she is, and always doing three things at a time, there's enough of her present in any moment to cry over other people's joys. And you were the first one to call it, I said. When he got me the computer, remember?

And the Bobbies? she asked; Your Mom is happy to have them as *mishpuchah*?

Mom has loved Ariel since I first brought her home from high school, so the two of them stood in the kitchen talking, Ariel munching on fruit she'd brought as she told Mom her plans to become a psychotherapist. They were soon joined by Flo, the natty red sweater she's been wearing for years stretched tight across her belly. Ariel put her hands there, a thing which strangely I have no desire to do. When the baby comes out, then it'll be real; for now, it is still just Flo's belly. Mom looked a little woozy with all the change, which I think is funny since she's spent my whole life telling me to embrace it. She asked Florence if she'd been taking care of herself with that penetrating Mom-stare of hers, and rather a dash too much doubt in her Okay, well, that's good, when Flo said she was trying; I could see Flo shrink under Mom's gaze for a moment, before closing herself off and dismissing Mom's unspoken judgments.

Paul didn't come – he's exhausted all the time, working fiendishly. And they've been shuttling between Paul's parents' condo and Flo's folks' house; mostly at the condo because Paul's mom is in China (that's another whole story; his dad lives there most of the year). But it's far from ideal – when his mom is there it's the three of them plus the neurotic dog and deranged cat (it'll come for cuddles then turn on you and scratch) in that flimsy shoebox of a Queen West atrocity (which Paul by turns berates and adores: It's a piece of shit! Why did they sell their house? It's swank, trendy, you know; the prices are still going up on places like that).

The other night, Florence told me as she escaped the kitchen with her glass of cranberry juice, The dog ate my bagel. In the night I get up and the only thing I want is a bagel and to go back to sleep, but I can't go back to sleep 'til I've eaten the fucking bagel. So I toasted the bagel, so tired you know but so hungry too? And I put butter on it and I'm eating one half and the other half is on a plate on the coffee table, and Gentry ate it right off my plate. And it was the last one, she laugh-wailed, a husky Janice Joplin vocal. I know it's a small thing man, but at the time, I tell you. I love dogs, you know, always had dogs, and I've never felt an animus toward a dog the way

I did that night. It's a fucked-up dog, man; she's been following me around, like, with her head literally attached to my hip, you can't shake her. It's a little much, you know?

What is, being pregnant? asked Michelle, who came to join us by the stereo which Flo had just commandeered for her Britney Spears, ignoring Ty's ferocious eye-rolling.

Oh, yeah maybe that too. I was talking about Paul's mom's poodle who we've been looking after. But being pregnant? It would be nice to stop feeling sick – they say most people stop after three months but it hasn't really, yet. But it's not that bad. I'm lucky, you know, I get to sit down at my job, and it's not that busy this time of year.

In the hall I heard Mike telling Noam about some slides from *Star Wars* he'd recently found when he was going through his stuff, getting ready to leave. It's the one, Mike was saying, Where Luke says There's nothing to see, I grew up here, and Hans Solo says Yeah well you're going to die here… (I thought of when he found it, just before he proposed, and I had seen it as prophetic.) It ended up being fine with Mom and Flo; Flo went back to the kitchen for more juice and found Mom and Ariel talking about the demimondaine, I think because of an article Mom had seen recently about Colette, and Flo joined in because she's been reading *Of Human Bondage*. I nipped in for a glass and saw Mom listening to Flo saying something about Maugham's representation of prostitution; Mama had a slightly wary look in her eye, a something that said I hope you're gonna be all right, girl; but her face was raised and bright with admiration for Flo's perceptiveness and insatiable curiosity: *I think you will be* winning out over *I'm worried you won't*, which made me happy.

In the living room Michelle was exhorting Ty not to take up the whole couch, and I saw Jamie make an involuntary "oh goody, this crap again" face, so I took him outside for a smoke where he was happy because he could tell me about Fichte and recognition: something to do with educating each other, an argument about how we become human. We were soon joined by Michelle, however, so the conversation was friendly but stilted for a few moments before Jamie ducked back inside.

Sam, did he fuck that girl in Samba, she asked me.

Not that I know of, I said. He thought about it. But maybe he heard me when I pointed out that it's totally insane.

Fuck. Whatever. I don't even care. Actually yes I do what am I talking about. Sam, what am I doing? He's going to live in fucking Australia. I don't even trust him when he's here. And I know he has feelings for this girl, I can just feel it. But you know what? Never mind. I think he would have told me. He's been really good lately, about being honest and telling me what he's thinking and where he's going to be, and that kind of stuff. I guess I've said I'm gonna give it a try, so I'm gonna give it a try. Yeah. We're thinking I'll go meet him in Sydney when I finish my degree.

Inside, Mike was putting on the *White Album*, because he recently discovered he loves "Rocky Raccoon." Jamie walked up to him and asked him something about Foucault, and I heard Mike say something like, If you're going to talk about power he should be read, even though he writes like a black-turtleneck-wearing French intellectual.

Jamie protested something about Foucault's politics – his position on Iran, I think, and Mike said, Sure, but look at Sartre in Algeria.

He didn't know how to live, I said, walking up to them. Catching Mom's eye I smiled at her, saying, Mom thinks his life was fascinating, but I think it was horrible.

You think Sartre's life was horrible? said Jamie.

Kind of. Mom was just showing me this article about him and Simone de Beauvoir, and how they'd have these twisted sexual relationships with people; this one young girl, man, they just ruined her.

They set up interesting scenarios, said Mom, in her best goading good humour.

Yeah, which were supposed to prove some interesting philosophical point, or teach the unwitting victim something – but that's complete hypocrisy. Their whole thing was you choose, you choose, well how are you supposed to choose if other people are doing fucked up shit to you on purpose?

Well isn't the point, said Mike, That you can only choose to a limited degree because there are always circumstances you're unaware of? It's like we talk about all the time, right –

Yeah, but that is different from having a pair of mad philosophers fucking around with the small bit of choice a person does have. How can you preach equality and justice and self-consciousness, and then use your position of power as famous intellectuals to conduct human experiments designed to prove your theories?

I left Jamie and Mike to the conversation I had interrupted, and went to greet Eshe and Dave, who were divesting themselves of their layers in the hallway. On my way I passed Mom who said, as she often says, You should be writing this down. And I, as I always do, smiled and tapped my head.

In the morning I awoke to Mom listening to Bach and preparing to make chicken soup, one of her favorite combinations. I made some tea and helped her peel carrots, parsnip, parsley root. When it came time to *shoim* – the skimming that makes the soup clear – she said, You do it; gently, gently. But fast. Like this.

And I watched her nimble hand do in four swift movements what I'd been fumbling with for half a minute.

You'll get better. It takes practice. Here, wait a moment till more comes. She gave the pot a shake on its burner. Now try. That's it!

When the soup was simmering with its vegetables she watered the plants, saying hello to them, plucking off the dead bits. The sun was coming in, illuminating the leaves, and suddenly everything seemed to be going too fast. I wanted to keep Mom forever there in her housecoat, Bach on the stereo, tending her geranium with that pleased, absorbed face. I could barely breathe for thinking that there were a finite number of mornings like this. She looked over at me and said, dark eyes full of knowledge and love, Having a little mortality moment, are we?

And I took myself into her arms, let my head rest against her shoulder feeling young, protected and grateful.

Speaking of childhood and the future, here is a piece of synchronicity: yesterday Mike and I went to Bregmans, that restaurant around the corner from my place that's been there for probably forty years – Mom used to take me for brunch before a matinee at the Hyland or the Hollywood, small theatres long since lost to multiplexes. Anyway, my fiancé and I (!) went there for eggs and I said, You know what would be great? If I could get a job right here. Family business, probably batshit management but whatever.

Today I walked past, and there was a help wanted sign. How about that?

So, my dearest Joe. Happiest of New Years – health, joy, mental stimulation and peaceful contemplation be yours.

With immense love,
Samantha.

AFTERWARD

01/09/2006

Dearest Joe,

I just got in not long ago, but wanted to send a short thank you for the email. I've been sitting here responding to condolences. People are kind; they don't know what the situation was, but they know he was my father and that's reason enough to extend sympathy. I just read an email from one of my schoolmates, who told me how she had devoured Irving's books when she was a teenager. I think this weekend has shown me more about his life than anything I knew before; I can see now how he affected people, and how grateful they are.

He wanted to be an old-fashioned giant, you know – believed that poems could bestow immortality. He came from a time when it was still possible to tell that kind of story, and I think he should be remembered that way. Even though that desire to dominate and claim each living moment made him myopic – poetry filled his whole frame of vision, and caused him to make painfully wrong decisions. For reasons unknowable, his artistic ego depended on chaining doubt in an oubliette. Perhaps it's the need for this containment that makes so many artists difficult to live with, so erratic and stubbornly irrational.

It's horribly sad to think of Irving sitting in his wheelchair year after year, words seemingly inaccessible to him. It helps to think that people of my own generation still read him, that his work matters to them – his personality still radiating out from those words.

Yes, there was a lot of press and weirdly, it didn't bother me in the least to talk to them; I think it was too much for Mom – I walked out of the funeral into a flashing, microphone-protruding mob, turned around to look for her but she had vanished. Later she told me that she'd been behind me and seen that I could manage the many-armed beast of media, before turning around to the kind face of Leonard Cohen who must have seen her dismay, took her hand and pulled her toward another exit. I suppose the reporters knew to talk to me because I read the poem…. I was dead nervous, shaking on the podium, but as I got going it was easier. Mike said you couldn't tell I was nervous. It was good to have him there – a weird but appropriate beginning to our union. Though I think it rattled Mom a bit: the first major family event where Mike is involved; he and I in a room in the lovely old Hotel de la Montagne where Mom always stays; where we stayed together when I was eight and Bonnie, Thor and the kids came up for a weekend. Yesterday, when we met Mom for breakfast, she delighted in my enjoyment of the exquisite croissants just as she always would but I felt a distance, like she is trying too hard to let me go. Or perhaps she was just processing Irving's death, which has certainly been hard for her. As has all the Layton family drama, but that I shall save until we speak….

Anyway, I wanted Michael with me because, if this makes sense, he helps me to conceptualize my relationship to Irving outside of Mom; to have some sense of who he was to me apart from who he was to her. Mike and I stayed up late talking about Irving's life, and how strangely appropriate it is for him to die now, when our lives are changing so. I had just begun to read his memoir for school.

His death has not only helped symbolize the end of an era, but has materially contributed to the one now beginning. Irving left me money. How fucking wild is that? This man who I barely knew has left me an inheritance. Not a huge one, but not nothing either. Who knew poets could have savings? I actually got choked up when Max told me, felt like perhaps Irving had loved me in whatever way he could; then I felt kind of bad – what right do I have to this stranger's money? But then I thought about it and thought, hell, there was no child support, there was no support, period (which was partly my grandfather's fault, but…). Then I got to thinking how inheritance is kind of evil; then, that's absurd, only massive inheritances are evil. Mom thinks it's wonderful, and right that I should have it. I suppose it is a kind of redress; in any case I am very grateful. A nest egg, a wedding present.

The power wasn't turned off in the loft on New Year's Day. I don't know why, but it's still on. Things are getting packed up; we'll have a final party probably just before Mike goes on the 27th. I am so excited to live with him and so afraid to leave Mom. No more birthday cards waiting on the bathroom mirror when I wake up, no *New York Times* stacked on chairs, highlighter circles around articles I'll like. It's too sad; but what can I do? Onward we must go. Or, as csny says, *Rejoice, rejoice, we have no choice but to carry on.*

Two of my favorite moments from 2006 so far? In the subway: a smiling man carrying a young tree in a pot, the other passengers a wet mob eddying around him; we smiled at each other as we passed and I wondered what he was planning as he hustled along clasping to his chest this contained, resilient life. And: me on the can about to take a leak as Ty struts from the bathroom into the dark stairwell, arms over his head like Zorba the Greek, singing the chorus from a song Samba plays with the horns – *I would say Bella, Bella, oh, vunderbar, da na na na na ba dum! Ba dum dum dum…. Bei mir bistu shein, I must explain*

The death, or the rituals around it, spawned a new poem – perhaps I can read it to you when you call? I shall be by the phone at two o'clock to receive my birthday wishes….

xo, until the morrow

ACKNOWLEDGEMENTS

Thanks first to Halli Villegas and Tightrope Books; to Robin Read, Shirarose Wilensky, Heather Wood, and Myna Wallin. Immense thanks to everyone who appears in these pages, and to those who do not appear but are here. Thanks to Priscila Uppal; to Richard Teleky; and to Susan Swan: the years I studied under you made me love the crafts of writing and reading. Priscila, you encouraged me when I was a shyly eager first-year student; and you introduced me to David, who I also thank, not least for your outraged marginalia, but more for being a great brother. Susan, how can I thank you for guiding my first research for this project, and for showing the earliest, 776 page version of this book to Samantha Haywood? Sam, without you this book might still be a pretty dream, had you not believed so steadfastly in its reality. I carry with me everywhere the sense of my good fortune in having you as my agent. Thanks to York University, for the Master's funding and the program that allowed me to begin this book. To Professors Leslie Wood, Penni Stewart, Marcel Martel, Rishma Dunlop, Maureen Fitzgerald, and Marlene Kadar. Thanks to my classmates in the York Creative Writing Program. To every professor I've had the benefit of learning from as a graduate student, especially Cheryl Cowdy, for the encouragement, and Thomas Loebel, for flexibility about deadlines. To Richard Simpson for clarity. To Baba, for showing me the dark; and for telling me: hitch your wagon to a star, and if you get halfway there, you're lucky. To Ariel Garten, Michelle den Hollander, Elinor Keshet, Jesse Rock, Vanessa Scott and Noam Lior, Sean Dickson, Jedediah Smith, Jonathan Rothman, David Arcus, Shelagh, Aran, and Brianne Rafter, Max Layton, Marc Bernstein, Bonnie, Thor, Cari and Michael Borresen, Sheila Allen, Brian, Janice, and Grant Bobbie, Franceszka Kolatacz, Jory, Talia, and Josh Lane for community. To all past and present members of Samba Elegua, for joy. To Jamie Smith for the Hegel primer; Jake Wadland for his critical eye and his kindness. To Brianna Sharpe for early years with notebooks, Florence Shaw for her fascination. To Itay Keshet, the most astonishing rodeo clown, for taking me places I'd never go otherwise, and for giving me hard truths about an early version. To Joseph Clark, for the quiet and the fullness; your eyes grace all my days. Eshe Mercer-James, there's no proper thanks for the blessing of your friendship; the hours we spent on this book, and meandering this city, are some of the happiest I've known. To my mom, for her unfailing encouragement, for being the editor who catches what no one else does; for always asking the most important question – What are you trying to say? – and caring about the answer. Michael Bobbie, the only thanks I can give you is to try and live what you see when you look at me.